The Collected Writings of Walt Whitman

WALT WHITMAN

Notebooks and Unpublished Prose Manuscripts

VOLUME IV: NOTES

Edited by Edward F. Grier

 NEW YORK UNIVERSITY PRESS 1984

© 1984 BY NEW YORK UNIVERSITY

Library of Congress Cataloging in Publication Data
Whitman, Walt, 1819–1892.
  Notebooks and unpublished prose manuscripts.

  (The Collected Writings of Walt Whitman)
  Bibliography: p.
  Includes index.
    1. Whitman, Walt, 1819–1892—Diaries. 2. Poets,
American—19th century—Biography. I. Grier, Edward F.
II. Title. III. Series: Whitman, Walt, 1819–1892. Works.
1961.
PS3231.A36 1984   818'.303 [B]   83-24415
ISBN 0-8147-2991-6 vol. I.
ISBN 0-8147-2992-4 vol. II.
ISBN 0-8147-2993-2 vol. III
ISBN 0-8147-2994-0 vol. IV
ISBN 0-8147-2995-9 vol. V
ISBN 0-8147-2996-7 vol. VI
ISBN 0-8147-2989-4 (set)

PS
3202
G75
1984
v. 4

MANUFACTURED IN THE UNITED STATES OF AMERICA

CLOTHBOUND EDITIONS OF NEW YORK UNIVERSITY PRESS BOOKS
ARE SMYTH-SEWN AND PRINTED ON PERMANENT AND DURABLE ACID-FREE PAPER.

The Collected Writings of Walt Whitman

THE PREPARATION OF THIS VOLUME,

AND COSTS ASSOCIATED WITH ITS PUBLICATION,

WERE SUPPORTED THROUGH GRANT NO. RP-*1726–80 FROM THE

Editing and Publication Programs
of the National Endowment for the Humanities,

AN INDEPENDENT FEDERAL AGENCY.

CENTER FOR
SCHOLARLY EDITIONS
AN APPROVED EDITION
MODERN LANGUAGE
ASSOCIATION OF AMERICA

CONTENTS

The Collected Writings of Walt Whitman

Notes

I.   Proposed Poems.

A City Walk.

Manuscript not found. Text from *N&F*, 120 (Pt. III, #126; *CW*, IX, 141). First published by Bucke in "Notes on the Text of Leaves of Grass," *Conservator*, 7 (February, 1897), 186, with first three words in lowercase and period after "Walk." Possibly a projected prose piece rather than a poem, but, on the other hand, considering "S of M," sec. 8, ll. 154ff., "The blab of the pave . . . ," it may well lie behind those lines. Since it was a Bucke MS, the date is probably before 1860.

A City Walk — Just a list of all that is seen in a walk through the streets of Brooklyn and New York and crossing the Ferry.

Poem of Architecture.

Manuscript in Duke (15, #37). Inscribed in black pencil on white laid scrap, approx. 3½″ x 4¾″, conspicuous vertical lines in texture (cf. "Poem of Wisconsin"). In upper right corner, indecipherable oval embossing. A light waved line cancels "(Poem of Architecture" and may cancel the next entry. The reference is to "Literature of the Middle Ages," *Westminster Review* (Amer. ed.), 51 (July, 1849), 179–191, a review of M. Villemain's *Literature du Moyen Age*. The review is in Duke (Trent *Cat.,* 71), but WW's extensive markings are not particularly suggestive. Page 190, underlined in part by WW, digresses into praise for the expressiveness of medieval architecture over Gallo-Roman or modern. "Meats" has not been identified. The date is presumably 1849 or slightly later.

Poem of Architecture ?The Carpenter's and Mason's Poem (page 190 "Literature Middle Ages" (in Meats)

Poem of Pictures.

Manuscript not found. Text from *N&F*, 177 (Pt. IV, #116; *CW*, X, 32). Cf. "Pictures" and "Salut au Monde!" (1856). The date is probably pre-1855.

Poem of Pictures. Each verse presenting a picture of some characteristic scene, event, group or personage—old or new, other countries or our own country. Picture of one of the Greek games—wrestling, or the chariot-race, or running. Spanish bull fight.

Pictures.

Manuscript in Yale. Inscribed on rectos in black ink with emendations in black pencil, black ink, brown (?) ink, and blue crayon on homemade notebook of unruled white wove paper, 8″ x 6⁹/₁₆″. On p. 43 the embossed stamp of "Owen & Hurlburt So Lee Mass" is clearly visible at upper left. The stamp is faintly visible on pp. 36–42. The notebook is bound by a light blue ribbon at p. 45. The pagination printed here, except for that on clipped pages, is WW's in blue crayon on the top center of the leaf. The binding ribbon seems normally tight and does not suggest that 32 leaves were removed, but on the other hand it was probably retied. An earlier series of numbers also in WW's hand in black ink exists in the upper right corner of each recto running from 1 to 27. They have been deleted in black ink. Possibly WW was thinking of "Pictures" as part of a larger cluster when he inserted the blue crayon numbers and made the blue crayon emendations at the same time. No reason can be assigned for the clipped lines, and I have not been able to identify them in my admittedly casual examination of verse MS which are not part of this edition.

There are a number of related fragments or poems. "Poem of Pictures," as Holloway pointed out in his edition of "Pictures," is the earliest suggestion of the poem. He also reprints (9) a draft from N&F, 27: "O Walt Whitman, show us some pictures. . . ." Bradley and Blodgett (LG CRE, 649) have identified six fragments, which, however, are not among the clipped lines. They also print (ibid., 678) a MS, "Pictures," which they identify as a draft. In 1881 WW returned to the notebook and slightly modified the first lines to produce "My Picture-Gallery."

A number of parallels with published poems are indicated in the notes. Significant relationships with other notebooks and MS are also listed.

The MS seems to have been written later than 1850, the date assigned by Holloway. The only other uses of Owen and Hurlburt paper are "Spring of '59," "What name?" also 1859, and "Oct. 17, 1860." Obviously, however, other MS on this paper might be lost or unidentifiable. A curious line [53] about Lascars sacrificing money to the sea seems to be related to the careful note he made of this fact, as if it were new to him, in "June 23d '57." The line [48], "But there, see you, a reminiscence from over sea—a very old Druid, walking the woods of Albion," may be related to "I see where Druids walked the groves of Anglesey — I see in their hands the mistletoe and Vervain" from "Old theory started." Since Bucke says that the latter was written on surplus yellow flyleaves from LG (1855), "Pictures" may then be dated in 1855 at the earliest.

First printed by Emory Holloway in "Whitman's Embryonic Verse," Southwest Review, 10 (July, 1925), and in Pictures (NY, 1927).

33[1] [*Front cover*] Pictures.

> Break all this into *several* "Pictures"
>
> Walt Whitman[2]

34 [*Front cover verso blank; three stubs*] Pictures.

In a little house pictures[3] I keep,[4] many pictures hanging suspended—It is not a
    fixed house,

It is round—it is but a few inches from one side of it to the other side,

But behold! it has room enough[5]—in it, hundreds and thousands,[6]—all the[7]
    varieties;

—Here! Do you know this? This is cicerone himself;[8]

And here,[9] see you, my own States—and[10] here the world itself, rolling
    bowling[11] through the air;[12]

And there, on the walls hanging, portraits of women and men, carefully kept,

35 This is the portrait of my dear mother—and this of my father—and these of
    my brothers and sisters;

This, (I name every thing as it comes,) This is a beautiful statue, long lost, dark
    buried, but never destroyed—[13] now found by me, and[14] restored to the
    light;[15]

There five[16] men, a group of sworn friends, stalwart[17] bearded, determined,
    work their way together through all the troubles and impediments of[18] the
    world;[19]

1. Front cover pasted to stub. Possibly conjugate with p. 57 originally. Both reinforced by
pasted strips at fold.

2. Note and signature in black pencil to right of center.

3. Inserted in black pencil above "se" in "house" and "I"

4. Inserted in black pencil in wordspace: "¶" . Remainder of original first line here printed
as separate line.

5. Deleted in black pencil: "for" ; inserted in black ink above "m" in "room" and word-
space: "enough" ; inserted in black pencil in right margin: "—in it,"

6. Inserted in black pencil: comma; possibly deleted in pencil: dash.

7. Inserted in black pencil in right margin.

8. Cf. "My Picture-Gallery" (1881), which is closer to this MS than to "O Walt Whitman,
show us some pictures" (*N&F*, 27 [Pt. I, #64]).

9. Deleted in black pencil: "one after another,"

10. Deleted in black ink: "there" ; inserted in black ink above "ere" of "there": "here"

11. Inserted above "rolling" in black pencil.

12. Cf. "Salut au Monde!" (1856), sec. 4, l. 43.

13. Deleted in black pencil: "and"

14. Deleted in black pencil: "again"

15. One or possibly two verse lines clipped out.

16. Deleted in black pencil: "stalwart"

17. Inserted above "bearded" in black pencil.

18. Preceding six words inserted in pencil above "ough" in "through" and "the world;"

19. Lines deleted in black pencil:

And that is a magical wondrous mirror—long it lay clouded,
    but the cloud has pass'd away,

36 It is now a clean and bright mirror—it will show you all [*del. in black pencil*] things you
    can conceive of [*del. in black pencil*] or all you [*preceding two words ins. in black pencil*]
    [*two words del. in black pencil*] to behold;"

36 And that is a picture[20] intended for Death—it is very beautiful—(what else is
    so beautiful as Death?)[21]

37 There is represented the Day, full of effulgence—full of seminal[22] lust and
    love—full of action, life, strength, aspiration,

And there the Night, with mystic beauty, full of love also, and full of greater
    life—. the Night, showing where the stars are;

There is a picture of Adam in Paradise—side by side with him Eve, (the Earth's
    bride and the Earth's bridegroom;)

There is an old Egyptian temple—and again, a Greek temple, of white marble;

There are Hebrew prophets, chanting, rapt, extatic—and here is Homer;

38 Here is one singing canticles in an unknown tongue, before the Sanskrit[23]
    was,

And here a Hindu sage, with his recitative in Sanskrit[24];

And here the divine Christ expounds[25] eternal truths—expounds the Soul,

And here he[26] appears en-route to Calvary, bearing the cross—See you, the
    blood and sweat streaming down his face, his neck;[27]

And here, behold, a picture of once imperial Rome, full of palaces—full of
    masterful warriors;

And here,[28] the questioner, the Athenian[29] of the classical time— Socrates,[30] in
    the market-place,[31]

39 (O you with[32] bare feet, and bulging belly! I saunter along, following you,
    and obediently listen;)[33]

And here Athens itself,[34]—it is a clear forenoon,[35]

Young men, pupils, collect in the gardens of[36] a favorite master, waiting for him,

---

    20. Deleted in black pencil: "of" ; inserted above "of" and "Dea" in "Death" in black pencil: "intended for"

    21. Lower two-thirds of leaf—three or four lines—clipped.

    22. Inserted above "of" and wordspace in black pencil.

    23. "k" inserted in black pencil over "c"

    24. "k" inserted in black pencil over "c"

    25. Deleted in black pencil: "the"

    26. Deleted in black ink: "again"

    27. Cf. "Salut au Monde!", sec. 3, ll. 37–40.

    28. Deleted in black pencil: "arguing,"

    29. Preceding two words inserted above "stioner" in "questioner" and "of" in black ink.

    30. Deleted in black pencil: "this,"

    31. Line deleted in black pencil:

39   (O divine tongue! I too grow silent under your eclenchus,

    32. Preceding two words inserted above wordspace and "bare" and wordspace in black pencil.

    33. Following fifteen lines marked by pencilled bracket at left of each leaf. At left of first line is "Out?" in black pencil. On pp. 39 and 40 is also "out?" in black pencil.

    34. Deleted in black pencil: "of" ; inserted above "[del.] of" in black pencil: "—it is"

    35. Deleted in black pencil: "two thousand years before These States" . Comma not deleted, not printed here.

    36. Deleted in black pencil: "their" ; inserted above "of" and "[del.] their" in black pencil: "[del.] some [ins.] a favorite"

Some, crowded in groups, listen to the harangues or arguments[37] of the elder
    ones,
Elsewhere, single figures, undisturbed by the buzz around them, lean against
    pillars, or within recesses, meditating, or studying from manuscripts,
40 Here and there, couples or trios,[38] young and old, clear-faced, and of perfect
    physique, walk with twined arms, in divine friendship, happy,[39]
Till,[40] beyond, the master appears[41] advancing—his form shows above the
    crowd, a head taller than they,
His gait is erect, calm and dignified—his features are[42] colossal[43]—he is old, yet
    his forehead has no wrinkles,
Wisdom undisturbed, self-respect, fortitude unshaken, are in his expression, his
    personality;
Wait till he speaks—what God's voice is[44] that, sounding from his mouth?
He places virtue and self-denial above all the rest,
He shows to what a glorious height the[45] man may ascend,
41 He shows how independent one may be of fortune—how triumphant over
    fate;
—And here[46] again,[47] this picture tells a story of the Olympic games,
See you, the chariot races? See you, the boxers boxing, and the runners running?
See you, the poets off[48] there reciting their poems and tragedies, to crowds of
    listeners[49]?
—And here, (for I have all kinds,) here is Columbus setting sail from Spain on
    his voyage of discovery;
This again is a series after the great French revolution,
This is the taking of the Bastile, the prison—this is the execution of the king,
42 This is the queen on her way to the scaffold—those are guillotines;
—But this opposite, (abruptly changing,) is a picture from the prison ships of my
    own old city—[50] Brooklyn city[51];

37. Preceding two words inserted above "ues" in "harangues" and "of the" in black pencil.
    38. Deleted in black ink: "of men" ; inserted above "[del.] of men" in black ink: "young and old"
    39. Cf. "PLATO."
    40. Inserted in black pencil: comma.
    41. Deleted in black pencil: comma.
    42. Deleted in black ink: "grand,"
    43. Deleted in black ink: "and regular"
    44. Deleted in black ink: "it then," ; inserted above "then" in black pencil: "that,"
    45. Deleted in black ink: "young men" ; inserted above "ng" in "young" and "m" in "men" in black ink: "man"
    46. Inserted above wordspace in black ink.
    47. Deleted in black ink: "and again, that" ; inserted above "that" in black pencil: "this"
    48. Inserted above wordspace in black pencil.
    49. Preceding comma and four words inserted in black pencil above "and tragedies,"
    50. Preceding four words and dash inserted above wordspace and "of" and "Brook" in "Brooklyn" in black pencil.
    51. Deleted in black pencil: "my own old city;" ; comma corrected to semicolon in black pencil. Holloway (31) cites a line deleted from what became sec. 37 of "Song of Myself" (LG [1855], 42): "What sobers the Brooklyn boy as he looks down the shores of the Wallabout and remembers

And now a merry[52] recruiter passes, with fife and drum, seeking who will join his troop;[53]

And there is an old European martyrdom—See you, the crackling fire—See the agonized contortions of the limbs, and the writhing of the lips! See the head thrown back;[54]

43 And here is a picture of triumph—a General has returned, after a victory—the city turns out to meet him,

And here is a portrait of the English king, Charles the First, (are you a judge of physiognomy?)

—But[55] there is a[56] group on[57]

And here is a funeral procession in the country,

A beloved daughter is[58] carried in her coffin—there follow the parents and neighbors;

44 And here, see you—here walks the Boston truckman, by the side of his string-team—see[59] the three horses, pacing[60] stately,[61] sagacious, one ahead of another;

—And this—whose picture is this?

Who is this, with rapid feet, curious, gay—going up and down Mannahatta, through the streets, along the shores, working his way through the crowds, observant and singing?

And this[62] head of melancholy Dante poet of penalties—poet of hell[63]

But this is a portrait of Shakespear, limner of feudal European[64] lords—[65] (here are my hands, my brothers—one for each of you;)

the prison ships." Since the prison ships moved WW deeply and he mentioned them several times, this line from "Pictures" is not necessarily a source for "Song of Myself."

52. Inserted above wordspace and "re" in "recruiter" in black pencil.

53. Holloway cites a later version from N&F, 15 (Pt. I, #29):

Hear my fife! I am a recruiter,
Come, who will join my troops?

Following verse line clipped.

54. Preceding five words and semicolon inserted in black pencil. Cf. "Poem incarnating the mind" and "Song of Myself," sec. 33, ll. 833–834.

55. Original opening deleted in black pencil: "And" ; inserted above in black pencil: "—But"

56. Deleted in black pencil: "curious"

57. Remainder of line and possibly two other verse lines clipped. In left margin deleted "¶" and "+"

58. Inserted above wordspace in black pencil.

59. Deleted in black ink: "you"

60. Deleted in black pencil: "so"

61. Deleted in black pencil: "so"

62. Inserted and deleted in black pencil: "other Dante"

63. Entire line inserted between lines in black pencil after "But this" (now in following line), but correct location indicated by "¶" and a pointed bracket.

64. Inserted in left margin and above "lords" in black pencil.

65. Deleted in black pencil: "and this of Italian, melancholy Dante, poet of penalties—poet of hell—[preceding six words ins. above "[del.] Dante" and "here are"]"

45 —And there are wood-cutters, cutting down trees in[66] my north-east
   woods—see you, the axe uplifted;
And that is a picture of a fish-market—see there the shad, flat-fish, the large
   halibut,—there a pile of lobsters, and there another of oysters;
Opposite, a drudge[67] in the kitchen, working, tired—and there again the laborer,
   in stained clothes, sour-smelling, sweaty—and again black persons and
   criminals,
And there the frivolous person—and there a crazy enthusiast—and there a
   young man[68] lies sick of a fever, and is[69] soon to die;[70]
46 This, again, is a Spanish bull-fight—see, the animal with bent head, fiercely
   advancing;
And here, see you, a picture of a dream of despair, ([71]—is it unsatisfied love?)[72]
Phantoms,[73] countless, men and women, after death, wandering;
And there are flowers and fruits—see[74] the grapes, decked off with vine-leaves;
But see this!—see where, graceful and stately[75] the young queen-cow walks[76] at
   the head of a the[77] large drove, leading the rest;
And there are building materials—brick, lime, timber, paint, glass, and iron,
   (so[78] now you can build what you like;
47 And this black portrait—this head, huge, frowning, sorrowful,—[79] is
   Lucifer's portrait—the denied God's portrait,
(But I do not deny him—though cast out and rebellious, he is my God as much
   as any;)[80]

    66. Deleted in black pencil: "the" ; inserted above "in" and "[del.] the" and "woods" in
black pencil: "my north-east"
    67. Deleted in black pencil: "is"
    68. Deleted in black pencil: "lying" ; inserted above in black pencil: "lies"
    69. Inserted above wordspace in black pencil.
    70. Holloway (32) cites a later version in N&F, 12 (Pt. I, #16):

We effuse spirituality and immortality,
We put a second brain to the brain,
We put second eyes to the eyes and second ears to the ears,
Then the drudge in the kitchen—then the laborer in his stained clothes—then the black person,
   criminals, barbarians—are no more inferior to the rest.
The frivolous and the blunderer are not to be laughed at as before,
The cheat, the crazy enthusiast, the unsuccessful man, come under the same laws as any.

    71. Deleted in black pencil: "from" ; inserted above "[del.] from" in black pencil: "is it"
    72. Preceding two words and parentheses inserted in black pencil.
    73. Deleted in black pencil: dash; inserted in black pencil: comma.
    74. Deleted in black pencil: "you"
    75. Preceding three words inserted above "where the young" in black ink.
    76. Deleted in black ink: "graceful and stately" . Opposite "stately" , which is at the in-
dented left margin of the verse line, is a pencilled "X"
    77. Inserted above wordspace in black pencil.
    78. Inserted above "n" in "now" in black pencil.
    79. Deleted in black ink: "I think it"
    80. Holloway (32) cites a passage from N&F, 19 (Pt. I, #40):

I am a hell-name and a curse:
Black Lucifer was not dead;

And again the heads of three other Gods—the God[81] Beauty, the God
   Beneficence, and the God Universality, (they also[82] are mine,[83])
And there an Arab caravan, halting—See you, the palm trees, the camels, and
   the stretch of hot sand far away;[84]
[48][85] And there are my woods of Kanada, in winter, with ice and snow,
And here[86] my Oregon hunting-hut,[87] See me emerging from the door,[88]
   bearing my rifle in[89] my hand;[90]
But there, see you, a reminiscence from over sea[91]—a very old Druid, walking
   the woods of Albion;[92]
And there, singular, on ocean waves, downward, buoyant, swift, over the waters,
   an occupied coffin floating,[93]
49 And there, rude grave-mounds in California—and there a path worn in the
   grass,[94]
And there hang painted scenes from my Kansas life—and there from what I saw
   in[95] the Lake Superior region;
And here[96] mechanics work[97] in their shops, in towns—There[98] the carpenter[99]

Or if he was I am his sorrowful, terrible heir;
I am the God of revolt—deathless, sorrowful, vast; whoever oppresses me
I will either destroy him or he shall release me.

Cf. a dropped passage from "The Sleepers" (1855), *LG CRE,* 627.
   81. "G" written over "g"
   82. Inserted above wordspace in black pencil.
   83. Deleted in black pencil: "also" ; undeleted preceding comma not printed here. Holloway
(33) calls attention to "I know a rich capitalist," "81 Clerman," and "Chanting the Square Deific"
(1865). One or two verse lines clipped.
   84. Preceding two words and semicolon inserted above "sand" in black pencil. Redundant
semicolon not printed.
   85. Top third of leaf—one or two verse lines—clipped.
   86. Deleted in black ink: "is an" ; inserted above "[*del.*] an" in black ink: "my"
   87. Deleted in black pencil: "with a hunter" ; inserted above the wordspace in black pen-
cil: "See" ; inserted above "[*del.*] hunter" : "my"
   88. Deleted in black ink: "carrying" ; inserted above "[*del.*] carrying" in black ink: "bearing" ;
deleted in black pencil: "his" ; inserted above "[*del.*] his" in black pencil: "my"
   89. Preceding three words and semicolon inserted above "[*del.*] rifle" and punctuation in
black ink. Redundant semicolon not printed.
   90. Holloway (33) cites "Starting from Paumanok" (1860), probably referring to secs. 1 and
14.
   91. Preceding three words inserted above "iniscence" in "reminiscence" in black pencil.
   92. Deleted: "over sea" ; semicolon not deleted, not printed. Cf. "Old theory started" and
"Salut au Monde!", sec. 6, l. 95.
   93. One line (or possibly a continuation of this line) is clipped. Holloway (33) calls attention
to the same curious image in "I know a rich capitalist."
   94. One line clipped.
   95. Preceding four words inserted in left margin and above "the Lake" in black pencil.
   96. Deleted in black pencil: "are"
   97. Deleted in black pencil: "ing"
   98. Deleted in black pencil: "is"
   99. Deleted in black pencil: "shoving" ; inserted above "[*del.*] shoving" in black pen-
cil: "shoves"

shoves his jack-plane—[1] there the blacksmith stands by his anvil, leaning on[2]
   his upright hammer;
This is Chicago,[3] with railroad depots, with trains arriving and departing—and,
   in their places, immense stores of grain, meat, and lumber;[4]
50 And here are my slave-gangs, South, at work upon the roads, the women
   indifferently with the men—see,[5] how clumsy, hideous, black, pouting,
   grinning, sly, besotted, sensual, shameless;
And this of a scene afar in the North, the[6] arctic—those are the corpses of lost
   explorers, (no chaplets of roses will ever cap[7] their icy graves—but I[8] put a
   chaplet[9] in this poem, for you, you sturdy[10] English heros;)[11]
But here, now,[12] copious—see[13] you, here, the Wonders of eld, the famed Seven,
The Olympian statue this, and this the Artemesian tomb,
Pyramid this, Pharos this, and this the shrine of Diana,
These Babylon's gardens, and this Rhodes' high-lifted marvel,
51 (But for all[14] that, nigh[15], at hand, see[16], a wonder beyond any of[17] them,
Namely, yourself—the form and thoughts of a man,
A man! because all the world, and all the inventions of the world, are but food
   for the body and Soul of one[18] man;)[19]
—And here, while ages have grown upon ages,
Pictures of youths and greybeards, Pagan, and Jew, and Christian,

   1. Cf. "Song of Myself," sec. 15, l. 265.
   2. Deleted in black ink: "an" ; inserted and deleted above in black ink: [illeg.] "a great" "own" ; inserted in black ink above "on" : "his"
   3. Deleted in black ink: "my great city,"
   4. Holloway (34) cites "Mediums" (1860), l. 6.
   5. Inserted in black pencil: comma; deleted in black pencil: "you"
   6. Inserted above wordspace in black ink.
   7. Deleted in black pencil: "those" ; inserted above "[del.] those" in black pencil: "their"
   8. Deleted in black ink: "give" ; inserted above "[del.] give" in black ink: "put" ; deleted in black pencil: "you"
   9. Deleted in black pencil: "here" ; redundant comma not printed; inserted above "plet" in "chaplet" and "[del.] here" and "you" in black pencil: "in this poem, for you,"
   10. Inserted above wordspace in black pencil.
   11. Possibly a tribute to Sir John Franklin (1786–1847) and his men, who disappeared in 1845 while searching for the Northwest Passage. The fourteen-year search for their remains attracted much attention.
   12. Preceding word and comma inserted above wordspace in black pencil.
   13. A mark, possibly deleted, may be a comma.
   14. Inserted and deleted above wordspace in black ink: "of" ; deleted in black ink: "them" ; inserted above "[del.] them" in black pencil: "that"
   15. Original "er" smeared out; comma inserted in black ink; inserted above "er" in "nigher" and "see" in black pencil: "at hand"
   16. Inserted in black pencil: comma; deleted in black pencil: "you" ; redundant comma not printed.
   17. Preceding two words inserted above "nd" in "beyond" and wordspace in black ink.
   18. Preceding twenty-one words inserted on facing verso in black pencil. Text on p. 51, which had been heavily emended, reads: "What is [preceding two words del. in black pencil] because all [ins. in black pencil above deletion] the world, what are all the works of the world in comparison with one man—namely, with you?) [preceding sixteen words del. in black pencil] and all the inventions of the world are but the food of the body and the soul of one man;) [preceding twenty words and punctuation inserted above preceding deletion in black pencil]"
   19. Holloway (34) compares "A Song for Occupations" (1855) and "To You" (1856).

Some retiring to caves—some[20] in schools and piled libraries,
To pore with ceaseless fervor over the myth of the Infinite,
But ever recoiling, Pagan and Jew and Christian,
As from a[21] haze, more dumb and thick than[22] vapor above the hot sea;
52 —And here now, (for all varieties, I say, hang in this little house,)
A[23] string of[24] my Iroquois,[25] aborigines—see you, where they march in single
    file, without noise, very cautious,[26] through passages in the old[27] woods;[28]
                                    Picture[29]
Of[30] a husking-frolic in the West—see you, the large rude[31] barn—see you,
    young and old, laughing and joking,[32] as they husk the ears of corn;[33]
And there in a city, a stormy political meeting—a torch-light procession—
    candidates avowing themselves to the people;[34]
[53][35] And here is the Lascar I noticed once in Asia—here he remains still,
    pouring money into the sea, as an offering to demons, for favor;[36]
And there, in the midst of a group, a quell'd revolted slave, cowering,
See you, the hand-cuffs, the hopple, and the blood-stain'd cowhide;[37]
And there hang[38], side by side, certain close[39] comrades of mine—[40] a Broadway
    stage-driver,[41] a lumberman of Maine, and[42] a deck-hand of[43] a Mississippi
    steamboat;

20. Deleted by smearing: "to"
21. Deleted in black pencil: "thick"
22. Deleted in black ink: "ever rose" ; inserted in black ink, deleted in black pencil: "any
rising" ; inserted and deleted above "than" in black pencil: "ever rose" ; deleted in black pen-
cil: "from" ; inserted above "the" and wordspace in black pencil: "vapor above"
23. Deleted in black pencil: "cautious"
24. Deleted in black pencil: "the" ; inserted above "[del.] the" in black pencil: "my"
25. Deleted in black pencil: "the"
26. Preceding two words and comma inserted in black ink above "ise" in "noise" and
"thro" in "through"
27. Inserted above wordspace in black pencil.
28. Holloway (34) compares "Our Old Feuillage" (1860), ll. 48–52.
29. Inscribed in pencil in middle of leaf in line with "old woods"
30. Original beginning deleted in black pencil: "And here" ; inserted above wordspace in
black pencil: "Of"
31. Deleted in black ink: "room" . Two superimposed crosses in left margin opposite "room"
32. Deleted in black pencil: "husking" ; inserted above wordspace and "[del.] husking"
and "corn" in blue crayon: "as they husk the ears of"
33. Holloway (35) compares "Song of Myself" (1855), sec. 33, l. 755.
34. One verse line clipped from bottom of leaf.
35. One verse line and page number clipped from top of leaf.
36. WW notes this custom in a report of a conversation about China dated June 23, 1857.
See "June 23d '57."
37. Holloway points out (35) that this is developed in "Song of Myself," sec. 33, ll. 838–843.
Note, however, the earlier and different attitude towards slaves (50).
38. Corrected from "hand"
39. Inserted above wordspace in black pencil.
40. Deleted in black pencil: "the" ; inserted above "[del.] the" in black pencil: "a"
41. Deleted in black pencil: "the" ; inserted above "[del.] the" in black pencil: "a"
42. Inserted above wordspace in black ink. Deleted in black pencil: "the" ; inserted above
"[del.] the" in black pencil: "a"
43. Deleted in black pencil: "the" ; inserted above "[del.] the" in black pencil: "a"

54 And again[44] the young man of Mannahatta, the celebrated rough,[45]
([46] The[47] one I love well[48]—let others sing whom they may—him I sing, for a
    thousand years[49]!)
And there a historic piece—see you, where Thomas Jefferson[50] of Virginia sits
    reading Rousseau, the Swiss, and[51] compiling the Declaration of
    Independence, the American compact;
And there, tall and slender, stands[52] is Ralph Waldo Emerson, of New
    England,[53] at the lecturer's desk lecturing,[54]
And there is my Congress in session in the Capitol—there are my two Houses[55]
    in session;[56]
And here, behold[57] two war-ships saluting each other—behold the smoke,[58]
    bulging, spreading in round clouds from the guns sometimes hiding the ships;
55 And there, on the level banks of the James river, in Virginia,[59] stand the
    mansions of the[60] planters;
And here an old black man, stone-blind,[61] with a placard on his hat, sits low at
    the corner, of a street,[62] begging, humming hymn-tunes[63] nasally all day to
    himself and receiving[64] small gifts;[65]
And this, out at sea, is a signal-bell—see you,[66] where it is built on a reef, and
    ever dolefully keeps tolling, to warn mariners;

44. Deleted in black pencil: "a" ; inserted above "[*del.*] a" in black pencil: "the"
45. Holloway (35) points out "Song of Myself" (1855), sec. 24, l. 497: "Walt Whitman, an American, one of the roughs, a kosmos" (1855, p. 29).
46. Original beginning deleted in black pencil: "Here" ; inserted and deleted above in black pencil: "He" "Him"
47. Capital "T" written in black pencil over lowercase.
48. Deleted in black pencil: "here" ; redundant dash not deleted, not printed; inserted above "[*del.*] here" and "him I sing" in black pencil: "well—let others sing whom they may—"
49. Semicolon deleted in black pencil; exclamation point inserted in black pencil; parentheses inserted in black pencil.
50. Inserted above wordspace and "sits" in black pencil: "[*del.*] of of Virginia"
51. Deleted in black pencil: "then"
52. Preceding four words inserted above "there . . . Waldo" in black pencil.
53. Deleted in black pencil: "standing up," ; inserted in blue crayon and deleted above "[*del.*] standing up," in black pencil: "tall and slender"
54. Entire line inscribed in black pencil on facing verso. Location in text indicated by pointing fist and "X" in left margin of p. 54.
55. Capitalized in black ink.
56. One or two verse lines clipped.
57. Inserted above wordspace in black ink; deleted in black pencil: [*illeg.*]
58. Deleted in black ink: "rising" ; inserted above "[*del.*] rising" in black ink: "spreading" ; inserted above "smoke" in black pencil: "bulging"
59. Preceding two words inserted above wordspace and "stand" in black pencil.
60. Deleted in black pencil: "Virginia"
61. Deleted in black pencil: "is sitting" ; inserted above "blind . . . low" in black pencil: "with a placard on his hat, sits [*all in blue crayon*]"
62. Preceding three words and comma inserted above "corner" in black ink.
63. Inserted above wordspace and "nasally" in black pencil.
64. Deleted in black pencil: "the"
65. Preceding four words inserted above "lf" in "himself;" and space at end of line in blue crayon. Cf. "Song of Myself," sec. 37, ll. 957–958.
66. Deleted in brown (?) ink: "how" ; inserted above "[*del.*] how" in brown (?) ink: "where"

And this picture[67] shows what once happened in one of Napoleon's[68] greatest
  battles,
(The tale was conveyed to me by an old French soldier,)[69]
In the height of the roar and carnage of the battle, all of a sudden, from some
  unaccountable cause, the whole fury of the opposing armies[70] subsided—there
  was a perfect calm,
56 It lasted almost a minute—not a gun was fired—all was petrified,
It was more solemn and awful than all[71] the[72] roar and slaughter;
—And here, (for still I name them as they come,) here are my timber-towers,
  guiding logs down a stream in the North;
And here a glimpse of my treeless llanos,[73] where they skirt the Colorado, and
  sweep for a thousand miles on either side of the Rocky mountains;[74]
57 And there, on the whaling ground, in[75] the Pacific, is a sailor, perched at the
  top-mast head, on the look out,
(You can almost hear him crying[76] out, *There-e-'s white water,*—or *The-e-e-re-'s*
  black skin;[77]
But here, (look you well,) see here[78] the phallic choice of America, a full-sized
  man or woman—a natural, well-trained man or woman
(The phallic choice of America leaves the finesse of cities, and all the returns of
  commerce or agriculture,[79] and the magnitude of geography, and achievements
  of literature and art, and all the shows of exterior victory, to enjoy the
  breeding of full-sized men, or one full-sized man or woman, unconquerable
  and simple;)
{58}[80]—For all[81] those have I in[82] a round house hanging—such pictures have
  I—and they are but little,

67. Deleted in black ink: "tells" ; inserted above "[*del.*] tells" in brown (?) ink: "shows"
68. Inserted above "n's" in "Napoleon's" and "battle" in black ink: "great" ; added in black
ink: "est"
69. Cf. the similar narrative device of an old sailor used to tell the story of the battle between
the *Bonhomme Richard* and the *Serapis* in "Song of Myself," sec. 35, l. 899.
70. Inserted in space after "opposing" in black ink.
71. Inserted at left in black pencil.
72. Deleted in black pencil: "following"
73. There seems to be a printed lowercase "s" in pencil before this word.
74. One verse line clipped.
75. Pencilled "X" in left margin opposite the following words, which begin the run-over of
the line.
76. Inserted above "y" in "crying" in black ink: "ing"
77. Holloway (36) compares a passage on whaling in "A Song of Joys" (1860), ll. 73–85,
which he thinks must have come from WW's reading Melville. WW had reviewed *Omoo* in 1847,
but there were plenty of whalemen on Long Island. See, for example, "The Whale," which Bucke
dates 1856. Fist in left margin, pointing to next line, pencilled parenthesis before first word and
direction above line: "take this out a ¶ by itself" presumably referring to the two following lines.
78. Inserted above wordspace in black ink.
79. Deleted in black ink: "or" ; inserted above "[*del.*] or" in black ink: "and"
80. Top five-sixths of leaf clipped.
81. Deleted in black pencil: "such" ; inserted above "[*del.*] such" in black pencil: "those"
82. Deleted in black pencil: "the" ; inserted above "[*del.*} the" in black pencil: "a"

59 For wherever I have been, has afforded me[83] superb pictures,

And whatever I have heard has given me[84] perfect pictures,

And every hour of the day and night has given deposited with[85] me[86] copious
   pictures,

And every rod of land or sea[87] affords me, as long as I live,[88] inimitable pictures.

83. Deleted in black pencil: "such"; inserted above "[*del.*] such" in black pencil: "superb"

84. Deleted in black pencil: "its" ; inserted above "[*del.*] its" in black pencil: "perfect"

85. Preceding two words inserted in blue crayon above "has given" and wordspace.

86. Deleted in black pencil: "its" ; inserted above "[*del.*] its" in black pencil: "copious"

87. Deleted by smearing ink: "Yet" ; inserted in black ink and deleted above "aff" of "affords"
in black pencil: "still"

88. Preceding four words inserted above "me" and "inimit" in "inimitable" in black pencil.

And There Is the Meteor-Shower.

Manuscript in LC (Feinberg #705). Inscribed in black ink on two scraps of pink wove paper, possibly a wrapper used for *LG* (1855), pasted together, totalling 5⅞" x 4¹³/₁₆". On verso are draft lines of "Poem of the Farmer." On an adjoining scrap, in another hand: "notes & fragments Leaves of Grass 1st drafts p. 51." Printed, as the note indicates, *N&F,* 51–52 (Pt. I, #184; *CW*, III, 183). Bucke also prints a similar prose passage at the beginning, "The shower of meteors" and a final line no longer extant in the MS, which relates it to "Pictures." Bucke's note says the MS is "very early" and dates it in the "forties or fifties," but the paper suggests a date of ca. 1856. For another reference to the same meteor shower see "Other names of Venus." (Gene Edward Veith, Jr.)

And there is the[1] meteor-shower, wondrous and dazzling,[2] the 12th–13th Elev-
    enth Month, year 58 of The States[3] between midnight and morning.[4]
See you! the[5] spectacle of the meteors overhead.—[6]
See you![7] myriads, in all directions, some[8] with long shiny trains,[9]
Some rolling over each other like water poured out and falling—
    leaping, silent, white apparitions of the sky.
Such have I in the round house hanging—such pictures name I
    and they are but little[10]

1. Deleted: "wondrous"
2. Deleted: "12th night of" ; inserted and deleted: "on" ; inserted: "the" . All above "[*del.*] 12th"
3. WW is dating from 1776. The meteor shower occurred in November, 1833. See "The shower of meteors." As Bucke notes, WW was then 14½ years old. Deleted new line: "See you, (for two more than two [*preceding three words ins.*] hours"
4. Following new line indicated by paragraph symbol with a lighter-nibbed pen. Inserted above "the" : "See you!"
5. Deleted: "dazzling"
6. Inserted, brought down by line.
7. "See" added at left with a lighter-nibbed pen to set off a new line. "you!" inserted.
8. End of first scrap.
9. New line indicated by paragraph symbol. Lowercase "some" capitalized.
10. Final line from *N&F*. The MS has been trimmed and mounted.

Poem of the Drum.

Manuscript not found. Text from *N&F,* 179 (Pt. IV, #135; *CW,* X, 35).

Poem of the Drum. Cannot a poem be written that shall be alive with the stirring and beating of the drum? Calling people up? A reveille to ? ?

Sea-Cabbage.

Manuscript not found. Text from *N&F,* 174 (Pt. IV, #97; *CW,* X, 27). Notes for a poem, possibly "There Was a Child Went Forth" (1855), l. 38, or "As I Ebb'd with the Ocean of Life" (1860), ll. 9–13, but just as possibly for a separate, unwritten poem. No date can be assigned.

Sea-cabbage; salt hay; sea-rushes; ooze—sea-ooze; gluten—sea-gluten; sea-scum; spawn; surf; beach; salt-perfume; mud; sound of walking barefoot ankle deep in the edge of the water by the sea.

Poem of Names.

Manuscript in Virginia. Inscribed in pencil on white laid scrap, 2¾″ x 4⅞″. Cable stitch water mark. See "Poem of Young Men," which is on the same paper. Cf. the lists of distinguished characters, which WW drew up in his last years, e.g. "La Fayette Aaron Burr." The writing is that of the 1850s.

Poem of Names/
bringing in all persons names, men's and women's, worthy to be commemorated.

Living Pictures.

Manuscript in Virginia. Inscribed in black pencil on blue laid paper, approx. 7⅝" x 6". Cancelled by slash. On verso is "a cluster of poems." The text suggests "A Song for Occupations" (1855). The writing also suggests an early date. For example, WW uses the old long "s" in "less." First printed in *N&F,* 177 (Pt. IV, #116; *CW,* X, 31).

LIVING[1] PICTURES
Nowhere,[2] in the known world, can so many, and such beautiful living[3]

AMERICA
Here[4] different from any other country in the world all forms of practical[5] labour is[6] recognized as honorable.—The man who tends the President's horses, not one whit less a man than the President.—THE healthy, fine-formed girl who[7] waits upon the[8] wealthy lady, not less than the wealthy lady.—

HE who carries bricks & mortar[9] to the mason, not less than the mason,

THE MASON who lays the bricks, not one tittle less than the builder, who[10] employs him,

THE architect &[11] BUILDER of the house, no less than

1. Preceded by deleted "Life"
2. Preceded by deleted "Evening"
3. Deleted: "Pictures be seen as in the United States!"
4. Deleted: "labour is"
5. Preceding four words inserted above "the world labour"
6. Deleted: "mainly"
7. Deleted: "tends"
8. Deleted: "great"
9. Preceding two words inserted.
10. Deleted: "engages"
11. Preceding two words inserted above "BUILDER"

Something That Presents.

Manuscript not found. Text from *N&F,* 117 (Pt. III, #112; *CW,* IX, 135). The text is suggestive of "Song of Myself," sec. 43. Since this was a Bucke MS, it probably dates from before 1860.

Something that presents the sentiment of the Druid walking in the woods . . . of the Indian pow-wow . . . of the Sacramental supper . . . of the Grecian religious rites.

Write a New Burial Service.

Manuscript not found. Text from *N&F,* 56 (Pt. II, #6; *CW,* IX, 4). The liturgical intention suggests the 1850s.

Write a new burial service. A book of new things.

National Hymns.

Manuscript in Duke (14, #36). Inscribed in black pencil on white wove scrap of pocket ledger paper, 1¼" x 3⅜" (see "Poem L'Envoy"). Horizontal blue rules ⅛" apart and usual vertical red rules. The writing indicates a date before 1860. First printed *CW*, III, 268.

National hymns,[1] real American music,
The master's words, arrogant, fluent, final severe.—

1. Deleted: "the"

Poem of Sadness.

Manuscript in Duke (14, #36). Inscribed in black pencil on white wove paper, approx. 3⁷/₁₆″ x 6¾″. The writing and the fact that it was a Bucke MS indicate a date before 1860. First printed *N&F,* 170 (Pt. IV, #75; *CW,* X, 20), with addition of "Passage in every Lecture," which may have been cut off by a dealer.

Poem of Sadness Sorrow[1]

just a list string[2] merely
Sobs of the tempest, sobs of the voice

1. Written below "Sadness" . Below is deleted: "Sobbing"
2. Written under "list"

To the English.

Manuscript in Duke (15, #37). Inscribed in black pencil on flimsy, white wove scrap approx. 2¼" x 4". The writing indicates a date before 1860. The text is suggestive of "Salut au Monde!" (1856).

To the English and the French of Canada—to the Scotch, the Irish, the German and the Scandinavian

Poem of the Trainer.

Manuscript not found. Text from *N&F*, 175 (Pt. IV, #99; *CW*, X, 28). Since this is a Bucke MS, the date is probably before 1860.

Poem of the Trainer.

Poem (Idea).

Manuscript not found. Text from *N&F,* 173 (Pt. IV, #89; *CW,* X, 25). First printed by Bucke in "Notes on the Text of Leaves of Grass," *Conservator,* 7 (February, 1897), 185. Since this was a Bucke MS, the date is probably before 1860.

Poem (idea). "To struggle is not to suffer."
Bold and strong invocation of suffering — to try how much one can stand.
Overture — a long list of words — the sentiment of suffering, oppression, despair, anguish.
Collect (rapidly present) terrible scenes of suffering.
"Then man is a God." Then he walks over all.

Poemet Leaf.

Manuscript in Duke (17, #40). Inscribed in black ink on flimsy, white wove scrap, approx. 4¼" x 2⅝", cut or torn along all edges. First fifteen terms in two columns, the first ending with "Hymn," the second with "Capricea," both closed by a rule; others in single column. The sequence of sonnet terms is also closed by a rule. A red check mark opposite the last three entries is probably Bucke's to indicate that they had been copied. It seems that WW was playing with words rather than titles. First printed by Bucke in "Notes on the Text of Leaves of Grass," *Conservator,* 7 (February, 1897), 185, later in *N&F,* 177 (Pt. IV, #121; *CW,* X, 33). Since it was a Bucke MS, the date is probably before 1860.

Poemet   Leaf   Chant   Song   Poem   Psalm   Hymn/   warble   carol   cav-
    atina   ballad   Thought   Caprices   Fantasia   Capricea/
Sonnet-Trio   Sonnet-Quinto   Sonnet-Duo/
Melange   Canticles.   Songlet

Indian Summer.

Manuscript not found. Text from *N&F,* 169 (Pt. IV, #62; *CW,* X, 17). A note for one of a number of projected special editions or versions of *LG.* In *CW,* Bucke substituted italics for quotation marks. Since it was a Bucke MS, this probably was written before 1860.

Indian Summer (in "Leaves for the Sick")—a jaunt, a long, slow, easy ramble—(the idea of ease and of being firmly and friendlily supported)—the idea of . . .

For Dropping.

Manuscript not found. Text from *N&F,* 104 (Pt. III, #72; *CW,* IX, 109). Since this was a Bucke MS, it is likely to date before 1860.

For dropping. Poem—embodying the sentiment of perfect happiness, *in myself* body and soul being all right—regardless of whatever may happen.

Poem of the Universalities.

Manuscript not found. Text from *N&F,* 142 (Pt. IV, #183; *CW,* IX, 190). The blank after "Love is universal among" is filled by "[men]" in *N&F,* by "men" in *CW.* Since this was a Bucke MS, the date is probably before 1860.

Poem of the Universalities. Poem of the Universal likenesses of all men—humanity. Though the times, climes, differ, men do not so much differ. There *is* a universal language. What is heroic is universal among men. Love is universal among   . Liberty is—justice is—the hatred of meanness is—etc.

Poem of the Longings of Friendship. Pictures of Friendship—the hankering for friends—the memory of only a look—the boy lingering and waiting.

In the West.

Manuscript not found. Text from *N&F,* 142 (Pt. III, #184; *CW,* IX, 190). Since it was a Bucke MS, this probably was written before 1860. See "Poem L'Envoy" for further Western poems.

In the West—a vision—? Poem of vision of future. Depicting the West a hundred years from now—two hundred years—five hundred years. (This ought to be a splendid part of the poem) (?poem of Ohio?)—it ought to lay in the colors and draw the outlines with a large, free and bold hand.

—Poem of Ohio.

Manuscript in Duke (15, #37). Inscribed in black ink on soft-textured, tan wove paper, approx. 5⁵/₁₆″ x 4⁵/₁₆″. Entries in column, divided by lines across the leaf, as in "Poem of Wisconsin." See "Poem L'Envoy" for further Western poems. This probably was written before 1860. First printed by Bucke in "Notes on the Text of Leaves of Grass," *Conservator,* 7 (February, 1897), 185.

—Poem of Ohio, Kentucky,
          Indiana and Illinois/
?Poem of Ohio./
?Poem of Kentucky./
?Poem of Illinois—&c &c./
?Poem of Massachusetts/

                    Prairie Poem/

The Carpenter's Poem./
Poem of Brooklyn.

Poem of Language.

Manuscript in Duke (15, #37). Inscribed in black ink on soft, tan wove paper. (Cf. "Poem of Fruits & Flowers" and "?Poem of The Husband.") Approx. 4″ x 5″. The writing and the fact that it was a Bucke MS suggest Whitman wrote this before 1860. First printed in *N&F,* 179 (Pt. IV, #133; *CW,* X, 35).

Poem of Language/

How curious —/
The immense variety of languages—
—The points where they differ are not near as[1] remarkable as where they resemble—all resemble[2]/
The simple sounds—/
Music

---

1. Deleted: "numerous" ; inserted above: "remarkable"
2. Preceding ten words in hanging indentation.

Secrets.—Secreta.

Manuscript in Duke (15, #38). Inscribed in black ink on flimsy white wove scrap, approx. 3½″ x 6¼″. Pointing hand at left of first entry. Rules across leaf. Since it was a Bucke MS, the date is probably before 1860. First printed in Bucke's "Notes on the Text of Leaves of Grass," *Conservator,* 7 (February, 1897), 185.

Secrets.—Secreta

? *theme for an immense poem*—collecting, in running list, all the things done in secret./

Poem
    Vocabularium
? names—terms—phrases—glossary—list/

—Poem of a Proud.

Manuscript in Duke (14, #36). Inscribed in black ink on yellow wove paper, approx. 2¼″ x 4¾″. (Cf. *"Poem (bequeathing"* and "Poem of the Devil.") "Bully for you, Manhattan" is a separate entry. Although there is a MS on yellow paper as late as 1879 (*"Sunday '79"*), most of the yellow paper MS appear from the writing and subject to be early. Bowers, xli*n*13, reports having seen yellow wrapper stock from *LG* (1855). See also "Old theory started." The writing, the paper and the fact that it was a Bucke MS indicate that this was written before 1860. First printed *N&F,* 172 (Pt. IV, #83; *CW,* X, 22).

—Poem of a proud, daring joyous expression—for Manhattan island!
Bully for you, Manhattan!

Banjo Poem.

Manuscript in Duke (15, #38). Inscribed in black ink on a coarse-textured, white wove scrap, approx. 1⅛″ x 2⅞″. At about the time of this note, WW declared that the banjo should be conspicuously used in American opera ("Memorials," 1854–1859?).

Banjo Poem

Poem for of My Adherence.

Manuscript in Pennsylvania. Inscribed in black ink on irregularly brownish (faded?) wove scrap, 5¼" x 4¼". The phrase "the good old cause" was used by both Milton and Wordsworth. First printed *N&F,* 55 (Pt. II, #5; *CW,* IX, 4). Since it was a Bucke MS, the date is probably before 1860.

Poem for of my adherence of adherence to[1] *the good old cause of* /
the "good old cause" is that in all its diversities, in all lands, at all times, under all circumstances, —which promulges liberty, justice, the Cause of the people as against infidels and tyrants/[2]
Poem of the People/
represent the People, so copious so simple, so fierce, so frivilous

1. The preceding four alternate readings are inserted one above the other above "for the"
2. Rule across leaf.

Poem of Poets.

Manuscript in Duke (14, #36). Inscribed in black pencil on a soft, tan wove scrap, approx. 2⅛″ x 5⅞″ (Cf. "Poem of Fruits & Flowers.") The writing and the fact that it was a Bucke MS indicate this was written before 1860. First printed N&F, 169 (Pt. IV, #67; CW, X, 18).

Poem of Poets (now?)[1] in all lands/
describing—all the different phases of the expression of the poetical sentiment in all lands

1. Question mark above word in MS.

Poem as in Visions.

Manuscript in Duke (15, #37). Inscribed in black ink on blue laid paper, approx. 7¼" x 5⅝". On the same sheet are pasted two clippings describing Puget Sound, labelled "2" and "3" in the right margins. Neither seems related to the MS text. Since it was a Bucke MS, this probably was written before 1860. First printed *N&F,* 167 (Pt. IV, #53; *CW,* X, 15).

Poem

As in Visions of——at night—
All sorts of fancies running through the head

Poem Of Young Men.

Manuscript in Duke (15, #38). Inscribed in black pencil on white laid scrap, approx. 2⅝" x 4¹⁵/₁₆", with "cable-knit" pattern in texture (cf. *"Poem* of Names"). The "flirt," presumably a vessel cruising in Southeast Asian waters, has not been identified. The writing and the fact that this was a Bucke MS suggest that this was written before 1860. First printed in Bucke's "Notes on the Text of Leaves of Grass," *Conservator,* 7 (February, 1897), 185.

Poem of Young Men/
The Sumatra young man, curious, handsome, manly, gentle, that
    came aboard "the flirt"/
Young men in all cities

? Poem of The Husband.

Manuscript in Duke (15, #38). Inscribed in black ink on tan, soft-textured wove scrap, approx. 3⁷/₁₆″ x 5⅝″ (cf. "Poem of Language"). Line drawn almost entirely across leaf at top; text in column. The text may relate to "Children of Adam." The writing is not dateable (other than before 1873), but the fact that this was a Bucke MS suggests WW wrote it before 1860. First published N&F, 165 (Pt. IV, #42; CW, X, 11).

?Poem of The Husband
?Poem of The Wife.—
?Poem of The Husband and The Wife.—
?Poem of Marriage

Poem of Fruits & Flowers.

Manuscript in Duke (15, #37). Inscribed in black ink on soft tan, wove paper (cf. "Poem of Language"), approx. 2¹¹/₁₆″ x 5⅞″. Entries separated by rules completely across leaf. The writing and the fact that it was a Bucke MS suggest this was written before 1860. First printed N&F, 171 (Pt. IV, #80; CW, X, 21).

Poem of Fruits &¹ Flowers./
Poem, of Forms,² Sounds, Colors, Tastes and³ Perfumes./
Poem of (?Laughter Joy)⁴

1. Inserted above wordspace between "Fruits" and "Flowers"
2. Inserted above "Sou" in "Sounds"
3. Preceding two words inserted above "Colors,"
4. "Joy" written above "au" in "Laughter)"

Poem of Wisconsin.

Manuscript in Duke (15, #37). Inscribed in black ink on white laid paper, approx. $8^5/_{16}''$ x $3^{15}/_{16}''$. Entries in column separated by rules across leaf. Red ink check mark at upper right by Bucke. See "Poem L'Envoy" for other Western poems. For similar paper see "Poem of Architecture." First printed by Bucke in "Notes on the Text of Leaves of Grass," *Conservator,* 7 (February, 1897), 185. This probably was written before 1860.

Poem of Wisconsin/
Poem of Missouri/
Poem of Texas/
Poem of Lake Superior/
Poem of the[1] Rifle./

for Western Edition/[2]

1. Deleted: "Hunter"
2. In smaller writing to the right of leaf.

In a Poem.

Manuscript in Duke (14, #36). Inscribed in black ink on white laid paper with conspicuous vertical lines in texture, 1¼" x 6". The writing suggests that this was written before 1860. First printed *N&F,* 169 (Pt. IV, #66; *CW,* X, 18).

In a poem make the thought of *"What will be the result of this years hence?"*

Poem? The Cruise.

Manuscript in Duke (15, #38). Inscribed in black ink on flimsy, white wove scrap, approx. 2¼″ x 3¼″. Since this was a Bucke MS, this probably was written before 1860. First printed in Bucke's "Notes on the Text of Leaves of Grass," *Conservator,* 7 (February, 1897), 185.

Poem?
The Cruise
? A Cruise

Poem Ante-Dating.

Manuscript in Duke (15, #38). Inscribed in black ink on white laid paper with conspicuous vertical lines in texture, approx. 2″ x 6″. The writing and the fact that it was a Bucke MS suggest this was written before 1860. First printed *N&F*, 169 (Pt. IV, #68; *CW*, X, 19).

Poem ante-dating, anticipating, prophecying   great results—those that will be likely to exist a hundred years hence

(In Poem of Existence.

Manuscript in Duke (13, #22). Inscribed in black ink on two faded, white wove leaves, approx. 6¼″ x 9″ each. The writing suggests an early date, possibly before 1860. Triggs prints it (*CW,* III) in a more conventionally poetic layout. The actual layout, which is here followed as closely as practicable, suggests a more proselike quality. First printed *CW,* III, 263–264.

(in Poem of Existence[1]
We call[2] one the past, and we call another the future
But both are alike the present/
It is not the past, though we call it so,—nor[3] the future,
        though we call it so,[4]
All the while it is the present only—[5] both future and past are
        the present only.—/

The curious realities now everywhere—on the surface of the
earth,—in the interior of the earth
        What is it? Is it liquid fire? Is it fire? Are there
            living creatures in that[6] solid?—[7]Is there not
            toward the core, some vast strange stifling vacuum?
            —Is there any thing in that vacuum? Any[8] kind of
            curious flying or floating life with its nature[9]
            fitted?—
The existences on the innumerable stars, with their varied
degrees of perfection, climate, swiftness

1. At upper left, line curving at left and below in addition to single parenthesis.
2. Deleted: "it" ; inserted above: "one"
3. Beginning of new line deleted: "And it is not"
4. Beginning of new line deleted: "It is" ; inserted and deleted: "Really to at," above the deletion and "all"
5. Deleted: "that" ; inserted following the deletion: "both" ; deleted: "pa" on the line following.
6. Preceding six words written above "fire . . . fire"
7. Deleted: "Is it some"
8. Deleted: "living thing" ; inserted above: "kind of curious" and "flying or floating life" above "with its na" in "nature"
9. Deleted: final "s"

—Some probably are but forming,[10] not so advanced as the
earth—(Some are no doubt more advanced—[11]

There[12] is intercommunion,[13]
    One sphere[14] cannot know another sphere,[15]
        (Communion of[16] life is with life only, and of what[17] is after
           life[18]
        (Each sphere knows itself only, and[19] cannot commune beyond
           itself,[20]
        Life communes only with life,
        Whatever it is that follows death,

10. Deleted: "—others"
11. Beginning of new line deleted: "(I should not wonder if the"
12. Deleted: "The" "Then" ; "there" capitalized.
13. Beginning of new line deleted: "Nothing can"
14. Deleted: "ch[?]"
15. Beginning of new line deleted: "The" ; inserted: curved line enclosing the three MS lines
of the phrase; "communion" capitalized.
16. Inserted and deleted: "what we call life" above "of life"
17. Deleted: "is call"
18. Beginning of new line deleted: "Each I think" . At some point a curved line was drawn
to left of this false start and the succeeding line.
19. Deleted: "h"
20. Beginning of new line deleted: "Wh"

Poem of the Farmer.

Manuscript in LC (Feinberg #705). In black ink on two irregular, white wove scraps pasted together. On verso: "and there is the wondrous." No date can be assigned, but the "Poem of——" formula suggests a date before 1860.

Poem of the Farmer[1]

whale—(the sperm whale[2]

1. Entry cancelled by slant line.
2. On second scrap. A good deal has been trimmed off at left.

A Poem Theme.

Manuscript in Duke (36, #28). Inscribed in black ink on bright green, wove paper, approx. 4⁵/₁₆″ x 5″. Rules across leaf. Pasted on the leaf is a clipping of a quotation attributed to Aristotle which observes that if people who had always lived underground, in dwellings however splendid, were allowed to see the sky, sun and stars they "would believe that there were gods, and these, so great things, are their works." The green paper is brighter than the wrapper stock for *LG* (1885). Since it was a Bucke MS, this probably was written before 1860. First printed in *N&F*, 175 (Pt. IV, #101; *CW*, X, 28), and incompletely in *N&F*, 149, and *CW*, IX, 202.

A[1] Poem theme Be happy/
Going forth, seeing all the beautiful perfect things—/

1. Deleted: "whole"

Poem (Bequeathing.

Manuscript in Duke (14, #36). Inscribed in black ink on yellow wove paper, approx. 4⅜″ x 6⅛″. (Cf. "—Poem of a proud.") The italicized words are in three lines, indented to make room for a pointing hand, which was evidently written first. The writing and the fact that it was a Bucke MS suggest this was written before 1860. First printed *N&F,* 175 (Pt. IV, #102; *CW,* X, 28).

Poem (bequeathing to others a charge) what poems are wanted—including a long list culled from the MS scraps.—

Poem of Kisses.

Manuscript in Virginia (Barrett). Inscribed in black ink on a faded white wove scrap, 1⅞" x 3¾". The sort of topic and the fact that it was a Bucke MS suggest WW wrote this before 1860. First printed in *N&F,* 174 (Pt. IV, #96; *CW,* X, 27).

Poem of Kisses—the kisses of love —of death—of betrayal—

In Poem.

Manuscript in Virginia (Barrett). Inscribed on small, white wove scrap. The MS probably relates to "Poem of Kisses." The writing indicates a date before 1860.

In Poem Song[1] of kisses

The hot[2] kiss of the new husband to the bride —and the kiss of the bride to the husband

1. As alternative above "Poem"
2. Inserted in wordspace between "The" and "kiss"

Poem of the Black Person.

Manuscript in Duke (14, #36). Inscribed in black ink on white laid paper, 7¾" x 6¼", torn along right edge. The final seventeen words, after the single parenthesis, are written in hanging indentation. The small writing and the fact that it was a Bucke MS suggest WW wrote this before 1860. First printed on Bucke, "Notes on the Text of Leaves of Grass," *Conservator,* 7 (February, 1897), 185.

Poem of the Black person

infuse the sentiment of a sweeping, surrounding, shielding, protection of the blacks——their passiveness—their character of sudden fits—the abstracted fit— (the three picturesque blacks in the men's cabin in the Fulton ferry boat—their costumes—dinner-kettles/ describe them in the poem.—

Poem, As in.

Manuscript in Duke (15, #38). Inscribed in black ink on white wove scrap, approx. 3″ x 5⅝″. The left margin is irregularly indented. The text probably relates to "By Blue Ontario's Shore" (1856).

Poem, as in a rapt and prophetic vision—[1] intimating—*the Future* of America[2]

1. Deleted: "depic"
2. Preceding two words written in two lines at right below *"the Future"*

The States.

Manuscript in Duke (9, #20V). Inscribed in black pencil in column on white wove scrap, approx. 6″ x 3⁷/₁₆″. On recto an early draft for "In Paths Untrodden" (1859). Since it was a Bucke MS the date is probably in the 1850s. First printed in Bucke, "Notes on the Text of Leaves of Grass," *Conservator,* 7 (February, 1897), 185.

The States
Praries[1]   Prairie Psalms? (Psalms ?(praise)[2]   Prairie Spaces   Prairie Babes
Prairie Daughters? sons[3]   ? Prairie Oaks   ([4]commence with a proto[5] with the word
"Perennial/ Babes of The States/ Prairie Airs   American Chants. {Amer-
ican}[6] Chorus

1. Preceded by a pointing hand.
2. "?(praise)" written below "(Psalms" . Possibly the last three words are meant to be can-celled by a large X somewhat above them.
3. Written below preceding words.
4. Large curved line running slightly under "Perennial"
5. The dictionary definitions of the prefix "prot, proto" illuminate WW's concept of poetry as organic and rational by adding suggestions of the primitive, basic, ancestral. Cf. "Proto-Leaf."
6. WW used ditto marks.

Whole Poem—Poem of Insects?

Manuscript in Duke (15, #37). Inscribed in black ink on green wove paper, approx. 3⅜″ x 4⅞″. Rules across leaf. A John Arkhurst, taxidermist, is listed at 9½ Prospect in Brooklyn directories, 1854–1857, 1862–1866. See "Rel ?outset" and "The scope of government." for further notes for this poem. Since the paper is probably wrapper stock for *LG* (1855), the date is probably between 1855 and 1857. First printed in *N&F,* 173 (Pt. IV, #91; *CW,* X, 25).

Whole poem
—Poem of Insects? /
Get from Mr. Arkhurst the
names of all insects—/
interweave a train of thought
suitable—also trains of words/

A Volume—(Dramatic Machinery.

Manuscript in Duke (17, #40). Inscribed in black pencil on pink wove paper, approx. 4¼″ x 5¼″. "Alb" is possibly WW's formation from the ancient Latin name for Britain: "Albion," as in "perfidious Albion." Cf. "Old theory started." The paper indicates a date not much later than 1856. First printed in *N&F,* 124 (Pt. III, #140; *CW,* IX, 149).

A volume—(dramatic machinery for localities, characters, &c) —running in idea and description through the whole range of recorded time —Egyptian, Hindostanee[1] Assyrian, Greek, Roman, Alb, Gallic, Teutonic,—and so down to the present day—

---

1. Inserted above "Assyrian"

? Poem of Different Incidents.

Manuscript in Virginia (Barrett). Inscribed in black ink on pink wove scrap, approx. 4⅝" x 5". The MS indicates WW's habit of depersonalizing characters. Cf. *"Companions."* The paper indicates a date not much later than 1856. First printed in *N&F,* 164 (Pt. IV, #36; *CW,* X, 10).

? Poem of different Incidents—
      characters—Men &
      Women—without giving
proper[1] Names—As/
There was ———/[2]
There was ———

1. Inserted in left margin and above "N" in "Names"
2. This and the following line are in column and may be verse. Each line is completed with a series of dashes.

Poem L'Envoy.

Manuscript in Duke (15, #38). Inscribed in black pencil on small scrap of pocket-ledger paper cut or torn at left from binding, with vertical red rules of the conventional sort. Blue rules ⁵/₁₆″ apart. On verso: "Vegetable not wood." Hanging indentation. The meaning of "L'Envoy" is not clear; perhaps the general sense is of a message or an ambassador, perhaps more specifically, since WW was taken in by the myth of the West, a farewell message from the effete East to the vigorous West. Other proposals for "Western" poems are in "Poem of Wisconsin," "In the West," "(written for the voice)," "Poem of Ohio," "Railroad Poem," "Poem of the Woods," "One Song," "I have found my authority," and his notes on his reading about the West. Most small ledger paper, white, but not identical, is early, e.g. "Poem incarnating the mind," "The regular old followers," "talk with Mr Jo Reeves." This particular MS, judging from the verso "Vegetable not wood," was probably clipped out of "[*illeg.*] Dick Hunt," possibly p. [*173*], and would thus be dated 1857.

Poem L'Envoy
—From one state to
    another—from the
    East to the West
    —from Massachusetts
       to Texas &c[1]

---

1. Preceding five words written in hanging indentation.

Poem of the Ancient (Earth.

Manuscript in NYPL (Berg). Inscribed with hanging indentation in black ink on a white laid slip, $1''$ x $3\frac{1}{4}''$. On verso, 1789 subtracted from 1857 and divided by "?" with result of 24; subtraction repeated and divided by 4 with correct result of 17. The date is probably 1857. First printed *N&F,* 175 (Pt. IV, #107; *CW,* X, 29) with omission of alternates.

Poem of the Ancient
 (earth heavens[1] to the Ancient
       (Heavens earth[2]

1. Inserted above "earth" ; parenthesis includes both words.
2. Inserted above "Heavens" ; parenthesis includes both words.

(How Will It Do.

    Manuscript in LC (#64, sheet #308). Inscribed in black pencil on tan wove scrap, 5⅝″ x 4⁷/₁₆″. All entries in hanging indentation. On verso printed announcement of the *Christian Examiner* for November, 1857. In the late 1850s WW was much concerned with the politics of slavery (see "Slavery—the Slaveholders"). The date is late 1857 or early 1858.

(How will it do for figure?)
Get a perfect account of the attack and taking of the Bastille
    (fire, blood, smoke, death, shouts, attack, desperation)[1]
    symbol of the attack[2] on slavery in These States—
The[3] masses of the north, stern and muscular
The enthusiasts not only of these lands, but of all lands.
The determined purpose—death does not stop it—it is filled
    up by others—and their death by others still.—

1. Deleted: [*illeg.*] in left margin.
2. Deleted: "the bulwarks"
3. Deleted: "stern"

(Written for the Voice).

Manuscript in Duke. Inscribed in pencil on irregular scrap of blue Williamsburgh tax blank. See "Poem L'Envoy" for other Western poems. The date is between 1857 and 1860. First printed (with slightly different reading) in *N&F*, 173 (Pt. IV, #90; *CW*, X, 25).

(written for the voice)[1]

Songs (with notes) with dramatic action, as, for instance a song describing the cutting down of the tree by wood-cutters in the West—the pleasures of a wood-life, &c

---

1. Parenthetical statement preceded by deleted *"vocal"*

Husking—"Fast Huskers."

Manuscript in LC (#79, sheet #749). Inscribed in black ink on blue Williamsburgh tax notice. Goodfellow's suggestions are written in column, each preceded by a dash. On verso deleted note in black ink: "Books have been [*two words del.*] sent by mail to all the addresses below & must have been recd. by this time." Unfortunately, there are only two Goodfellows listed in either NYC or Brooklyn, between 1857 and 1861. The less unlikely is James, a shoemaker, at 300 Myrtle Ave., Brooklyn. Since the list of topics does not suggest a shoemaker, Appleton's *Cyclopedia* was consulted. Edward Goodfellow (1828–1899), an employee of the Coastal Survey, was found. According to the 1858 *Report* of the Survey, Goodfellow, who had literary interests, was in New York making astronomical observations in May and June of 1858. It is not impossible that WW should have fallen into conversation with an astronomer who knew he was a poet. The date is certainly between 1857 and 1860.

husking—"fast huskers"/ Mr. Goodfellow's suggestions about writing a pastoral poem—including/ —life in the American country—animals, their habits, their beauty—bees—the plants, the trees—the geology—(his illustration of the white & black ants in Africa.)—fox hunting—house-raising—the different crops—

What Name? Religious Canticles.

Manuscript in Duke (15, #38). Inscribed in black ink on white wove paper, torn along both left and bottom sides, 3⅜" x 6¹/₁₆". Embossed upper right parallel to right edge (original top?) "Owen & Hurlbut So. Lee Mass" (cf. "Spring of '59," "Oct. 17, 1860"). On verso are two and a half lines of "Hours Continuing Long, Sore and Heavy-Hearted." We do not know when WW began to use this paper, but clearly the date is approximately 1859–1860. First printed in Bucke, "Notes on the Text of Leaves of Grass," *Conservator,* 7 (February, 1897), 185.

What name[1] ? *Religious Canticles*
These[2] *perhaps* ought to be the *brain,* the *living spirit,* (elusive, indescribable,[3] indefinite)[4] of all the "Leaves of Grass."—[5]/ Hymns of extasy and religious fervor/

1. Written below line. Question mark at right of both words.
2. Pointing fist precedes word in left margin.
3. Deleted: "each"
4. Parenthesis written on two lines.
5. Pointing hand precedes this entry. Next line deleted: "saw that the histories of man" . "I" not deleted, not printed here.

Companions.

Manuscript in Duke (15, #38). Inscribed in black pencil on white wove scrap, approx. 3¾" x 5¹⁵/₁₆". The indentation is very irregular. It is generally agreed that WW portrayed his parents in *LG,* especially in "There Was a Child Went Forth," but nowhere else are individuals depicted. The writing is looser than that of MS identifiable as being of the 1850s, and despite the fact that this is a Bucke MS it may well belong to 1860 or later. First printed in Bucke, "Notes on the Text of Leaves of Grass," *Conservator,* 7 (February, 1897), 185.

Companions,[1]

(viz *Poems—Cantos*—of my various Companions—each one be celebrated in a verse by himself or herself

---

1. Inserted and deleted between heading and first line: "(? Walt Whitman"

Song of the Future.

Manuscript in Duke (15, #37). Inscribed in black ink on a scrap of blue Williams-burgh tax blank, text at top trimmed irregularly by WW (?). The paper, the style of writing, and the kind of emendation indicate that "of Death" (Duke 15, #37) is part of this MS. Date between 1857 and 1860. First printed *N&F,* 177, 171 (Pt. IV; #'s 117, 81; *CW,* X, 31, 22).

Song[1] of the Future—the song[2] of Democracy.—[3] the[4] songs of Women—the[5] song of young men—the[6] song of Life here, not elsewhere—[7] the[8] song[9] of Death — the[10] song of Immortality and Ensemble —[11]

1. Deleted: "the poem [*originally capitalized*]" ; preceding word inserted. Inserted and de-leted: "of songs" . Probably words trimmed by WW from left of leaf.
2. Deleted: "Poem" ; inserted: "song" . Asterisk not printed here since there is no referent.
3. Preceding four words and dashes inserted. Redundant first dash not printed here.
4. Deleted: "Poem" ; inserted above: "songs"
5. Deleted: "Poem" ; inserted above: "song"
6. Deleted: "Poem" ; inserted above: "song"
7. Preceding three words and dash inserted. Redundant dash not printed here.
8. Deleted: "Poem" ; inserted: "song"
9. New leaf.
10. Deleted: "Poem" ; inserted: "song"
11. Words trimmed by WW?

A Cluster of Poems.

Manuscript in Virginia (Barrett). Inscribed in black ink with broad-nibbed pen on blue laid paper similar in color and appearance to Williamsburgh tax blanks, 7⅝" x 6⅛". On verso is "Living Pictures." Written with hanging indentations. WW does not seem to have consulted a dictionary for his unusual use of Latin. The writing, the paper, the use of the word "cluster" (cf. "string" in "A string of Poems"), and the reference to "Calamus Leaves" seem to date the poem to the late spring of 1859. Bowers (lxx–lxxi) does not mention this MS, but gives evidence that the idea of a Calamus cluster occurred to WW at that time. See also: "Poems. A cluster (same)"; "Theory of a Cluster"; "Poems. A Cluster of Poems"; "A string of Poems." First printed N&F, 176 (Pt. IV, #115; CW, X, 31).

A cluster of poems, (in the same way as "Calamus Leaves") expressing the idea and sentiment of[1] Happiness, Extatic life, (or moods,)   Serene Calm   Infantum Juvenatum   Maturity—a young mans moods.   [2][:][3] Middle-age   Strong, well-fibred, bearded, athletic, full of love, full of pride & joy   Old Age   Natural Happinesses   Love, Friendship

1. Succeeding terms in indented column, lineation indicated by spaces.
2. Following passage, to "joy", written in hanging indentation behind a brace at left. To left of brace, a pointing fist.
3. Deleted: "A"

Poems. A Cluster of Poems.

Manuscript not found. Text from Bucke's "Notes on the Text of Leaves of Grass," *Conservator,* 7 (February, 1897), 185. WW used the word "cluster" in MS written before 1860 ("A cluster of poems"). Since this MS was also a Bucke MS, it is very likely that this was written before 1860. The reference to death is also suggestive of these years.

Poems. A Cluster of Poems, Sonnets expressing the thoughts, pictures, aspirations, &c., fit to be perused during the days of the approach of Death. that I have prepared myself for that purpose. Remember now ——— Remember the — ———.

Poems. A Cluster (Same.

Manuscript not found. Text from *N&F,* 165 (Pt. IV, #39; *CW,* IX, 11). See "A cluster of poems" for WW's use of the word "cluster." The use of the word "Sonnets" seems to date from just prior to 1860. "Calamus Leaves" is the title WW gave to the cluster of twelve poems first entitled "Live Oak, with Moss," which Fredson Bowers identified in the Valentine manuscripts. See Bowers, lxiv–lxvii, 92ff. The date is therefore 1859 or a little earlier.

Poems. A cluster (same style as of Sonnets like, as "Calamus Leaves,") of poems, verses, thoughts, etc. embodying religious emotions.

Cluster of Sonnet-Poems.

Manuscript in LC (Feinberg #496). Inscribed in black pencil on irregular, white wove scrap cut from a larger sheet. The writing suggests a date in the 1860s.

Cluster of Sonnet-Poems.

Leading *trait-idea*
The splendor & copiousness of
　　　These Days[1]:
[2]?(Would not that be a good name for them viz: "These Days."[3]

1. "D" written over "d" . Two words in large script centered as title.
2. Following entry at right of preceding line. Hand points to "These Days."
3. Query written at right margin.

Poems Identifying.

Manuscript in Duke (15, #37). Inscribed in black ink on blue wove paper, approx. 7⅞" x 5". Vertical blue rules ⁵/₁₆" apart. Paper may be identical with "Hannah Brush," and (my grandmother) "Torquato Tasso," both of which are 1859 or slightly later. The subjects of poems are in columns. First printed in Bucke, "Notes on the Text of Leaves of Grass," *Conservator,* 7 (February, 1897), 185.

Poems identifying the different branches of the Sciences, as for instance,[1]/
    Poem of The Stars   ? Astronomy[2]   ? Suns, planets?[3] & moons[4]
    Poem of Geology?[5] (not a good word)[6]   ?the processes of The Earth[7]
    Poem of Chemistry?[8]
    Poem of Arithmetic   Mathematics   Calculation   Figures—Exactitude—[9]/
    Poem of Musicians tenor,   soprano,   baritone,   basso.[10]/

1. Preceding eight words in hanging indentation.
2. Entry indented.
3. Question mark above word.
4. Preceding three words are a separate indented line, indented like "? Astronomy"
5. Question mark above word.
6. Parenthesis above and to the right. WW is possibly objecting to the Greek root, although the other, somewhat older, borrowings passed his censure.
7. Phrase indented.
8. Question mark above word.
9. Preceding four words in column under "Arithmetic" . "Figures—Exactitude—" written as one entry.
10. Preceding four words indented.

Write a Drunken Song.

Manuscript in Texas (Hanley). Inscribed in black pencil on white wove scrap. Bernard suggests that it is a note toward "One Hour to Madness and Joy" (1860), although the relationship seems remote. A date cannot be established. First printed Edward G. Bernard, "Some New Whitman Manuscript Notes," *AL,* 8 (March, 1936), 59.

Write *A Drunken Song* slashing—intoxicated—drunk with joy and high *exhilaration*——

Poem of Fables.

Manuscript in Virginia (Barrett). Inscribed in black pencil on Williamsburgh tax blank. The date is between 1857 and 1860. First printed *N&F,* 176 (Pt. IV, #112; *CW,* X, 30).

Poem of Fables
A long string, one after another, of Poetical Fables, as Dreams, Spiritualisms, Imaginations[1]/

last piece[2]/ (still another Death Song? Death Song with prophecie's

1. Cancelled lines:
   The trained runner
   The five old men/

   Now this is the fable of the
     mirror;
   The Mirror lay clouded, (enveloped)
     enmisted/

   Now [*ins.*] And this is the fable
     of a beautiful statue:
   A beautiful statue was lost
     but not destroyed/

   The runner suggests "The Runner" (1867). The old men suggest "Salut au Monde!" (1856), l. 10, and "Debris" (1860), ll. 30–32.
2. The slash-mark is WW's.

The Most Triumphant Jubilant Poem.

Manuscript in Duke (14, #36). Inscribed in black ink on light tan wove paper, approx. 5″ x 5¾″. The writing and the fact that this is a Bucke MS suggest a date before 1860. First printed in Bucke, "Notes on the Text of Leaves of Grass," *Conservator*, 7 (February, 1897), 185.

The most [1] *Triumphant Jubilant* [2] *Poem*
This ought to express the sentiment of all [3] great jubilant glee, of athletic sort,—for great deaths, devoirs, works—in battle—falling in battle—in martyrdom——for great renunciations——for love—*especially for the close of life*—(the close of a great true life,)—for friendship—

1. Inserted above wordspace between *"The"* and *"Triumphant"*
2. Preceding word inserted above *"Triumphant"*
3. Inserted above wordspace between "of" and "great"

Aspirations.

Manuscript not found. Text from *CW,* III, 276. The word "cluster" and the challenge at the end suggest "Whoever You Are Holding Me Now in Hand" (1860) from "Calamus." See "Theory of a Cluster." The date is probably 1859. First printed in slightly different arrangement in Bucke, "Notes on the Text of Leaves of Grass," *Conservator,* 7 (February, 1897), 185.

Aspirations.

"Keep the secret—keep it close."

A Cluster of Poemetta.   To my Soul.

To Friends
Did you think you knew me?
Did you think that talking and the laughter of me, represented me?

Poem There Can Be.

Manuscript in Duke (14, #36). Inscribed in black pencil on a white wove scrap, approx. 7⅞" x 6¼". On verso is the beginning of a letter to a Mr. Graham. The writing and the fact that this is a Bucke MS suggest WW wrote this before 1860. First printed *N&F,* 120 (Pt. III, #129; *CW,* IX, 142).

Poem

There can be no greatest and sublimest character[1] without having passed through sin.— Not the earth has now arrived[2] rotund[3] and compact, with all this beautiful life upon the surface, the trees, the running waters, the air the[4]

—after all the ?geological[5] any more than the divine man, when he becomes [*illeg.*][6] has pas

1. Deleted: "withough"
2. Deleted: "at this"
3. Deleted: "beauty a"
4. Deleted: "—af" . Blank space at end of this line and beginning of next.
5. Question mark above word. Phrase written above the succeeding three words.
6. Corner and word trimmed.

Thos Nelson & Sons.

Manuscript in Texas (Hanley). Inscribed in black pencil, blue pencil, and red ink on irregular white wove scrap, 6½″ long. Presumably "Illustrated Meditterranean" was a book published by Thos. Nelson & Sons, although the firm has not kept its records. WW was concerned with the word "wing-and-wing" in 1880 ("*At the Ferry houses*"). Since Nelson established its American branch at the Bleecker Street address in 1854, the date is after that year—the writing suggests a date in the 1850s.

Thos Nelson & Sons 42 Bleecker st N Y[1] Illustrated Meditterranean[2] for picture of Wing-and-Wing/ but the best idea will be to have a fleet of many boats, plenty of little ones making a big reversed[3]   on the water[4]

1. Name and address in black pencil.
2. Title in blue crayon.
3. Preceding in red ink. A large inverted "V" in red ink and black pencil follows.
4. Preceding three words in black pencil.

Idea of a Poem.

Manuscript in Texas (Hanley). Inscribed in black ink on a white wove scrap, 5″ x 3½″, in a variety of indentations within the two entries. At bottom of leaf the inverted figure "28" in an unknown hand. Bucke refers to "Leaves of Grass 15" ("Night on the Prairie") (1860). First printed *N&F,* 149 (Pt. III, #201; *CW,* IX, 202).

Idea of a Poem,/

Day and Night/namely celebrate the beauty of day, with all its splendor,—the sun—life—action—love—strength

Then Night with its beauty—(rather leaning to the celebration of the superiority of the night.)[1]

1. Upside down at foot of sheet in another hand: "28"

Poem of. . . .

Manuscript not found. Text from *N&F*, 171 (Pt. IV, #77; *CW*, X, 21). The ellipse is in the printed text. The address to Manhattan suggests *DT*, but no date is assignable.

Poem of . . . first line:
Manhattan, go in!

Railroad Poem.

Manuscript in LC (Feinberg #92). Inscribed in black ink on a white wove scrap, 7½″ x 4″, torn from a larger sheet. The proposed titles are in column separated by rules across the leaf. For other Western poems see "Poem L'Envoy." The date seems to be in the 1860s.

Railroad poem/
Poem of corn and meat —(pork, beef, fish/
Poem of mines/
Inland poem/
Poem of The Man's hand and the Woman's hand.—/
In[1] Western edition don't make it *too* west—[2] it is enough if there be nothing in the book that is distasteful to the west, or is meaningless to it—and enough if there be two or three pieces, *first-rate,* applicable enough to all men & women, but *specially* welcome to western men & women.—

1. Paragraph preceded by pointing hand.
2. Deleted: "namely, don't"

Write a Poem.

Manuscript in Texas (Hanley). Inscribed in black ink on a stiff, white wove scrap. With it is a long clipping from an unidentified Washington paper about Major General Winfield Scott Hancock's repulse of the charge led by Major General George E. Pickett (1825–1875) at Gettysburg. The *DAB* (XIV, 570) says Pickett had 4500 men; J.G. Randall, *The Civil War and Reconstruction* (Boston, 1937), 523, names three other units which supported him to the total of 15,000 men. For Hancock see also "Review—" and "Maj Gen Hancock." The date is probably shortly after Gettysburg, in July, 1863.

Write a poem on the theme the great charge & repulse of the Secesh 20000 strong under ?   July 3, '63, *at Gettysburgh*

Reminiscences '64.

Manuscript in Huntington. Inscribed in black pencil on white wove paper, 8″ x 5″, torn smoothly at left. Vertical blue rules ½″ apart. Black ink offset runs parallel with rules. The writing is very irregular, suggesting haste. It is with a bundle of notes labelled "Hospital Notes 1863." Possibly an early version of "for lecture," "The dead of This War," and, ultimately, "Where Lilacs Last in the Dooryard Bloom'd," sec. 15. First printed by Karl Adalbert Preuschen, "Walt Whitman's Undelivered Oration 'The Dead in this War,'" *Études Anglaises,* 24 (1971), 151.

Reminiscences '64

—I saw the bloody holocaust of the Wilderness[1] & Manassas[2]
I saw the wounded & the dead, & never forget them
([3]Ever[4] since have they[5] been[6] with me—they have fused ever since in my
     poems;—)
They are here forever in my poems/

How quick forgotten[7]

1. Deleted: "the Cro"
2. Preceding five words begin at left under the dash rather than being indented.
3. Deleted: "They have"
4. Capitalized over lowercase.
5. Preceding two words inserted above "nce" in "since" and "been"
6. Deleted: "fused"
7. Below at right in unknown hand: "x6" or "+6"

For Lecture.

Manuscript in Hungtington. Inscribed in black ink on two leaves of white wove paper: [*1*] 9⅞" x 7⅞", blue rules on verso; [*2*] 9⅞" x 7¾", blue rules recto and verso. Numbered in WW's hand. Miss Jean F. Preston, Curator of Manuscripts, says further that there is a mark and slight tearing as if the top right back of [*1*] had been glued to top left front of [*2*]. The final lines, beginning "bodies float down," were apparently written in haste, for they are blotted and there is an offset on [*1*] verso. Both leaves are heavily folded in the middle and have many pinholes. WW's lineation has been respected because of the fact that, since the MS is not only notes for a lecture but also for a "recitation," the style is markedly poetic. Cf. "The dead of This War," possibly a later version, in which the strong detail of this MS has been somewhat softened. As WW remarked, "The real war will never get into the books." Karl Adalbert Preuschen connects this MS with a lecture tour projected on June 9, 1863 (*Corr.*, I, 109 and *n*), but points out that the dates of the battles mentioned fall on both sides of this date and that the references to the prisons at Andersonville and Salisbury extend the work on the MS into October, 1864. First printed by Karl Adalbert Preuschen, "Walt Whitman's Undelivered Oration 'The Dead in this War,'" *Études Anglaises,* 24 (1971), 148.

for lecture[1]
Write a piece for address to Audiences—(Recitations[2]/

The Dead in this War.
—there they lie, strewing the fields & woods of the south—
The Virginia[3] peninsula then[4] Malvern Hills & Fair Oaks the banks of the
    Chickahominy/
The bloody[5] terraces[6] hills of Fredericksburgh—Antietam Bridge—The grisly
    ravines of[7] Manassas
——The prison-pens Andersonville, Salisbury, Belle Isle[8]

1. Pencil at upper left.
2. At far right in darker ink. Beginning parenthesis curls under the word.
3. Inserted above "penin" in "peninsula"
4. Deleted: "between the James River" ; inserted: "Malvern Hill & Fair Oaks" above "la" in "peninsula" and "there" and "[*del.*] between the"
5. Inserted in black pencil above "The"
6. Inserted in black ink above "hills"
7. Preceding four words inserted in pencil above "Manassas" . Miss Preston suggests the possibility of "ravens."
8. Line inserted in pencil above "grave yards of hospitals"

The grave yards of hospitals—the[9] great crop reaped by the mighty reapers,
typhoid, dysentery and inflammations

—the unknown dead—noble & beautiful young men   Hooker's battle of
Chancellorsville (see description) at night[10]

some lie at the bottom of the sea—some where they crawled to die alone in
bushes in clumps on the sides of hills —& there their skeletons[11] bleach white
& unheeded.

(2 —The dead, the dead—*our* dead—our young men, so handsome, so joyous,/
taken from us, the son taken from the mother, the brother from the brother,
the husband from the wife, the dear friend from the the friend/

bodies float down the rivers, & catch & lodge, (dozens, scores floated down the
Potomac[12] after the cavalry engagements following Gettysburgh when our
men pursued Lee)

9. Deleted: "results"
10. Preceding eight words inserted at right in blue crayon. Cf. "from Hooker's command."
11. Deleted: "ref"
12. Deleted: "in" ; inserted above: "after"

The Dead of This War.

Manuscript in LC (#8). Inscribed in black ink on verso of p. 3 of "Description of Articles," a military order form for miscellaneous supplies. Stiff, blue wove paper, 8″ x 5⅞″. The text is a variant on a Huntington Library MS, "for lecture."

The dead of This War/

The grisly ravines of Manassas.
The vast wide[1] burial pits at Andersonville & Salisbury
? Where did they bury the dead of Belle Isle/

the bleach'd bones of the dead. The tufts of hair, the[2] shreds &[3] fragments of
   Clothing & rusty buttons/

The grave yards of a thousand hospitals./

The camp-graves every where—the squads of graves—the single graves in the
   woods, or out in a field, or by the road[4]-side,

1. Inserted above: "burial pits at" "vast wide [*del*.] fearful"
2. Deleted: "fro"
3. Deleted: "button"
4. Written over [*illeg*.]

For National Patriotic.

Manuscript in LC (Feinberg #987). Inscribed in black ink on white wove scrap, 9¾"
x 5⅞", torn from larger sheet. The writing and topic suggest a date in the 1860s.

for National Patriotic American simple [:]¹
song chant march²/

first words See! see! see!/

another³ stanzas, (the preceding⁴ stanzas to ask some question,)/

Ay! Ay! ay!

1. Large brace encloses preceding entry in column.
2. Preceding three words in column.
3. Deleted: "verse" ; inserted above: "stanzas"
4. Deleted: "standing" ; remainder of entry in hanging indentation.

Subject for a Ballad.

Manuscript in NYPL (Lion). Inscribed in black ink on verso of white laid slip pasted in *LG* (1860), 109 ("Blue Book"). The song overheard is a misquotation or current variant of a line from the variously attributed, popular Civil War song: "John Brown's body lies a'mouldering in his grave." This must have been written before 1867, the date of the next edition of *LG*.

Subject for a ballad

The hand organ in the street
    ("Old John Brown is a mouldering in his grave"

Idea of Piece—Sword-Calls.

Manuscript in LC (Feinberg #180). Inscribed in black pencil on two leaves of white wove paper, $12^3/_{16}$″ x 7¼″ and 8″ x $4^{15}/_{16}$″. A third leaf, $12^3/_{16}$″ x 7¼″, is blank. The indentation is very irregular. Since the title is mentioned in "Emerson Idaho," it may have been pinned by WW with that MS. Mr. Feinberg dates this MS between 1863 and 1864.

idea of piece —*Sword-Calls.*[1]
    invocation to the sword in dialogue dramatic [:] form

first——invokes the sword

second —The sword answers him them it[2]

again   ?   invokes the sword.

        or[3] descriptive as

first so[4] & so—invoked call'd[5] the sword

        then

        the result — the sword came
—The sword came with keen edge/

so & so *Call'd the sword.*

The sword came, sadly and slowly
Weeping, trailing[6] low, down toward the ground/

1. Title in red ink.
2. "him" is above "them" ; "it" below.
3. Deleted: "more"
4. Deleted: "a"
5. Inserted.
6. Deleted: "the ground with slow"

The sword came, & the bayonet,
And the cannon responded, with long procession,
And[7] by swift horses, the cavalry on high-pomel'd saddles.

[2] *Joys of War*[8]   See Mass Cav. Man in Ward F[9]
                                                              Sword Calls[10]

On[11] my saddle seated, my sabre grasping
    With my sabre in my hand/
    &[12] h
Where[13] the sabres flash & clink
In[14] the fight of horsemen,[15] on their turning horses, glad I join
With[16] the cavalry I join on my saddle, with my reins in hand, with my pistol
    handy
Soon my blood is up[17] soon the fight grows deeper, deeper[18] sharp the cracking
    pistols,
Bloody gashes, angry curses, shouts, screams of wounded,

7. Deleted: "the Cavalry, with" ; inserted: "by"
8. Indented beginning of new line deleted: "A cavalry"
9. Preceding seven words in black pencil at right.
10. Preceding two words in red ink at right under preceding entry.
11. False start preceding this word deleted: "With"
12. False start preceding this word deleted: "With"
13. False starts preceding this word deleted: "When" "In"
14. False start preceding this word deleted: "When" . Inserted above "[*del.*] When" : "In" ;
deleted: "the fight, the" ; inserted above "[*del.*] the" : "the"
15. Deleted: "with" ; inserted: "on"
16. False start preceding this word deleted: "Glad I join with"
17. Deleted: "as"
18. Inserted above wordspace with preceding comma.

Poem of the Sunlight.

Manuscript not found. Text from *N&F*, 174 (Pt. IV, #98; *CW*, X, 27). Notes for a poem, just possibly "Give Me the Splendid Silent Sun" (1865).

Poem of the Sunlight—Sunshine. Poem of Light.

Voices, Recitatives.

Manuscript in NYPL (Berg). Inscribed in black pencil on white laid paper, approx. 4″ x 5″. On verso, address: "N Aubin 50 Broad Street Room 9 New York." Aubin was an engraver and is probably the same person who translated Victor Hugo's "L'Année Terrible" for WW ("D. W. Dwight"). The date is probably 1867 or after.

VOICES, RECITATIVES

THE RICH MAN'S JUST AWAKENED SOUL

as just awaken
 can I enjoy these
 —Now rise & troop around me

Poem (Subject).

Manuscript in Duke (10, #24). Inscribed in black ink on white wove paper, approx. 7″ x 5″. Blue rules ⅜″ apart. Hanging indentations. On verso of [2] an early draft of "Song of the Redwood-Tree," sec. 1. (1873). Photograph of [1] facing Trent *Cat.,* 20. See "The foregoing remarks" for the call of the oyster-peddler. The writing is very much like that of "Theme for Piece." The date is in the late 1860s.

Poem (*subject*) ? for recitation.

Something which in each verse shall comprise *a call* (local and native, sea or land, American, *wild*).[1]

As the[2] country gorl (or boy) toward sun-down letting down the bars and calling the cows out of the lot—Kush! Kush! Kush!/

Or the horses and colts, exhibiting an ear of corn with one hand and holding the halter behind out of sight with the other—Ku-juk! Ku-juk! Ku-juk!/

Or the watch at mast-head of the whaler[3] looking out for the whales—There she blo-o-o-ws![4]/

[2] Or the quail whistling (whistling) Phoo! Phoo! Phooet!/

What are the peculiar calls of drovers, with a great heard of cattle?/

What are —if any —some of the peculiar calls of raftsmen?/

How would the calls of a man driving oxen do? What are those calls?/

Don't attempt too close or vivid a rendering of the calls—a mere trick—leave an easy margin—more poetical

---

1. Parenthesis at right. In left margin: "75 x 4 = 300 − (?)30."
2. Deleted: "call of the"
3. Preceding three words inserted above wordspace and "head" and right margin.
4. Deleted from "blows" : "ows" ; inserted above "[*del.*] ows" in "blows" : "o-o-ws!"

{3} For the 3-stanza-piece of out-door cries:/

First, there she blows—there she blows./

Second, Cu-juk! c' juk! c'juk! or Co! Co! Co!/

Third, Here goes your fine fat oysters—Rock Point oysters—here they go.

One[?] Song.

Manuscript in Virginia (Barrett). Inscribed in black ink and pencil on white wove scrap, 9″ x 5⁵/₁₆″. Possibly there are notes for at least two poems here: a pastoral song entitled "Come Philander" and a patriotic song. WW began to think of the nation as a mother in the late 1860s.

One[?] song—Come Philander/
Three verses[1]
    one for North,
    [one] [for][2] South
    [one] [for][3] West

See the[4] silver constellation
Every[5] one in its[6] path a-rolling[7]
Shine, & Shine, & shine[8] forever
On[9] and on they roll forever

2d or 3d verse[10]
   See! See! See!
On & on
Here to you! & here to you!
And here[11] for once

1. Following three phrases in indented column.
2. Ditto marks in MS.
3. Ditto marks in MS.
4. Deleted: "golden" ; inserted above: "silver constellation"
5. At beginning of line, deleted: "Ro" ; inserted: "every"
6. Blank space followed by deleted "rolling" ; inserted above space and deletion: "path a-rolling"
7. Deleted false start on next line: "Ro" above "Sh" in "Shine"
8. Preceding two words inserted above "ne," in "Shine," and "for" in "forever"
9. Deleted: "w"
10. Phrase begins at edge of leaf.
11. Deleted: "to"

Sisters[12] chords of life entwining in their rings
Orbs of[13] life a-rolling

Mother![14]
      ?[15] Children![16] over all[17]
See the Mother! See the children![18]
Northern, Southern, Eastern, Western,[19]

                    Missouri[20]
Children links of equal[21]

12. Long blank space following; inserted in pencil: "[*del.*] tr chords of life entwining" above "in their rings" and the deletions; deleted: "so" ; deleted below: "in ther"
13. Deleted in black pencil: "love" ; inserted in black pencil above: "life" ; deleted: "forever"
14. Black pencil; deleted: "still to yours" ; inserted and deleted in black pencil above: "all to you are equal"
15. Deleted: "O"
16. Black pencil.
17. Black pencil. Possibly belongs with "Mother!" in preceding line.
18. Line in black ink.
19. Line in black ink.
20. Pencil.
21. Pencil.

Other-Leaves.

Manuscript in LC (#120). Inscribed in black pencil on white wove paper, approx. 8⅛" x 5". Vertical blue rules ½" apart. Although the entries may well be trial titles, this MS has been included because WW seems to be circling around a poem. "Flanges" was a word WW used several times in the 1870s and later. See "Flanges of Fifty Years" (LC #78, sheet #650), "?Flanges of Five Years" (LC #78, sheet #647) and the 1876 Preface. The date is probably in the 1870s.

Other-Leaves
Dust-and-Spray/

The sense of something[1]
—as of Flanges
  Margins
  Coruscations
  —Fringes
  —Extraneous
  —trailing afterwards

Successions
Progeny—
Line[2]

Progeny[3]
Lineaments,
Series[4]

[2] The procession/
Lines & Marches
trains

 After

 Follow[5]

1. Following nouns in this entry are in column.
2. In column.
3. Deleted: "Lines" . Hyphen connecting "Lines" and "Progeny" not deleted, not printed.
4. In column.
5. In column with considerable space between entries.

The Soul's Procession.

Manuscript in Virginia. Homemade notebook of twenty leaves of folded paper, self-covered, fastened with pink ribbon through fold and brass paper fastener as described below, 8″ x 5⅜″ overall. Paper of two sorts: [1], [1–14, 27–40]: white laid paper, 10⅛″ x 8″ (before folding), blue rules ½″ apart, at upper left embossed stamp of Philp and Solomon's; [2], [15–26]: white laid paper, 11¼″ x 8¼″ (before folding), blue rules ½″ apart, red-blue-red left margin 1¼″ from edge. Paper for [2] also was used for pasted-on [9–13], which are approx. 6″ x 3½″. The enclosed clipping, dated 1869, gives the earliest date; the citation of Louis (?) Agassiz is inadequate to establish a more specific date. The very irregular writing in [9–13, 17–19] suggests, however, a date after WW's stroke.

[1] *The Soul's Procession*
WW [1]

[3; 2 blank] [2] affords a field for many bold & fine pictures & panoramic groupings & movements—
—finally ending in a flight suggesting the greatness but indefiniteness of the

[7; 4 blank, 5–6 stub] [3] In Soul's Procession/

Strong picture of *man* (? the soul.) contending with the elements—as, for instance, the captain of a ship at sea (the Soul personified as the captain of a ship at sea)
I [4]
My ship sails the sea in a storm

[9; 8 blank] [5] *The Soul's Procession*

The idea—after carrying the Soul through all experiences
tableaux Situations
Sufferings heroism [6]

1. Cover, Paper 1. Title in black ink; initials in black pencil.
2. Black ink, Paper 1.
3. Black ink, Paper 1. Inserted unidentified newspaper clipping dated (by WW?) 1869 narrates the partial destruction of the steamship *Periere* in a storm at sea, which inspired this leaf.
4. Deleted line: "I am the captain" . "I" inadvertently (?) not cancelled.
5. Pasted-on scrap of Paper 2, 6″ x 3½″. Black pencil. The fact that [9–13] present a sequence of achieved verse in a fairly distinctive handwriting suggests that WW used at least two "notebooks" in planning the poem and pasted this sequence into the present one.
6. Preceding four words in column in center of leaf.

Especially[7] *AT SEA* wrecks storms
picture[8] of a ship in a storm at sea/

—then

The Soul stalks on by itself
swims on—sails on like a sufficient splendid solitary ship by [*11; 10 blank*][9]
   itself—There is space enough—/
There are the orbs of the worlds, in space, with ample room enough
& there are the orbs of Souls, also swimming in space
Each one composite complete in itself
And the spirit of God holding them together
[*13; 12 blank*][10] The orbs of the suns & worlds[11] swim in space,
But[12] souls[13] swim in the Spirit of God in[14] greater[15] space[16]

[*15; 14 blank*][17] *The Soul's Procession*

[*17; 16 blank*][18] The general idea—passing through various experiences
                                    transmigrations
                                    gradiations[19]/

the[20] beginnings & successions of animated life—according to Agassiz— Animal
Life p. 53 Webster[21]/

As in the long chain of endless developement & growth in the physical[22] world,
   (yet with a curious oneness) the interminable[23] material process[24]

7. Preceded by a pointing hand in left margin.
8. Preceded by a pointing hand in left margin.
9. Pasted-on leaf of Paper 2, as on [9].
10. Deleted with vertical stroke:
[*del.*] See'st
I [*del.*] saw [*ins.*] knew the great greater [*ins. and del.*] er idea of Space
But I knew the idea of still greater Space
[*del.*] The Spa
11. Preceding five words inserted above "orbs swim in"
12. Deleted: "the"
13. Originally lowercase.
14. Preceding five words inserted above "in greater space"
15. Inserted above "ter" in "greater" and deleted: [*illeg.*]
16. An illegible letter is cancelled below at the left.
17. Folded leaf of Paper 2, 11¼" x 8¼". [*15–26*] are separately fastened with a brass cotterpin
and the entire gathering is fastened to [*1–14*]—[*27–40*] by a pink ribbon.
18. Black pencil. Entries in hanging indentation.
19. Preceding two words in column at right under "experiences"
20. Deleted: [*illeg.*]
21. Probably Louis Agassiz (1807–1873), *The Structure of Animal Life,* NY, 1866, 1868, 1874.
In the editions of 1866 and 1874, which a cursory collation shows to be printings rather than
editions, p. 53 describes the coral polyp by comparison to the sea anemone. The lecture is entitled
"Remote Antiquity of Animal Life as Shown in the Coral Reefs." On January 24, 1868, WW heard
Alexander Agassiz, Louis' son, lecture "on the succession of organized beings in geological times"
(*Corr.,* II, 14*n*). "Webster" has not been identified.
22. Deleted: "&[?]"
23. Written above "material"
24. Since this and the following lines distantly approach the cadence of WW's verse, hanging
indentation or verse overrun of the MS has been followed.

So in the ? ethereal world an endless spiritual[25] procession of growth
[19; 18 blank][26] The material is all for the spiritual—they[27] curiously blend.
And[28] the spiritual is for the body—and[29] they[30] also blend[31]/

    Make a succession of splendid[32] gorgeous stately pageants or moving
panoramas[33]/ involving the best & latest versions of the truths of Modern Sci-
ence—Astronomy, Geology, Ethnologhi[?] or History the succession of races &
empires

[21; 20 blank][34] The successive developments of all the growths of the earth—
from its nebulous condition—all through its meteorological & geological growth &
formation[35]/
The grand procession of universes & stars
—The Constellations
—make a procession of them—

[23; 22 blank][36] —All these shows are for the mind, to form &[37] give identity &
character to the spiritual identity, the real Being, which is immortal,[38]/
term—the chemical Being
?—the super-chemical Being

                    [25; 24 blank] query ?[39]

Perhaps the best plan will be (staccato) to make a staccato strain of picture-verses
or groups—expressing in strong florid poetry—[40]leading points in *History*[41] as of
the different races & empires—wars some few Characters

---

    25. Placement obscure, since it is inserted between the lines below "? ethereal" and
above "endless procession"
    26. Paper 2.
    27. Deleted: "They" . Since this is at the left margin, it appears that WW decided to reduce
the remaining words to a half line and inserted "they" , which stands at the end of the line above.
    28. Inserted above "The" . WW neglected to reduce "The" to lowercase.
    29. Inserted above dash before "they"
    30. Deleted: [illeg.]
    31. Two preceding lines in black pencil; following entries in black ink above a horizontal ink
line across leaf.
    32. Deleted: "&"
    33. Short line from left.
    34. Black ink, hanging indentation.
    35. Short line from left.
    36. Hanging indentation.
    37. Preceding two words inserted above "to give"
    38. Deleted: "&"
    39. A wild variety of indentations in following entry.
    40. Deleted: "the" ; inserted and deleted above: [illeg.]
    41. In larger letters.

The Wars [42]

The *greatest philosophy* [43] & *poets* & great *artists*

Religious Leaders, [44] prophets & [45]

[27; 26 blank] [46] Then at the end/

What other ? O Soul/

intimate the procession continuing *for ever* /

most of it through regions & experiences unknown [47]

—and still from stage to stage
From life to life, higher & [48] higher
From orb to orb continuous the journey

[29; 28 blank] Piece on *Greenwood Cemetery* [49]

various verses

then at end

Methinks I hear the chorus of the dead, & see the faces/

42. In larger letters.
43. In larger letters.
44. Preceding two words in larger letters.
45. "r" written over "pro"
46. Reverts to Paper 1; [27–28] is conjugate with [14], etc. Apparently fragmentary lines of verse.
47. Preceding three lines in blue pencil.
48. Inserted in wordspace between "higher" and "higher"
49. In Brooklyn. See "A Letter from Brooklyn," March 21, 1851, *UPP,* I, 240.

a[50] triumphant Song of Life—the real life/

full of exultation—new scenes untellable

{40;30–34 *blank; 35–36 cut out, 37–39 blank*}
{*Back cover, fold over from* {1} *turned upside down, inscribed in black pencil of varying intensity, at random*} car 55　3–20　7,50　M st 9 am　1,50　1.50 3 20　7:50　9 at M

50. Original first word deleted: "full"

Principal Personages.

Manuscript in LC (#24). Inscribed in black ink, except as noted, on white wove paper, as described. A soft brown cardboard cover sheet, 11¼″ x 9″, is lettered *"The Cru-sades"* in blue crayon in another hand (?), followed by a small label in black ink "Walt Whitman Mss." and in Bucke's (?) hand "Notes for a proposed poem on the Crusades." In upper right corner is a label of Harnden Express of Boston.

The MS is accompanied by a seven-page letter dated January 21, 1869, from a Julius Sing of 251 F St., Washington (?). Sing thanks WW for a copy of the *Atlantic Monthly* containing "Proud Music of the Storm" and goes on to suggest and outline a poem on the Crusades in terms which evidently appealed to WW. Unfortunately Sing is not in the Washington directories, nor has any person of that name been located in biographical or bibliographical sources. A long newspaper clipping of 1871 about the Children's Crusade is also in the file.

Almost as curious are the versos of several leaves which contain cancelled copies in Whitman's hand, with one exception, of letters between Charles Francis Adams, Minister to England during the Civil War, Earl Russell, British Foreign Minister, and W. H. Sew-ard, Secretary of State. All the correspondence relates to a Confederate privateer, *Georgia*. The correspondence, assuming WW did not have access to the archives of the Department of State (which the scrap in a copyist's hand suggests), was published in 1865 in *House Executive Documents, 38th Congress, First and Second Sessions*. Since he went to the trouble of copying them, he must have been interested in the *Georgia* case, but no connection has been found. The copies were used as scrap after January, 1869, for the writing of notes on the Crusades. The copy of a review from an 1844 *North British Review* [106R] is in WW's hand of the 1860s, but he may have had the clipping for years. The 1871 clipping about the Children's Crusade probably indicates a continuing interest. The date is probably 1869 or a little later.

[*102R*[1]*; V*[2]] principal personages of the crusades[3]
Peter the Hermit   St Louis, king of France   Godfrey, (he is the Agamemnon[4])
Richard Cour de Lion   Saladin   Tancred (fierce & tender as Pelides[5])   The popes—(Sylvester, Hildebrand, Urban, &c.)

1. Black ink on white laid paper, 6¼″ x 7⅛″. Red-blue-red margin at right. Blue rules ½″ apart on verso.

2. On verso cancelled beginning of letter from Earl Russell to Charles Francis Adams, August 8, 1864, in WW's hand, concerning the *Georgia*. Continued on [*105V*]. In upper right corner in another hand: "10"

3. The names are in column, divisions here indicated by spaces.

4. Modern historians do not credit Godfrey with the position of leadership in the First Cru-sade which this implies.

5. Achilles, son of Peleus.

[*103R* [6]; *V* [7]] *For an idea*   put in this point STRONG   that the great redeeming movement, revolutions of the world [8] have been those (Such as the Crusades, & our own great war) [9] Which have been mainly for *an Idea*

[*104R* [10]; *V* [11]] Oft has the tale been told   Crusades [12]

&c &c &c

. . . . but never linked (but never yet [13] for the   (Never for thee America [14]
Again [15] narrate [16]
Recall the [17] fervor, & the mighty deeds.
The tumult of the [18] nations, swarms of knights & kings.
The [19] whole [20] Crusades [21]
To link [22]
To link them it [23] on the chain
That leads to thee America

[*105R* [24]; *V* [25]] The number of the Crusades is generally computed to be *eight* — (there were other feints & slighter attempts, however,)

6. Black and red ink on white laid paper, 8⅛″ x 8″. Red-blue-red margin on right. Printed in Glicksberg, 162.

7. On verso, fragment of conclusion of Adams to Russell, May 9, 1864. In a copyist's hand.

8. Deleted: dash.

9. Parenthetical statement in red ink.

10. Black ink on white wove paper, 10″ x 8″. Blue rules ½″ apart.

11. On verso, a sort of table of contents in column, cancelled. The references are to letters in *House Executive Documents, 38th Cong.* The first is in error. Pt. 1, 199, is a London newspaper report of a Commons debate held on March 27, on the fitting out of Confederate privateers, but in Pt. 1, 231, is a letter from Adams to Seward, of April 8, 1863, forwarding correspondence with Russell about the ship *Japan,* later *Georgia.* All the other references are to correspondence in ibid., 2nd Session, Pt. 2, about the *Georgia,* some of which WW copied, as identified here by cross references to this MS. Part 1, 1863, April 8, 1863. p. 199   Part 1, 1864, May 9, 1864. p. 743 [*103V*]   Part 2, 1864, June 7, 1864. p. 100 [*not copied*]   July 27, 1864. p. 256 [*108V*]   Aug. 18, 1864. p. 277 [*109V–110V*]   Aug. 8, 1864. p. 278 [*102V, 105V*]   Sept. 8, 1864. p. 298

12. In upper right corner.

13. Inserted above "for"

14. Two fragmentary lines at right inserted at an angle with loop at left and below. Beginning of new line deleted at left: "—But"

15. Deleted: "I"

16. Cancelled line: "Recall the famous deeds"

17. Deleted: "mighty"

18. Deleted: "k[?]"

19. Meaningless line between words.

20. Space for six- or seven-letter word.

21. Beginning of new line deleted: "Link"

22. Beginning of following line deleted: "Lin"

23. Inserted above as alternate.

24. Black ink on white wove paper, 8⅛″ x 6⅛″. Red-blue-red vertical margin at right, blue rules ½″ apart.

25. On verso continuation of Russell to Adams, Aug. 8, 1864 [*102V*].

—The Crusades fill up nearly 200 years—yet with wide breaks or gaps (58 years divide the first from the second) between the second & third 200 years

[*106R blank*][26] North British Review, May 1844 Michaud's Hist. Crusades "And surely none can think of those files of horsemen who obeyed the summons of the Eremite Peter the hermit[27] & the Hierarch, the Pope[28] without a dazzled mind The tens of of thousands starr'd all over with the cross, covered with morion & helmet, glittering with breastplate & greave, their spears like a moving wood; their targes like a golden sea; their standards like a canopying rainbow—mounted on barbed & caparison'd steeds; the oriflamme unfurled & streaming out from all its folds; the cry of St. Dennis on every tongue; the anointing & benison & shrift of the church; the equipage of kings' gorgeous tents & queens pavilions; the lines of pursuivants & heralds—of[29] sumpters, armorers, &c; the acclaim of the multitude on their departure[30]/[31] The analogy between all this & the exciting scenes at the breaking out of our own war][32] the acclaim of the multitude on their departure—; the first clarion-peal which put the advance of these masses on the march; the sudden burst of all their music—[*107R; V blank*][33] the deep and measured, or more likely wild tumultuous tread of all these moving squadrons[34]

open the foregoing by)[35] ([36]specifying some fine locality—the[37] broad plains of   ?   of a fine forenoon—as starting forth upon their great campaign/

[*108R*[38]*; V*[39]] Peter the Hermit

Peter of Amiens, a monk, a hermit, who had become a priest, as the reaction of a gay & military life   enthusiastic, learned, yet vehement & sinewy—[40] laid his scheme before pope Urban

26. Black ink on white wove paper, 8½″ x 6¼″. Red-blue-red horizontal margin at bottom, vertical blue rules ½″ apart.
27. Preceding three words above "Eremite" , possibly WW's clarification of the author's elegant variation.
28. Preceding two words above "Hierarch" , possibly WW's clarification of the author's elegant variation.
29. Deleted: "sumters"
30. Slash and following entry through the terminal square bracket in red ink. Pointing hand in left margin.
31. Pointing hand.
32. WW's bracket.
33. Paper and ink as in [*106*], 8⅛″ x 6⅜″.
34. No quotation marks, but evidently quotation ends here.
35. Written in column at left in front of long, single, closing parenthesis.
36. Long, single, opening parenthesis.
37. Deleted: "brad" "brad" . Capital "O[?]" above second "brad"
38. Black ink on white wove paper, 8½″ x 7½″. Red-blue-red margin at left, blue rules ½″ apart. A variety of indentations.
39. Cancelled conclusion of letter from Adams to Russell, July 27, 1864.
40. Deleted: "lade[?]"

[*109R*[41]; *V*[42]] Bring in the cause of Crete & Greece—as embodying the *great idea*—opposed to which, to-day, are the commercial,[43] trading, & balance of power notions of France & England/

The Crusades opened up maritime spirit, knowledge & experimental[44] daring which led to the discovery of America, through the Italian & Spanish navigators —& thus *tells momentously on this day & land*

[*110R*[45]; *V*[46]] Trace the connection down even to America, to-day/ An unbroken chain of sequence, causes & effects, runs through the progress of[47] history & man/

All great emotions, agitations, &c[48] produce the mightiest[49] ameliorating[50] results/

The Crusades of the 12th & 13th centuries are tallied by the American war of the 19th//

? Begin by
    ? Often has the tale been told
? Oft has the tale been told

---

41. Black ink on white wove paper, 10⅝" x 8". Red-blue-red margin at left, blue rules ½" apart. A variety of indentations.
42. Part of cancelled letter from Adams to Seward, August 18, 1864. Illegible pencilled inscription upper left corner. Letter concluded on [*110V*].
43. Deleted: "&"
44. Inserted above "& daring"
45. Black ink on white wove paper, 11" x 8". Red-blue-red margin at right, blue rules ½" apart. Hanging indentations, except in first and second entries.
46. Cancelled conclusion of Adams to Seward, August 18, 1864 [*109V*].
47. Deleted: "man"
48. Deleted: "do good"
49. Deleted: "ameliorating"
50. Deleted: "ef"

Penitenzia.

Manuscript in LC (Feinberg #866–877). Inscribed in black ink, except where noted, in two homemade notebooks and a separate sheet. The title is in red ink on the outside cover of both notebooks. Notebook #1: white wove, 7¾" x 5", vertical blue rules ½" apart, embossed "Philp & Solomon" and held together by brass fastener. Notebook #2: white wove, 7¾" x 5", held together by paste. Separate sheet: white wove, 9¾" x 7¾". Entries in hanging indentation.

The evidence for the dating is not definitive. The evidence from the references to photographs, for example, is inconclusive. WW was photographed by Kurtz in 1860 and in 1879 (Henry Saunders, *Whitman Portraits* [Toronto, 1928]). William Kurtz (b. 1834), regarded as the leading American photographer of the 1870s, invented the "Rembrandt" style of photographic portraiture with its experiments in lighting and shadows (Robert Taft, *Photography and the American Scene* [N.Y.: Macmillan, 1938], pp. 336–342). Although an 1879 portrait by Kurtz of WW with the J. H. Johnston children has his "eyelids drooping" (Saunders, #67), a more likely possibility is the unattributed Saunders #14, a *"head* with eyelids drooping," dated 1861. Although the photographer is unidentified, he may have been Kurtz. Tarisse and his portrait of WW have not been identified and both photographs may no longer be extant. Notice that WW may be working on two separate poems: "Penitenzia," on Kurtz's portrait with the eyes closed ("eyelids drooping"), and "on the photo by Mr. Tarisse," in which WW is gazing out of the depths ("Thou forth from the shadows peering").

The reference to a second volume to *LG* on [*13*] is also inconclusive. In the Preface to *As a Strong Bird on Pinions Free* (1872), WW stated his conviction that LG was complete and that the "surplusage" composed thereafter should be made a second volume (*Prose 92*, I, 458–459). Each of the poems mentioned on [*13*], except *DT*, was printed in the *Passage to India* pamphlet of 1871, appended to some issues of *LG* (1871). *DT* had been printed separately in 1865 and had been appended to some issues of *LG* (1867), but was not worked into the plates of *LG* until 1871. *LG* (1876)—"The Author's Edition"—was indeed issued in two volumes (with portraits), with the plates of *LG* (1871) used for Vol. I, and the *Passage to India* pamphlet, *DV,* and other pieces organized into Vol. II, *Two Rivulets*. However, since WW on [*13*] is thinking of individual poems, rather than an already printed pamphlet, he is probably planning *LG* (1871) and the *Passage to India* pamphlet. The paper, from Philp and Solomon, a Washington stationer, confirms a date before 1873, when WW moved to Camden. The "advent of Grant" and the Transcontinental Railroad, alluded to on [*4*], would refer to 1869. This, then, was probably written between 1869 and 1871. Portions first printed in Furness, pp. 190–191. (Gene Edward Veith, Jr.)

[*Outside front cover*] PENITENZIA
[*Notebook #1, 1*] for [:][1] part in L of G[2]
Collect the good portraits—Kurtz's head with eyelids drooping/Tarisse's head/
Make poems to match.

Penitenzia.[3]

O[4] sight of shame & poem
O beautiful thought one[5]—a [*illeg.*][6]
   Hollow[7] soul [*illeg.*] destructive [*illeg.*] despairingly[8]
O [*illeg.*]
O fear [*illeg.*] disguise
O [*illeg.*]
O fearful sight [*illeg.*] court[?] soul

[3[9]; 2 *blank*] Mask ? Veil[10] with the lids thine eyes, O soul!
x x x Retire within thyself

[5; 4 *blank*] Mask with the lids thine Eyes, O soul/[11]
Droop—droop thine eyes O Soul
Be not abased
Veil—veil thy?[12] strong perceptions
Musing
retire within thyself

[7[13]; 6 *blank*] I sing the un   accomplished
I sing the dark vast[14] unknown/
As the night shows the myriads
(Piece "The fire on the ground burns low,[15])

    1. Brace pointing right.
    2. Deleted false start of line: "th"
    3. This and the remaining entries on this page in red ink, with [*illeg.*] inscriptions in pencil
underneath and between the writing in ink.
    4. Deleted: "life" ; inserted above: "sight"
    5. Inserted.
    6. In pencil as noted above. Feinberg's transcript (in LC) reads "comrat[?]"
    7. Deleted at beginning of line: "To"
    8. The two preceding words may be meant to be read as separate lines or notes for develop-
ment of "Hollow soul"
    9. Pasted-in ledger sheet.
    10. "? Veil" written above "Mask" in pencil.
    11. Following four lines in pencil.
    12. "?" above.
    13. Leaf written in black pencil.
    14. Written above "dark"
    15. "Night on the Prairies" (1860), l. 2.

[9 [16]; 8 *blank*] Let the piece "Droop—droop thine eyes, O Soul"—convey the idea of a trance, yet with all the senses alert—only a state of high exalted musing— —the tangible & material with all its shows, the objective world, suspended or[17] surmounted,[18] [11 [19]; 10 *blank*] for a while, & the powers in exaltation, freedom, vision— —yet the *senses* not lost contenaried[?]/ Then chant, celebrate[20] the the unknown, the future hidden spiritual world   the real reality

[13; 12 *blank*][21] qu?—Whether to make a new Vol. of these pieces, including *Whispers of Heavenly Death*[22]—que?— Whether to finish up[23] Leaves of Grass in one Vol/[24] Drum Taps in another[25]   Carol of Harvest for 1867[26]   Ethiopia Saluting[27]/ —Whispers &c. in another[28]

[15; 14 *blank*] good to bring in *lecture or reading.*[29]

beauty[30]
series of comparison/
not the beautiful youth with features of bloom & brightness/
but the[31] browned old farmer & father/
not the soldiers trim in handsome uniforms marching off to sprightly music with
    measured step/
but the remnant returning, thinn'd [17][32] out./
not the beautiful flag with stainless white, spangled with silver & gold
But the old rag[33] just adhering to the staff, in tatters—the remnant of the many
    battle-fields./

16. Page in hanging indentation.
17. Preceding two words inserted above "world surmounted"
18. Deleted: "or"
19. Both entries in hanging indentation.
20. Inserted above "chant, the"
21. See headnote.
22. The title of a poem published in *Broadway Magazine* (October, 1868), later the title of a cluster of thirteen poems first printed in the *Passage to India* pamphlet (1871). Hanging indentation.
23. Deleted: "t"
24. Hanging indentation.
25. *DT* had been published separately in 1865, had been appended to *LG* (1867) and was worked into the plates of *LG* (1871).
26. A poem first published in the *Galaxy* (September, 1867) and printed in the *Passage to India* pamphlet.
27. "Ethiopia Saluting the Colors" (written in 1867) was part of the *Passage to India* pamphlet. Hanging indentation.
28. Hanging indentation.
29. Remainder of the leaf in pencil.
30. Deleted false start precedes entry: "be" . This and remainder of passage on beauty first printed in Furness, 51–52.
31. Deleted: "scarr"
32. WW continued on rectos, then returned to a verso [16], since he was at the end of the notebook.
33. Possibly "rug"

not the beautiful [34] girl or the elegant [35] lady, with   ?   complexion
But the mechanic's wife at work, or the mother of many children, middle-aged
   or old/
[16] Not the [36] vaunted scenery of the tourist, picturesque,
But the plain landscape, the bleak sea shore, or the barren plain, with the com-
   mon sky & sun, or at night the moon & stars. [37] [18] [38]

[*Notebook #2, 1*] *Veil with the* their [39] *lids* thine *eyes, O Soul*

Sentiment of the piece [40] abstraction Meditation Penitence
? qu——three (or more) stanzas of interrogatory character

Penitenzia [41]/
for portrait with hat [42]
Under Behind [43] that mask of shade   ?   heavy shade [44]

[*3; 2 blank*] Veil with the lids

Eyes, droop thy li [45]

(It)
Penitenzia
   The drooping of the eyelids generally accompanies humility—indicates pen-
itence—see the Roman Catholic devotees—& specimen pictures of the saints, &c.

[*4*] [46] photo by Mr. Tarisse

As apostrophising the depths
Look out from the shadows Thou who—&
? qu   Lookest out from the shadows

   34. Deleted: "g"
   35. Preceding two words inserted above "or lady"
   36. Deleted: "famed so"
   37. This entry written sideways, in hanging indentation.
   38. A few [*illeg.*] words inscribed upside down in pencil.
   39. Written above "the" as alternate reading.
   40. Following three words in column.
   41. Word in red ink. Following twelve words in black pencil.
   42. Unidentified. A Kurtz photograph of 1860 (Sanders, #13) shows WW in a hat, but the
eyes are gazing askance rather than drooping.
   43. Inserted above "Under" as an alternate reading.
   44. Preceding two words and question mark below "shade"
   45. Deleted new line: "O penitence Repentance"
   46. Deleted false starts: "On the portrait" "On Mr Tarisse's" on two lines to the left of "photo
by Mr. Tarisse"

On   [47](leading[48] events of the day in America Europe (Spain & Cuba)[49] —
          Advent of Grant[50] abolition of Slavery[51] Pacific Railroad[52] (*Moral*[53]
          events & characterization[54] as well as physical & political[55]
Thou who, in[56] the shadows returning
Lookest[57] from thence out[58] on the world
Lookest out on the land—

[5] (on my portrait
Tarisse's

Thou[59] *forth from the shadows peering*
  From shadows deep & dark I peer
Tell, how

(photograph'd[60]
by Mr. Tarisse)
From Shadows[61], deep & dark I peer[62] Out[63]
On Nature,[64] on my comrades dear
Curious/
Peering[65] from
Tell, how, forth[66] from those[67] shadows peering,
[6] Thou, who, peering from shadows deep Can y
Do you too[68] form a poem of this book
Telling what[69]

    47. A long space intervenes after "On" . The following three lines are in a very heavily indented column.
    48. Inserted above "events"
    49. Cuba was in rebellion against Spain from 1868 to 1878.
    50. Grant was president between 1869 and 1877.
    51. The Thirteenth Amendment to the Constitution was ratified on December 18, 1865.
    52. The first transcontinental railroad was completed May 10, 1869. WW celebrated the opening of the transcontinental railway in "Passage to India" (1871).
    53. Deleted: "events as"
    54. Deleted: "well as"
    55. Preceding ten words written at right of preceding entry, enclosed by a curved line.
    56. Deleted: "loo from" ; inserted: "in" above "from"
    57. Deleted: "out on the"
    58. Inserted in the wordspace between "thence" and "on"
    59. Deleted: "than" ; inserted and deleted above: "there" ; inserted and deleted above: "there [*not del.*] on"
    60. Deleted: "on my" before "(photograph'd" . Deleted after "(photograph'd" : "bt"
    61. Deleted: "deep" before "deep"
    62. Deleted, possibly as beginning of new line: "Peer"
    63. Deleted line: "Forth on the world, my race, my comrades dear" above "On Nature . . . dear"
    64. Deleted: "man," ; inserted above: "on"
    65. False start of the line deleted: "Tell"
    66. Inserted above wordspace between "how," and "from"
    67. Inserted above "shad" in" shadows"
    68. Deleted: "be"
    69. End of second notebook.

                    [*separate sheet*] (The portrait
Mask[70] with their lids thine eyes, O Soul![71]
The standards of the light & sense shut off[72]
To darkness now retiring,[73] from thy[74] thy inward abysms.
How curious, looking thence,[75] aloof appears the appear thy world comrades,[76]
    this[77] visage[78]
Appears aloof[79] thy[80] life, each passion, each event.[81]
And thy[82]
The objective world behind thee left,

70. Deleted: " 'd "
71. Deleted: "Think of [*del. in blue crayon*]
Pass to the unaccomplish'd hover [*del. in ink*]
Pass to [*del. in blue crayon*] the vast unknown. [*del. in ink*]
The objective world behind thee leave [*ins. above* "leave"] left [*ins. below* "leave"] afar
Droop, droop thine eyes, O Soul!
Exalt thyself to musing— speed
    thy flight! (thy slough dropt from thee,)
The objective world behind thee leave. / [*Preceding three lines cancelled by two slanting strokes of
    black ink.*]
Drooping thy
Droop, droop thine eyes!
Light & the senses abdicated, veiled, shut off, [*preceding three words inserted*]"
72. Preceding line inserted amidst the previous deletions.
73. Deleted in blue crayon: "aloof in" ; inserted and deleted in blue crayon: "aloof" ; de-
leted: "to"
74. Preceding two words inserted.
75. Inserted and deleted in blue: "aloof" above "appears" ; inserted in blue above: "aloof"
76. Deleted in blue crayon: "[*ins.*] appear thy comrades" ; inserted: "comrades"
77. Deleted: "the"
78. Deleted: "of thyself visage"
79. Deleted in blue: "appears,"
80. Deleted: "own"
81. Preceding line inscribed at left, marked by paragraph sign.
82. Deleted: "own life, passions, and body."

America to the Old.

Manuscript in LC (#117, sheets #1368–1370). Described in LC *Cat.* as originally "5 p. on 10 l. (5 blank)." It was a homemade notebook held together by a pin. Only three leaves have been mounted. Inscribed in black pencil on white laid paper, 5″ x 3⅞″, blue rules ⅜″ apart. Dating is difficult. LC *Cat.* places it in a group of undated notebooks. The "Genius" ([*1037R*]) suggests the "Phantom" of "By Blue Ontario's Shore" ("Poem of the Many and One," 1856) or of "As I Ponder'd in Silence" (1871). Egyptian priests and/or music appear in "Proud Music of the Storm" ("Proud Music of the Sea-Storm," 1869). The appreciation of Old World Bards is most clearly expressed, with a reference to Egyptian priests, in "Old Chants" (1891), but the writing will not support so late a date. Nat Bloom was a friend from NY Bohemian days with whom WW was in touch as late as the 1870s ("Add*resses*"). Unfortunately his street address is illegible. See "Mrs H. J. Wright." The writing suggests a date in the 1860s or 1870s.

[*1368R*] *America to the Old World Bards*
Be thy task for once to thank in my name, the old World Bards
And be thy task to speak,[1] in my name, to preserve the antique poems.
[*1369R; 1368V blank*][2] * Let them[3] pass
Let the phantoms walk through the roads of thy soul
Call up the great ?pale[4] procession
* Let them[5] pass—let after me the shadows walk through thy very soul[6]/

After the above as 1st stanzas (or Canto)[7]
 —The second
must be a strong Invocation[8]/

Then the poems
 appear (are acted)[9]

1. Deleted: "to"
2. This line, preceded by an asterisk, and the line following are crammed at the top of the leaf. The third line, also with an asterisk, is crammed in after the second. It is not possible to tell the intended order of the lines.
3. Deleted: "walk"
4. Preceding two words were written in the right margin, "?pale" above "great"
5. Deleted: "pass" "walk" ; inserted: "pass"
6. Preceding eight words inserted above "the [*illeg.*] as"
7. Hanging indentation.
8. Hanging indentation.
9. Hanging indentation.

{*1370R; 1369 blank*} Let the last stanzas of the 1st Canto be the voice of the Genius (But the identity of that a little veiled, vague) & the words in italic

{*1371R; 1370V blank*} The charms work—the ?/

Time falls back—

I hear the old Egyptian—the priests of   in the temples[10] of Memphis & Thebes The[11] singers singing before the Pharaos

{*1372R; 1371V blank*} Nat Bloom [*illeg.*] p.o. 320 Broadway.[12] {*1363R and V blank*}

10. Deleted: "of"
11. Deleted: "Musicians" ; inserted above "sicians" in "Musicians" : "singers"
12. In blue crayon. See *"Bloom."*

Light.

Manuscript in LC (#45, sheet #122). Inscribed in black ink on soft, wove, gray-brown paper, $9^{13}/_{16}''$ x $6''$. Cf. paper of "*Note* A * While." The ink is blurred because the paper is very porous, but the writing seems to indicate a date in the late 1860s or the 1870s. WW used "ostent" in "Eidolons" (1876), l. 21, and "Shakspere-Bacon's Cipher" (1891), l. 5.

Light

Lives, waters, light and darkness

Yet
And then behind these/
These voices[1] to the ostent,[2]
when the night deepen'd[3]
And[4] from its stillness
   Came the enclosing voice of all

1. Inserted.
2. Original first word in next line deleted: "wh"
3. Three lines deleted: "While latent of " "all another voice" "the enclosing voice"
4. Deleted: "n the" ; inserted above "n" : "from"

[*Illeg.*] the [*Illeg.*] I See.

Manuscript in LC (#119). Inscribed in purple crayon on top-bound notebook paper with rounded lower corners, approx. 6¼″ x 4⅛″. As LC *Cat.* points out, there are sketches for two poems. WW used this sort of notebook between 1870 and 1890.

[*Illeg.*] the [*illeg.*] I see
Life light and the in-bound tides[1]

?only   only through ye,
Through death and[2] waning[3] day and the ebb's depletion
Life, light, and the inbound tides

[*3; 2 blank*]   ? Whirl
To morrow's sailing[4]
  fleets with

pennants of [*illeg.*]
  And the

The
And over the rolling waves the Steamship[5] [*illeg.*] and the trailing pennant of smoke

alternation [*4 blank*]

1. Preceding lines and lines clipped at top cancelled with vertical stroke.
2. Deleted: "the"
3. Deleted: "light" ; inserted above: "day"
4. Deleted: "and coming" at beginning of next line.
5. Reduced from plural to singular.

Poem of the Woods.

Manuscript in Texas (Hanley). Inscribed on verso of engraving from *Sartain's Magazine* entitled "Won't You Come Along," by J. Bannister from an original by Andre. A pretty peasant lass in tall hat with ribbons and an unlaced bodice stands with one foot on the gunwale of a small boat, inviting the spectator to accompany her. *Sartain's* expired in 1852. The writing, however, is the loose script of WW's later years. First printed by Edward G. Bernard, "Some New Whitman Manuscript Notes," *AL,* 8 (March, 1936), 60–61, who suggests it was written during or just after his 1879 trip to Colorado.

Poem of The Woods.   (Poem of the Prairies)[1]
for Chicago edition

names of western trees—and of all American trees—/

sentiment of the woods/

    large, broad, fresh,—/
the smell of the woods in the morning—/

pictures of the woods in winter—in summer—/

the human[2] characters one meets in the woods—identical with the woods—
the lonesome hut—the hunting-hut—the hunter—the curious character of the
hunter—the very old hunter, with

The singular wild pleasure of being[?] alone in the woods—

1. Written in upper right corner.
2. Inserted above "char" in "characters"

Idea of New Poem.

Manuscript in Texas (Hanley). Inscribed in black ink on white wove paper, 9¼" x 5¼". Although the text is not even a sentence, it is written as three entries with hanging indentations. Below the text is pasted a clipping from a Philadelphia newspaper, "King Ludwig's Latest Whim," which describes plans to move monumental religious statues to a mountain peak overlooking Oberammergau by means of a "street locomotive." The contrast between traditional devotion and modern technology evidently moved WW. Since Ludwig II was deposed as King of Bavaria in 1886, this must have been written between 1873 and 1886. First printed by Edward G. Bernard, "Some New Whitman Manuscript Notes," *AL,* 8 (March, 1936), 51.

Idea of New Poem

a poem expressing the attitude of modern thought, progressivism science &c, toward the antique Myths, Christianity Art, Bibles, &c

Make a Poem.

Manuscript in Texas (Hanley). Inscribed in black ink on irregular, gray wove scrap. The loose writing is that of WW's later years, perhaps the 1880s.

Make a poem, (piece
   the *central theme of which should be*[?]
The *Untellable,*
That which can not be put in fine words,
Nor in any words or statement or essay, or poem[1]
Of Heroism, Of poetry, the life &[2] best[?][3]   of both, Of Eloquence, of

1. Start of new line deleted: "The best"
2. Preceding two words inserted above "the best"
3. Deleted: "the"

Summer Rivulets.

Manuscript in LC (#78, sheet #634). Inscribed in black ink on white laid scrap. Vertical blue rules ⅜″ apart. The three titles are written in a centered column rather widely spaced. The writing suggests a late date. "By the road-sides" suggests a relationship, at least in time, with the cluster title of 1881.

Summer Rivulets
By the road-sides
Evening Dews
write a little piece strongly recognizing the affiliations of many of my poems—with simple natural objects—grass, rain, the open (?head it *names*) ? note to one of the names

Poem As to.

Manuscript in LC (#78, sheet #639). Inscribed in pencil on white wove scrap with marks of having been walked on. Blue rules ½″ apart. The very irregular writing suggests a very late date.

Poem as to my book/
Idea that though personally in solitude I am travlling all over the world, &c

To the Liquid.

Manuscript in LC (#78, sheet #612). Inscribed sideways, in column, with considerable space between entries, in black pencil on verso of sheet of white wove notepaper, 8¼" x 5⅞". Watermarked "Whiting Paper Co." Blue rules ½" apart; letterhead "Special Agent Treasury Department." Letter is a breakfast invitation for 9 A.M. on Sunday, dated May 14, 1884. The signature is illegible. Charles W. Eldridge, one of WW's 1860 publishers, was in the Treasury Department. WW had written him May 7 for help in obtaining a picture of Father Taylor (*Corr.*, III, 369–370).

To the liquid
To the
   As I sat
To the music of ebb-tide ripples softly [1]
Alone
To the ripples [2]
Idly I float

1. A raised slanting mark before the beginning of the line.
2. Deleted: "flo" , "Floa" , "Idly floating" above "Idly I float"

Drift Sands.

Manuscript in LC (#41, sheet #90). Inscribed in black ink on a white wove scrap, approx. 7¼" x 8". Vertical blue rules ⁵/₁₆" apart. On verso is a cancelled letter from L. H. Bartlett, June 8, 1883. WW proposed "Drifts & Bubbles" as a title for *LGTR* (1876). He also experimented with Sands and Sand Drifts and Drifted Sands at 61, 62, 63, 64, 65, that is, in 1880–1884. The lines themselves do suggest old age. This MS and other trial lines date, therefore, from 1880–1884. A number of trial titles related to these poetical fragments also exist, but are not published here. As LC *Cat.,* 12, suggests, these MS were probably intended for a poem "Drift Sands."

Drift Sands.

As half-caught echo from the twilight[1] shore

As we[2] float idly,[3] in the twilight ebb echoes from the shore,

Ripples, and

As[4] echoes[5] from the shore

Ripples and

Edges[6] and glints of sand and[7] ripples from the shore,

As we float idly on.

1. Inserted above "the shore"
2. Deleted: "to drift" ; inserted above: "float"
3. Deleted: "glint" ; inserted: "in the twilight ebb" above the deletion and "echoes from the shore"
4. Inserted above.
5. Not reduced to lowercase in MS.
6. Deleted: "Ripples" ; inserted above: "Edges"
7. Deleted: "echoes" ; inserted above: "ripples"

As Half-Caught Echoes.

Manuscript in LC (#41, sheet #91). Inscribed in red ink and black ink on white wove scrap, approx. 4⅞″ x 7¾″. The scraps of verse, which are in smaller writing, were possibly written later than the three trial titles. For dating see "Drift Sands."

/ As half-caught echoes, ripples, glint of sands,
While we drift idly by.[1]

Drift-Sands.
Moments and Minutes.— No
Scintilla at 65[2]

As[3] a half-caught[4] echo, glint of sands, or ripple
While we drift idly[5] down the ebb
As idly[6] drifting off the river's[7] passing glimpses,
Those[8] half-caught river & echoes

1. Both lines, including rules above and below, in red ink.
2. Three titles in black ink in column as indicated by spacing.
3. Inserted. Following "A" not reduced in MS.
4. Deleted in red ink: "glimpses[?]" "ripples[?]," "and [*illeg.*]" . Inserted in red ink: "echo, glint of sands, or ripple"
5. Inserted above wordspace between "drift" and "[*ins.*] down" . Deleted: [*illeg.*]; inserted below: "[*del.*] on [*ins.*] down the ebb," . The following two lines are heavily indented.
6. Inserted above "dr" in "drifting"
7. New line deleted: "We pass half-caught and[?]" ; present line continued on insertion: "passing glimpses"
8. Deleted: "passing" . About half a line left vacant; text begins again on indented line. Deleted: "passing" ; inserted: "half-caught" above the deletion and "river"

Drift Sands As We.

Manuscript in LC (#41, sheet #92). Inscribed in black ink on white wove scrap. WW experimented with this title in 1860 and again in the 1870s and 1880s ("Sands and Drifts"). The writing indicates a late date. Cf. "Drift Sands."

Drift Sands

As we float idly[1] with the ebb
Echoes[2] and glints of sand and[3] twilight on the shore.

1. Deleted: "idly on the twilight" ; inserted above: "with [*del.*] on the" above "[*del.*] on the" and "tw" in "twilight"
2. Deleted: "Ripples" ; inserted above: "Echoes"
3. Deleted: "echoes from" ; inserted: "twilight on" above "and" and "[*del.*] echoes"

Drift Sands Ripple.

Manuscript in LC (#41, sheet #93). Inscribed in black ink on white wove scrap, approx. 3¾" x 7¼". Vertical blue rules ⅜" apart. Cf. "Drift Sands."

Drift Sands

Ripple[1] and glint of sand and[2] jutting the shore.
As[3] we float idly[4] by.

1. Deleted: "Echoes" ; inserted above: "Ripple"
2. Deleted: "ripples on" ; inserted: "jutting" above "[*del.*] ripples"
3. Deleted: "While" ; inserted above: "As"
4. Deleted: "on" before "by"

Notes and Flanges.

Manuscript in LC (#41, sheet #94). Inscribed in black ink, black pencil, and red ink on white wove scrap, approx. 2¼" x 7¹³/₁₆". Blue rules ⁵/₁₆" apart. "Flanges" (in the figurative sense) was apparently a WW coinage of his later years. Cf. the trial titles "?Flanges of Five years" and "Flanges of Sixty-Five" (LC #78, not published). For dating see "Drift Sands."

Notes and Flanges.—No. 1.
"Ripple, and¹ passing river, and² half-caught glimpse
As we sail idly,"
Ripples and glints. No [*illeg.*]³

1. Deleted in pencil: "broken" ; inserted in pencil and deleted in ink above: "passing" ; inserted in ink above the deletions: "passing"
2. Deleted in pencil: "passing" ; inserted in pencil above: "just caught" ; deleted in ink: "just" ; inserted in ink above: "half"
3. Preceding entry in red ink.

Ripple, and Echoes.

Manuscript in LC (#41, sheet #95). Inscribed in red ink on white wove paper, approx. 4½" x 7". Vertical blue rules ¼" apart. Cf. "Drift Sands."

Ripple, and echoes from the
Ripple,[1] and drift upon the shore, and resume[2]
As I drop float[3] down the ebb,
And

As I float sail[4] idly down the twilight ebb,
Ripple, and drift upon the sunset[5] shore, and half-caught[6] echoes
As I sail, idly.

1. Deleted: "and resumé,"
2. Preceding two words inserted above "the shore" . Probably "resumé" was intended.
3. Inserted as alternate above "op" in "drop" and "d" in "down"
4. Inserted as alternate above "float"
5. Inserted above "the" and "s" in "shore"
6. Preceding two words inserted above "echoes"

After Reading a Ballad.

Manuscript in LC (#78, sheets #644 R and V, 645, 646). Inscribed in black pencil and purple crayon on inside of opened envelope [*644 R* and *V*] postmarked Oct. 18, 1890. [*645* (not found) and *646*] are detached back flaps, which were apparently attached to the sealing flap when the MS was inscribed. Date after late October, 1890. Reproduced, Furness, facing 30.

After reading a Ballad

from Walter Scott.[1]

after reading[2] a *Ballad from Walter Scott*[3] [*illeg.*] ballad[4] [*illeg. del.*] Walter Scott

1. In black ink. Deleted in black ink below: "An" above "[*del.*] *The*" in *"The ancient ballad reciting."* Deleted below *"The . . . reciting"* : "An"
2. On sealing flap. Inserted in purple crayon.
3. Preceding five words in black ink. Entry runs over on detached side flap, [646].
4. Deleted on [646]: "reciting"

Full Tide and Ebb.

Manuscript in LC (#78, item #642). Inscribed in black ink on white laid paper, 8¼″ x 5⅛″. Chain lines 1″ apart. Probably a half-sheet of note paper. There is probably some relation to "He went out with the tide" and "another note" to "An Ended Day" (1891). The date is probably 1891.

Full Tide and Ebb.
Make three stanzas of about ?16 or[1] 17 lines each/ the first the flood
    second   ebb
    third[2]/
with note at bottom on Wash hospitals

1. Written or inserted above "17"
2. Description of the three stanzas in column.

The Mandolin.

Manuscript in Texas (Hanley). Inscribed in hanging indentation on white laid scrap. Blue rules ½" apart. *"The Mandolin"* is in black ink, the other two phrases in blue crayon. No date can be assigned, although the writing is sprawling and WW used blue crayon in his later years.

The Mandolin
? a kind of large guitar   ? brass strings

Who Shall Write.

Manuscript in Texas (Hanley). Inscribed in black pencil on white wove scrap. The writing and the subject, the sky, often commented on in *SD,* suggest a late date. On verso in WW's hand: "James L. Giffins."

Who shall write—who tell—who paint—the lessons of one mere day and night—the picture of the sky? If I were younger & well, I should lay out a poem, a whole book about them.

Bubble, Bubble.

Manuscript in Texas (Hanley). Inscribed in black pencil on white wove scrap. Cancelled by WW. No date can be assigned.

Bubble, bubble—*flup! flup!*—the big kettle is going it wild!

II. Explanations.

And As Here.

Manuscript not found. Text from *N&F,* 167(Pt. IV, #55; *CW,* X, 15). Since this was a Bucke MS, the date is probably before 1860.

And as here in this article, which is written to present truthfully and plainly one side of the story indispensable to the examination, (now just seriously beginning) of Walt Whitman's writings, may here perhaps not improperly be given in the brief, spinal idea of Walt Whitman's poetry.

[*Illeg.*] of These Poems.

Manuscript in LC (#79, item #765V). Inscribed in black pencil on white foolscap sheet, 7⅜" wide, badly wrinkled and torn. On recto in black ink, two stanzas from William Collins's "Ode on the Passions": "But O how altered was the tone . . . Shook thousand odors from his dewy wings.—" There seems to be little or no relation between recto and verso. Writing indicates a date in the 1850s or earlier.

[*Illeg.*][1] of these poems [*illeg.*] drawn to the element of sympathy [*illeg.*] should say it was sympathy.— if to pride [*illeg.*] should[?] say it was pride.— If to then love of the [*illeg.*] we should say it was the love of the body.— If to then spiritualism we say it is then spiritualism.— Not one instant is the soul forgotten, nor immortality forgotten, nor eternity forgotten.[2]

He demands[3] reality of literature. He will have nothing splendid or pretty or startling or new or talented, but honest truths.— If they are at the roots, he says, there is a live growth;[4] else all is of no avail.— There[5] can be no romances or fancy works, no grotesque ornament, no put on politeness

1. This and the other illegible and questioned passages in this paragraph are caused by the tattered state of the top of the MS.
2. Deleted paragraph: "Who is there that is not touched on the lips with a kiss?"
3. Deleted: "a"
4. Deleted: "but all"
5. Deleted: "must"

Otherways, They Remain.

Manuscript in LC (#63). Inscribed in black ink on pink wove scrap with pin holes at the center. The stationery, perhaps from the wrapper of the second issue of the 1855 *LG,* suggests a date between 1855 and 1857. The first two-thirds of the leaf is cancelled by two vertical lines: "Through the spirit of [*preceding four words ins. above* "Such a" *and* "w" *in* "work"] Such a work/ [*del.*] begun [*ins. above* "[*del.*] begun"] done Could this be done—our could it be [*preceding eight words del.*] —Such a work of This [*preceding five words ins.*] even generally [*del.*] understood [*ins. above* "understood"] acknowledged as [*del.*] necessary [*ins. above and del.*] needed necessary [*ins. above* "our"] to be done,— our lot would be [*preceding two words del.*] is [*ins. above* "ld" *in* "would"] severed once and forever [*preceding three words ins.*] from [*del.*] forever [*ins. and del.*] unworthy [*del.*] The dependence once and forever and We would too then [*preceding eight words del.*] through such a [*illeg.*] meaning [*del. illeg.*] become a live power These States [*preceding two words ins. above* "power"] see that the incumbency when [*illeg.*] that they [*preceding seven words brought down from a balloon*] take [*illeg.*] in The [*preceding four words del.*] universe of mind [*preceding three words del.*] the universe [*illeg.*] [*preceding three words ins. above*] of mind [*preceding two words inserted below line*]/" This cancelled passage is rewritten in "Through the spirit."

Otherways, they[1] remain[2] with doors barred against[3] the voice of namely our own voice[4] salvator,—[5]still it remains too rude,—[6]still nothing but our own.

1. Preceding two words inserted over deleted "Meanwhile an"
2. Deleted: ", at use" ; inserted and deleted above: "[*illeg.*],"
3. Deleted: [*illeg.*]
4. Preceding six words inserted above "salvator"
5. Deleted: "The [*ins.*] it is" ; inserted above: "still it remains"
6. Deleted: "The [*ins.*] it it" ; inserted: "still" above "n" in "nothing"

Through the Spirit.

Manuscript in LC (#63, #304). Inscribed in black ink on white wove scrap with blue lines ⅜″ apart. Since the text is a version of the deleted passage at the top of "Otherways, they remain," it probably also was written between 1855 and 1857.

Through the spirit of such[1] means, such[2] works,[3] These States ascend once and forever from unworthy dependence to stand in[4] the like[5] original vast[6] power in the[7] universe of mind,[8] as they stand[9] in the political[10] universe.—

1. Deleted: "a world"
2. Deleted: "a"
3. Deleted: "we see our lot would be [*preceding two words ins.*] [*illeg.*]" ; inserted above deletion and "over" : "These states ascend"
4. Preceding three words inserted above the following: "and [*illeg.*] The States [*illeg.*] [*ins. and del.*] standing as [*illeg.*]"
5. Deleted: [*illeg.*]
6. Preceding four words inserted above "[*del.*] as [*illeg.*] power in"
7. Deleted: "universe" ; inserted and deleted over "[*del.*] universe" : [*illeg.*] ; inserted over "of mind" : "universe"
8. Dash deleted.
9. Deleted: "amidst[?]"
10. Deleted: [*illeg.*]; inserted over deletion: "universe"

—"Even Now Jasmund.

Manuscript in Duke (35, #26). Inscribed on recto and verso in pencil and ink, where noted, on pink wove paper, 9⅝" x 5¾". The left edge shows evidence of having been glued on to a printed surface. A scrap of white wove paper, 1⅜" x 3¾", and a newspaper clipping are pasted on recto; on verso is pasted a scrap from an unidentified school text of Ossian. The width of the type page is 3⁵/₁₆". C. Carroll Hollis, in "Whitman and William Swinton: A Co-operative Friendship," *AL,* 30 (1959), 436, identifies the quotation from Schele De Vere as being from a copy, now in the Feinberg collection and once owned by William Swinton, and dates the entry as being from 1856 to 1858, when Whitman and Swinton were close. Notice also, of course, the dates mentioned in the text for various entries. See also Stovall, *AL,* 26 (1954), 345, and "Ossian—? for Note Preface." First published in *N&F,* 73, 96–97 (Pt. II, #70; Pt. III, #48, #49, #50; *CW,* IX, 43, 93–94).

[1]—"Even now Jasmund, the people's
poet, prefers to sing in Provençal."

De Vere's Comparative Philology
1853.

Pythagoras was very beautiful, and lived to a great age.— He was of athletic tastes, a boxer, a dancer, wrestler, runner, &c.— He delighted in music and[2] perfumes—wore his beard long,[3]

Sept. '56
"Leaves of Grass," must be called *not* objective, but altogether *subjective —"I know"* runs through them[4] as a perpetual refrain. [:][5] Yet the great Greek poems,[6] also the Teutonic poems, also Shakespeare and all the great masters' have been objective epic[7]—they have described characters, events, wars, heroes, &c—

1. Asterisk and fist pointing down, at the upper left, referring to a newspaper clipping pasted at the bottom of the leaf on the presentation of a crown of gold to the Provençal poet, Jacques Jasmin (1798–1864). Clipping marked by asterisk and Whitman's notation: "early in '57"
2. Deleted: "dancing" ; inserted above: "perfumes"
3. "Sept. '56 . . . refrain." is inscribed on a pasted-in scrap. See William A. Little, "Walt Whitman and the *Nibelungenlied,*" *PMLA,* 80 (1965), 562–563.
4. Deleted: "all, like"
5. Through "also Shakespeare" to right of a brace opposite "Sept. '56 . . . refrain." Remainder across leaf, connected by line.
6. Deleted: "and"
7. Inserted in ink in wordspace above the dash.

[2] Jas Macpherson 1737—1796

Ossian, (The real Ossian, if ever there were one is put down at 300 or 400 B.C.)[8]
Ossian bosky shield—wooden[9] shield[10] very likely a myth altogether[11]

The Irish swear that Ossian belongs to them—that he was born, lived, and wrote in Ireland

---

8. Parenthetical material inserted in ink over [illeg.] in pencil.
9. Inserted over: [illeg.]
10. Fist pointing to the following phrase.
11. Clipping from James Macpherson's *Poems of Ossian:* "Sect. CCLXXIV.—The Sun," ll. 1–10. From the vocabulary exercise on the recto of this clipping, it appears to be from an unidentified school text.

*Shakspeare and Walter Scott.

Manuscript in Duke (49, #35). Inscribed in black pencil with emendations in black ink, as noted, on a blue, wove, Williamsburgh tax blank. At the upper left is an asterisk which probably connected this MS with another not now identifiable. At the upper right is a circled "1" possibly in another hand. First published *N&F,* 91–92 (Pt. III, #34; *CW,* IX, 84). The date must be 1857 or a little later.

*Shakspeare and Walter Scott are indeed[1] limners and recorders—as Homer was one before, and the greatest perhaps of any[2] recorder.—[3] All belong to the[4] class who depict characters and events;[5] and they are masters[6] of the kind.—

I will be also a master, after my own kind,[7] making the poems of emotions, as they pass[8] or stay—the poems of freedom, and the exposé of personality— singing in high tones, Democracy and the New World of it through These States.—

1. Deleted: "the" ; inserted: "limners and" above "[*del.*] the" and "recorders"
2. Preceding three words inserted above "est" in "greatest" and "record" in "recorders"
3. Deleted: "They" ; inserted in pencil above and deleted in black ink: "Those now named" ; "all" written over as "All" in ink.
4. Deleted: "masters of the"
5. Deleted: dash.
6. Deleted: "among their" ; inserted: "of the"
7. Succeeding ten words written over erased pencil entry. Deleted: "of"
8. Deleted: "and" ; inserted above: "or"

The Poetry of Other Lands.

Manuscript in Duke (27, #37). Inscribed in black ink on verso of fragment of Williamsburgh tax blank, approx. 3⅝" x 4¼". First printed in *N&F*, 175 (Pt. IV, #100; *CW*, X, 28). This was written between 1857 and 1860.

The Poetry of other lands lies in the past—what they have been.[1] The Poetry of America lies in the future—what These States and their[2] coming men and women[3] are certainly to be.

1. "in the . . . been" probably added later on two lines above "[*del.*] American" and "The Poetry of" . Deleted: "American"
2. Deleted: "f"
3. Deleted: "of there" "cer"

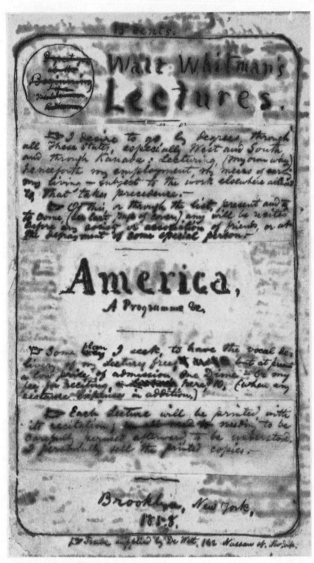

WALT WHITMAN'S LECTURES. Trent Collection, Rare Book Department, William
R. Perkins Library, Duke University, Trent *Cat,* 58. Recto. See pp. 1436–1437.

WALT WHITMAN'S LECTURES. Trent Collection, Rare Book Department, William R. Perkins Library, Duke University. Trent *Cat,* 58. Verso. See pp. 1437–1438.

Walt Whitman's Lectures.

Manuscript in Trent (57, #37). Inscribed in black ink with emendations in black ink and black pencil on recto and verso of a leaf of pink wove paper, approx. 6″ x 3⅝″. The leaf is made of two pieces of paper of the same dimensions pasted back to back to form a single stiff sheet. The paper is probably from leftover wrappers for *LG* (1855).

The general appearance of the recto is as of printer's layout. The text, with the exception of the price and the distributor's name, is enclosed in a rectangular frame approx. ⅜″ from top, right, and bottom edges, narrowing from ³/₁₆″ at top left edge to ⅛″ at the bottom left. There are short rules between the title and the first paragraph and the subhead, "America . . ." ; between the subhead and the third paragraph, and between the fourth paragraph and the place and date. The verso, which is very closely written, has no special characteristics.

WW revised the MS at least three times. The first revision, in ink, was probably made in the course of composition; the second, deletions and insertions in black pencil, was probably done later; the third, again in ink but involving pencil revisions, was made still later (see *nn* 21, 28).

What Whitman had in mind for this painstaking arrangement is not clear. Bucke, Harned, and Traubel (*CW*, I, liv) believe it to have been intended as the front cover of a book. Allen (219) calls it a "circular" and thinks that the price was that of the printed lectures. On the face of it, it does look like a circular, but in that case why did not WW put the price and distributor in paragraph four? Very possibly WW thought of it as a pamphlet, although it would have been a very small one, hardly more than a single sheet.

Allen also notes the anomaly that in 1858 WW was fully occupied as editor of the Brooklyn *Daily Times,* a position he held until June, 1859. But there is no reason to think that he would not have dropped journalism for prophecy in a moment had he thought it feasible.

The manuscript was first printed in *CW,* I, liv–lvii. I am much indebted to Mr. Jan Tor Hall, William L. Perkins Library, Duke University, for his careful examination of the MS and his contributions to these notes. See illustration in this edition.

[*1*] 15 cents.[1]

Walt[2] Whitman's
Lectures.[3]

———

1. Above the frame.
2. Inside the frame. In a circle to left of title: "I greet you at the Beginning of a great career. R. W. Emerson" deleted in ink.
3. Entire title handlettered; "Lectures" somewhat larger than preceding words, as is "America" below.

I[4] desire to go, by degrees, through all These States, especially West and South, and through Kanada: Lecturing, (my own way,) henceforth my employment, my means of earning my living—subject to the work elsewhere alluded to, that takes precedence.—

Of[5] this, or through the list, present and[6] to come, (see last page of cover,) any will be recited before any society or association of friends, or at the defrayment of some special person.—

America
A Programme, &c.[7]

Some[8] plan I seek, to have the vocal delivery of my lectures free;[9] but at present a low price of admission, One Dime— Or my fee for reciting,[10] here, $10, (when any distance expenses in addition.)

Each[11] Lecture will be printed, with its recitation;[12] needing to be carefully perused afterward, to be understood. I personally sell the printed copies.—

Brooklyn, New York
1858.

Trade[13] supplied by De Witt, 162 Nassau st. New York.[14]

[2] *Notice—Random*[15] *Intentions—Two Branches*.

Henceforth[16] two co-expressions.— They expand, amicable, from common sources, but each[17] with[18] individual stamp, by itself.—[19]

4. Preceded by a small fist pointing right.
5. Preceded by a small fist pointing right.
6. "to" is written at end of the line and at the beginning of the next.
7. Title handlettered. "America" in large letters.
8. Preceded by small hand pointing right. Deleted in ink: "way" ; inserted above in ink: "plan"
9. Deleted in ink: "to cost [*illeg.*]" . Entire reading not clear. Semicolon probably inserted.
10. Deleted in ink: "a Lecture" . Not clear.
11. Preceded by a small fist pointing right.
12. Deleted in ink: "for all need to"
13. Preceded by a small fist pointing right.
14. Below the frame.
15. Inserted above in ink on pencilled arrow.
16. Original opening "Now and" deleted in ink; "henceforth" capitalized in ink.
17. Deleted in ink: "with its" ; inserted above in ink and deleted: "of"
18. Inserted in pencil.
19. Preceding two words inserted in ink on a caret, although they are at the end of a line.

First, POEMS,[20] Leaves of Grass, as of *Intuitions,* the Soul, the Body,[21] (male or female)[22] descending below laws, social routine,[23] creeds, literature, to celebrate[24] the inherent, the red blood, one[25] man in himself, or one[26] woman in herself— Songs of thoughts and wants, hitherto repressed[27] by writers.— Or[28] it may as well be avowed, to give the personality of Walt Whitman, out and out, evil and good—whatever he is[29] or thinks, that sharply set down, in a book[30] the Spirit commanding it; if certain outsiders[31] stop puzzled, or dispute, or laugh, very well.—

Second, LECTURES,[32] as of[33] Reasoning, Reminiscences, Comparison, politics,[34] the Intellectual, the Esthetic, the desire for Knowledge,[35] the sense of richness, refinement, and beauty in the mind, as an art, a sensation—from an American point of view.—[36]Also, in Lectures, the meaning of Religion, as a statement.— Every[37] thing[38] from an American point of view[39]

Of the above,[40] (so far, only the beginning) both would increase upon themselves.—[41] By degrees to fashion for These States,[42] two athletic volumes, the first to speak for the Permanent[43] Soul, (which speaks for all, materials too, but can be understood only by the like of itself—the same being the reason that what is[44]

20. Double underscoring in black pencil.
21. Words in ink within following parenthesis deleted in pencil: "a man, a woman" . Present reading inserted above in pencil.
22. Deleted in ink: "passing heedlessly through" ; inserted in ink: "descending" above "[*del.*] passing" and "below" above "[*del.*] through"
23. Comma probably obscured by insertion in following line.
24. Deleted in pencil: "a human being," ; inserted in pencil and deleted in ink: "what is" above "[*del.*] human" ; inserted in ink: "the" above "[*del.*] being"
25. Deleted in pencil: "male" ; inserted above in pencil: "man"
26. Deleted in pencil: "female" ; inserted above in pencil: "woman"
27. Inserted in ink above "to" in "hitherto" and "by"
28. Deleted in ink: "in plain" ; deleted in pencil: "Leaves of Grass give" ; inserted below the line in ink: "it may as well be . . . to give" . Deleted in pencil above deleted "in plain" : "to give" ; above deleted "Grass give" : "in [*illeg.*]" ; inserted above and deleted in pencil: "in a book"
29. Indecipherable mark of punctuation heavily deleted in ink.
30. Preceding three words inserted in pencil above "down the"
31. Deleted in ink: "rage" ; inserted in ink: "stop puzzled, or" above "rs" in "outsiders" and "disp" in "dispute"
32. Underscored in pencil.
33. Deleted in ink: "*Knowledge* (or the desire for knowledge,)"
34. Inserted in pencil above "n," in "Comparison," and "the"
35. Preceding four words inserted in ink above "Esthetic, the sense"
36. Preceding six words inserted in pencil.
37. In pencil, deleted in ink: "all" ; inserted to the left in ink: "Every"
38. In ink over "this" in pencil.
39. Preceding six words inserted in pencil above "as a statement" . WW apparently wrote first in pencil and revised in ink.
40. In ink, deleted in pencil: "two" ; inserted in pencil: "(so far, [*del. in ink*] beginning" ; inserted in ink: "only the beginning)" above "both would increase up" in "upon"
41. Deleted in pencil: "not at any time finished, any more than any live operation of nature is—but unfolding, urging onward and outward."
42. Deleted in ink: "(it may as well be avowed),"
43. Inserted in ink above "the Soul"
44. Deleted in pencil: "musical"

wisdom music[45] to one is gibberish to another.)[46] But the second, temporary[47] shall be the speech of the attempts at[48] Statements, Argumentation, Art. Both to[49] illustrate America—[50]illustrate the whole, not merely sections, members—throbbing from the heart, inland, the West, around the great Lakes, or along the flowing Ohio, or Missouri, or Mississippi.

Curious, much advertising his own appearance and views, (it cannot be helped)[51] offensive to many, too free, too savage and natural,[52] candidly owning that he has neither virtue or knowledge—such, en passant,[53] of Walt Whitman,[54] his own way, to his own work—because that, with the rest, is needed—because on less terms how can he get what he has resolved to have, to himself, and to America?

45. Inserted in pencil above "m" in "wisdom" and "to"
46. Illegible mark of punctuation deleted in ink.
47. Inserted in ink above "cond" in "second" and "shall"
48. Deleted in pencil: "Knowledge" ; inserted in pencil: "Statements"
49. Deleted in pencil: "identify" ; inserted in pencil above: "illustrate"
50. Deleted in pencil: "identify" ; inserted in pencil: "illustrate" above the deletion and "A" in "America"
51. Parenthetical phrase in ink inserted above "ws . . . to"
52. Deleted: "never restraining his egotism,"
53. Two words inserted in ink over pencil blur.
54. Deleted in ink: "determined to proceed after" . Possible insertion and deletion above: "determined"

List of Things Recognized.

Manuscript in NYPL (Berg). Inscribed in black ink on two strips of soft yellow paper, approx. 11¾" x 4½" and 4¾" x 4¼" each, pasted one above the other. Bucke, *N&F*, 148*n*, dates it to "the pre-poetical era in Whitman's life," but evidence of other MS on lectures and oratory suggests this was written in the late 1850s. The yellow paper may be leftover wrapper stock from *LG* 1855 (Bowers, xl*in*). Although the Atlantic cable failed after a month and was not relaid until 1866, it was completed August, 1858. First printed *N&F*, 148 (Pt. III, #199; *CW*, IX, 200–201).

List of things[1] recognized by[2] my lectures./

The Texan Ranger
The Boston truckman
The young men and women too of Philadelphia—Baltimore[3] Cincinnati, Chicago, St. Louis, Charleston, New Orleans,/

Above[4] all I recognize the localities and persons of my own land—[5]

The Kentuckian, The Tennessean, the Kanadian, the Californian the Alabamian, the Virginian the Californian/
The lumberer of Maine, the oysterman of Virginia, the corn-gatherer of Tennessee, (look in Census—or rather List M.S/[6]

I recognize in America the land of materials—the land of iron, cotton,[7] wheat, beef, pork, fish and fruit—[8]

---

1. Deleted: "present"
2. Deleted: "the spirit of"
3. Preceding two words inserted above "of Cincinnati"
4. Line preceded by a fist pointing right.
5. The preceding twelve words are in a smaller hand than the rest of the text and may have been inserted.
6. The preceding seven words in a smaller hand inserted on two lines at right. The single parenthesis is followed by a fist pointing right.
7. Inserted above "wh" in "wheat"
8. Entire entry in small writing.

I recognize all the great inventions, machines, and improvements of to-day, the ten-cylinder press, printing[9] thirty-thousand sheets an hour—the electric telegraph that binds continents and threads the bottoms of seas—the track of railroads[10]— the cheap newspaper[11]—[12]

—the idea that the common[13] American mechanic, farmer, sailor, &c.[14] is just as eligible as any to the highest ideal of dignity,[15] perfection, and knowledge, (I sometimes think an independent American workingman[16] is more eligible than any other.)

9. Deleted: "twenty-thousand"
10. Comma deleted.
11. Period deleted.
12. End of first strip of paper.
13. Inserted above "Americ" in "American"
14. Deleted: "can occupy"
15. Inserted above and deleted: "happiness" above "perf" in "perfection"
16. Deleted: [*illeg.*]

This[?] Has Made.

Manuscript in LC (#73, sheet #457V; #63, sheet #288V). Inscribed in black pencil on white wove scrap, originally approx. 4⅞" x 8", later divided vertically. Cancelled. On recto of left-hand scrap (LC, #73, sheet #457V) is "go into the subject." This scrap is cancelled with blue crayon. The writing of "this[?] has made" is smoother than that of "go into the subject." The words "organs and acts" are used in "Starting from Paumanok" (1860), sec. 12, l. 166. The writing does not rule out a date slightly before 1860.

this[?][1] has[2] made his[3] poem of the complete human form, in[4] the faith[5] that it is God's highest[6] work, & perfect masterpiece[7] and that[8] those of its organs and acts[9] tacitly yielded as vile, are not[10] in reality vile,[11] but[12] believing that they too are[13] to be mentioned and faced, and to be openly treated in literature.

1. First line trimmed at top. Deleted: [*illeg. illeg.*]
2. Deleted: "boldly[?]"
3. Deleted: "the complete body" ; inserted above: "his poem of [*ins.*] the complete"
4. Deleted: "his poem, with entire in the entire [*preceding three words ins. above* "with entire"]"
5. Deleted: "and proce" above "highest"
6. Deleted: "[*ins. above* "pe" *in* "perfect"] most perfect [*illeg. ins.*]" ; inserted: "highest" above "work"
7. Preceding three words inserted above "and that"
8. Deleted: "org"
9. Deleted: "though"
10. Deleted: "so"
11. Preceding word and comma inserted above "ity" in "reality"
12. Deleted: [*illeg.*] ; inserted above: "believing"
13. Deleted: "[*illeg.*] good"

Poems.

Manuscript in Duke (46, #25). Inscribed in black pencil on verso of a blue Williamsburgh tax blank, 8⅝″ x 4½″. This must therefore have been written in 1857 or after. The coupling of poems and lessons suggests "Walt Whitman's Lectures." First printed in *N&F*, 57–58 (Pt. II, #18–19; *CW*, IX, 8–9).

Poems[1]

Hasting, urging, resistless,—no flagging, not even in the "thoughts" or meditations—florid—spiritual—good, not from their direct but indirect meanings—to be perceived with the same perception that enjoys music, flowers, and the beauty of men and women—free and luxuriant—/

Lessons[2]

Clear, alive, luminous,—full of facts—full of physiology—acknowledging the democracy,[3] the people——must have an alert character, even in the reading of them/

—The enclosing theory of "Lessons," to permeate All The States, answering for All, (no foreign imported models,)—*full of hints*, *laws*, *& informations*, to make a superb American Intellect and Character in any or all The States—

Also[4] the strength, Command & Luxuriance of Oratory

1. The body of the text is inscribed on the right two-thirds of the page. "Poems" and "Lessons" are inscribed in the left third approximately opposite the third line. A vertical line, perhaps intended as a bracket, extends from the first line of the text to the right of "Poems"; a horizontal line two-thirds of the way from the left divides the two entries; a vertical line the full length of the body separates it from "Lessons."
2. See *n* above.
3. Semicolon corrected to comma.
4. A hand pointing right marks this paragraph.

I Say That.

Manuscript not found. First published in *N&F,* 55 (Pt. II, #3; *CW,* IX, 3). Since it was a Bucke MS, it probably was written before 1860.

I say that if once the conventional distinctions were dispelled from our eyes we should see just as much.

I do not expect to dispel them by arguing against them, I sweep them away by advancing to a new phase of development where they fail of themselves.

Introductions to *Leaves of Grass*.

The eleven manuscripts pinned into the front and back flyleaves of the paperbound *LG* (1855, 2d issue,) are among the most interesting of WW's MSS.

The best introduction to their study is that by Furness (118–126), which should be read by every student. Aside from telling the curious story of their disappearance and their rediscovery by the literary executors, Furness correctly emphasizes (124–125) the way WW cannibalized his manuscripts. WW borrowed freely, and the relations among them are complex. It is, further, as Furness points out, difficult to date any one of them with great confidence. For example, "Introduction" (No. 1) can be dated in part to May, 1861, yet has passages written later and "I commenced Leaves of Grass" (No. 11) can also be dated in part to 1861 and in part to 1870.

As Furness points out, there was a larger problem, for WW never wrote an introduction to the *Leaves* which he would accept. A much-tamed version of the 1855 Preface was buried in *Complete Prose Works,* as were some of the later prefaces. At the time he was working on these introductions he was writing "Criticism" and the later "Introduction to the London Edition," which he never printed. In the attempt represented by these manuscripts, he worked over the same cluster of ideas eleven times, yet worked them over in different ways so that they fall into three distinguishable, if not distinct, groups: "one for an 'Introduction?' (or 'Introductory Notice' or 'Advertisement') for *Leaves of Grass;* another for an 'Inscription to the Reader at the entrance of *Leaves of Grass';* and a final record of Whitman's own appraisal of his work, together with proposals for its continuance and extension."(Furness, 120). In the first group we can place "Introduction" (No. 1), *"Introduction"* (No. 3) and "Introductory" (No. 4). In the second group, all in verse, are "To the Reader at the Entrance of Leaves of Grass" (No. 2)," Inscription to the Reader at the entrance of Leaves of Grass" (No. 5), "Thus wise it comes" (No. 6), INSCRIPTION at the entrance of Leaves of Grass"(No. 8), "Meantime, plans failing" (No. 9) and "The Epos of a Life" (No. 10). The third group comprises "(Some good points)" (No. 7) and "I commenced Leaves of Grass" (No. 11). Of course, all of this painful effort was not lost. The manuscripts of the second group were distilled into "One's-self I Sing" (1867); ideas and even language from the others appear in *Democratic Vistas* and in "As a Strong Bird on Pinions Free" (1872). Yet as WW was rejecting these manuscripts, he was following the possibilities of the second group. In *LG* (1872) he printed for the first time the cluster called "Inscriptions."

The introductions are printed here in the order indicated by Furness's analysis. The reader should remember that the numbers were assigned either by Oscar Lion, who obtained the MSS from Traubel, or by Furness, or by the New York Public Library. They are used here only to distinguish between almost identical titles.

Dec. 23. 1864.

Manuscript in NYPL (Lion). Introduction #1. Homemade notebook of white laid paper, 7¾" x 4¾", tied by light blue silk ribbon through holes in center fold. The actual leaves are pasted on stubs of an earlier notebook, some of which, as noted, have illegible inscriptions. Inscription in black ink with black-pencil and blue-pencil emendations. First three leaves numbered on recto by WW. The whole was pasted down to *LG* (1855, 2d issue), iii, by WW.

The extraordinary form of the notebook—sheets pasted on stubs—may indicate not so much parsimony as intensity of the revision, since the pasting otherwise would have been more trouble than the manufacture of a new notebook. The endorsement of December 23, 1864 on [*1*] suggests WW's satisfaction, as does the amount of the revision and the use of paste-overs. At least four levels of revision of the original inscription in black ink seem to be present: (1) current deletions and insertions in black ink, (2) deletions and insertions in black pencil at some later time (the most frequent), (3) deletions in pencil and insertions in black ink, (4) the solitary emendation in blue pencil.

The date is obviously prior to December 23, 1864, and almost certainly is 1861. WW inadvertently omitted the date when pasting the notebook together, [*13*], but his reference to writing on his birthday and the close relationship to "Introduction No. 3," "*Introduction.*" May 31, 1861, indicate a date of 1861 for this more developed statement. Since the third edition had been printed in the summer of 1860, it may be an introduction to the unpublished *Banner at Day-Break*, which was announced sometime after June 16, 1860 (Allen, 267), or, possibly, for a projected fourth edition of the whole *Leaves*.

First printed in Furness 127–130, with a photograph of the cover facing 126. Furness's block paragraphs are not indicated in the MS.

[*1*]¹Dec. 23. 1864 Good—& must be used

Introduction.

[*3;*²2 See *n*13 below.] I claim that, in literature, I have judged and felt every thing from an American point of view³—which is no local standard, for America to me, includes humanity & is⁴ the universal⁵

1. Actually the outside front cover. The title, in black ink, is centrally placed. WW's approbation is in black ink at the top and to the right. The entire leaf is pasted on a stub.
2. WW numbered this leaf, "2"
3. Pencilled entries noted in appropriate places in [*3*].
4. Pencil. Inserted from [*2*] where it is indicated for insertion by an asterisk and a small fist: "—which is. . . . the universal" Deleted in pencil: "and made a poem from the same."
5. Deleted: "the the"

America,[6] (I have said to myself,) demands one Song, at any rate, that is bold, modern, and all-surrounding as she is herself. Its[7] scope like hers, must[8] span[9] the future & dwell on it as much as on the present or the past. Like her it must[10] extricate itself from the models of the past, and, while courteous to them must be sung[11] from the depths of its own native spirit exclusively. Like her, it must bring to the van, and hold up at all hazards, the banner of inalienable rights, and the divine pride of man in[12] himself.[13] It must pierce through the shifting envelope of costumes & formulas,[14] and strike perennial[15] born qualities and organs, which always have meaning deeper than even[16] any theories of morals or metaphysics, or any conventional distinctions whatever[17]. . . . . Hitherto the geniuses of nation have been listening to poems in which natural humanity bends low, humiliated. But the genius of America cannot listen [5; [18] 4[19]] to such poems. Erect and haughty must the chant be, and then the genius of America will listen with pleased ears. . . . . The meaning of America is Democracy

6. Hanging indentation. Cf. "America (I to myself have said)" for a variant.

7. Deleted in ink: "spirit aim" ; inserted and deleted in black pencil: "aim" ; inserted in pencil: "scope"

8. Deleted in pencil: "have" ; inserted in pencil: "span"

9. Preceding three words and ampersand inserted in black pencil. Deleted: "more than" ; inserted in black pencil: "as much as on"

10. On a paste-over: "be sung . . . her,"

11. End of paste-over.

12. A third paste-over, which continues to end of leaf.

13. On [2] the following in pencil and ink but cancelled: "*It must pierce through the [ins.] shifting envelope of costumes and strike born qualities and organs, which have meaning deeper than any theories of morals or metaphysics, [del. in pencil] and [ins. in pencil] or the distinctions of good and bad [preceding seven words in black ink]." Obviously a draft for revision of the text under the facing paste-over, but discarded.

14. Preceding two words inserted in pencil.

15. Inserted in ink.

16. Inserted in ink.

17. Inserted in pencil.

18. WW numbered this leaf "3." Entire leaf pasted on a stub.

19. On [4] a series of notes entirely in pencil which seem to relate to [5]:
* The labor [illeg.] [del.] hands mechanics, farmers, boatmen and men and women in factories only needs to be siezed upon by [two words del.] the poets the right

(*2) Let me then, for (I feel that it must be so) saturate

[Three words del.] I will have [three words ins.] Let me saturate my poem [two words ins.] saturated bodily animal robustness and health, [two words del.] and owning [three words ins.] and own the complete physiology

(*2) [Del.] And Let me, [three words del.] too Also let

3)* [Two words del.] I desire [ins. and del.] would to give [del.] A general photograph of modern times [del.] and inclusive of commerce, inventions, and manly trades—and of the crowded tableaux of cities, and of continents, in the tone of large toleration, now prevalent, that [del.] embrace accepts all the [del.] varieties races and [del.] races of the globe such that I would put in [del.] also I will have [illeg.] a poem saturated with bodily robustness and health.

The final[20] meaning of Democracy through many transmigrations[21] is to press on through all[22] ridicules,[23] arguments, and ostensible failures, to put in practice the idea of the sovereignty, license, sacredness of the individual. This idea isolates, for reasons,[24] each separate man and woman in the world;—while the idea of Love fuses and combines the whole.[25] Out of the fusing of these twain, opposite as they are, I seek to make a homogeneous Song—([26] A third idea also, is, or shall be put there,[27] namely Religion—the idea which, purifying[28] purifies all things[29] gives endless[30] purpose an[31] destiny and growth to a man, or woman,[32] and in him or her[33] condenses the drift[34] of all things.[35] These[36] for the main result[37], which though I do not touch in my book,[38] is the purpose of all, namely the Unknown, which fills time, & is as pure as the known. . . . . The employment and personnel of mechanics, farmers, boatmen, [7; 6 note][39] laborers, and men and women in factories, must be seized upon with decision by America's bards[40] to be by them[41] saturated with[42] fullest charges of electric illumination[43] and to be held up forever with enthusiasm and dignity. Our highest themes are thus at hand.[44] Current, practical times[45] are to be photographed[46] embracing the war,

20. Inserted in pencil.
21. Preceding three words inserted in pencil. Cf. "Democratic Vistas," *Prose 92*, II, 374–375, ll. 397ff.
22. Deleted in ink: "failures"
23. Deleted in pencil: "and"
24. Preceding two words inserted in pencil. Deleted in ink: "for identity's and [*del. in ink*] perf freedom's sake"
25. Deleted: "The twain are in the following Song [*over* "chants"]" . Inserted and deleted in pencil: "If" . Cf. "Democratic Vistas," *Prose 92*, II, 381, l. 612.
26. Preceding eighteen words inserted in pencil.
27. Inserted in pencil.
28. Dash deleted in ink.
29. Inserted in pencil: "things" . Deleted in ink: "other" . Inserted and deleted in pencil: "other" . Deleted in pencil: "ideas and things, and"
30. Deleted in pencil: "meaning"
31. Originally "and"
32. Preceding two words inserted in pencil.
33. Preceding two words inserted in pencil.
34. Inserted and deleted: "to gro"
35. End of a paste-over. The following twenty-two words are brought down from the top of the leaf on an arrow. It is not clear whether they are meant to precede or follow the dots.
36. Deleted in ink: "and all"
37. Inserted in ink: "result" . Deleted in ink: "purpose" . Inserted and deleted in ink: "plan[?]"
38. Preceding three words inserted in ink.
39. Black ink; pencil emendations. Not numbered by WW. Pasted on a stub, illegible pen and pencil entries on verso of stub. [6] inserted in [9] according to WW's directions.
40. Deleted: "and must be" . Inserted in pencil over inserted and erased "I say [*illeg.*]" : "to be"
41. Preceding two words inserted in ink.
42. Deleted: "their" ; inserted and deleted: "our"
43. Deleted: ";—must" ; inserted and deleted: "and to"
44. Sentence inserted in pencil.
45. Deleted in pencil: "must" ; inserted in pencil: "are to"
46. Deleted in pencil: "including" ; inserted in pencil: "embracing the war,"

commerce, inventions, Washington, Abraham Lincoln[47] the mechanics[48] and the[49] great work now going on, the settlement of this Western World the great railroads, &c[50]—embracing indeed[51] the races and locations of the whole world.——[52] . . . .[53] Prevalent poems cast back only facial[54] physiognomy, a part. In the following chant, the apparition of the whole form, as of one unclothed before a mirror is cast back.[55] The teachers of the day teach, (and stop there) that the unclothed face is divine. {9; 8 *blank*}[56] It is indeed; but I say that only [57]the unclothed body,[58] diviner still is fully divine.[59] These Leaves image that[60] physiology—not apologizing for it, but exulting openly in it, and taking it to myself. . . . . I know the rectitude of my intentions, & appeal to the future.[61] I seek, by singing these, to behold & exhibit[62] what I am as specimen to all—[63] these material, aesthetic and spiritual relations, I am[64] & tally the same in you whoever you are[65] The[66] Body[67] merged with & in[68] the soul & the Soul merged in the Body,[69] I seek. For once, anyhow, needs that tantalizing[70] wonder, to go or seek to go[71] in a poem, in perfect faith in itself—not as it might be, or as it is fancied in conventional[72] literature to be, but as it actually is, good and bad, as maturity[73] and passions youth, sex, experience, & the world,[74] turn it out. A living,

47. Names inserted in ink.
48. Deleted: "&c. ; with" ; inserted: "and [*del.*] all"
49. Deleted in ink: "mighty" ; inserted in ink: "great"
50. Preceding four words inserted in pencil. Deleted in pencil: "and" ; inserted in pencil: "embracing"
51. Deleted in ink: "with"
52. Deleted in pencil: ", in [*del. in ink*] the that tone of the [*del. in ink*] large toleration that accepts them all" . Inserted: ".—"
53. Deleted: asterisk.
54. Inserted in ink.
55. Deleted: "We are taught" ; inserted: "The teachers . . . teach"
56. Black ink, pencil emendation. Pasted on stub. Illegible writing in ink on verso.
57. Inserted in ink.
58. Deleted in ink: "is"
59. Preceding three words inserted in ink.
60. Deleted in ink: "divine"
61. Inserted from pencilled [6] on authority of WW's inserted note: "?* 2 pages back" . See *n*39. Deleted in pencil: "?(I know the rectitude of my intention and appeal to the future,"
62. Preceding two words inserted.
63. Preceding four words and dash inserted in pencil.
64. Deleted in pencil: "&" . WW neglected to delete a period.
65. Preceding nine words inserted in pencil. Cf. "Poem of You, Whoever You Are" (1856), now "To You (whoever you are)."
66. Deleted in ink: "joined"
67. Deleted in ink: "with"
68. Preceding four words inserted in ink.
69. Preceding seven words inserted in ink.
70. Deleted in ink: "nonpareil and wonder" ; deleted in pencil: "study" ; inserted in pencil: "wonder"
71. Preceding four words inserted in ink.
72. Inserted in ink.
73. Inserted in pencil above "maturity" and deleted in ink: "body and soul"
74. Preceding six words inserted in ink; "sex" inserted.

flush, eating and drinking man, the mould—and as[75] from that, without wincing, to mould a book. . . . . Not but that[76] modesty and[77] [*11; 10 blank*][78] delicatesse ?decorum[79], and what proceeds[80] from them & accumulates[81] in literature &c.,[82] are important. But that, in literature, &c.[83] we were all lost without redemption, except we[84] retain the[85] sexual fibre of things, and simplicity, and acknowledge, as supreme above[86] those pictures and plays, man, nude and abysmal, and[87] indifferent to mere[88] conventional delicatesse.[89] Here then, (make or break,[90] for me it must be so,)[91] I sing the[92] complete physiology.[93]

[*13; 12 blank*][94] this introduction on my birthday, after having looked over the poem, as far as accomplished. So far, so well; but the most and the best of it, I perceive, remains to be written—the work of my life ahead, which[95] if all prove propitous I would yet do. . . . . . All as is appropriate to me. Of the[96] crowds of poets, current or on record, with performance popular and[97] appropriate to them— they[98] to their use, (which is great,)—I,[99] perhaps alone, to mine. I do not purpose[1]

75. Inserted in pencil.
76. Deleted in pencil: "sentimentalism" ; inserted in pencil: "modesty"
77. Deleted in pencil: "conventional"
78. Pasted on stub. Not numbered by WW.
79. Inserted in pencil.
80. Deleted in ink: "accumulates out of" ; inserted in ink: "proceeds from"
81. Preceding two words inserted in ink.
82. Deleted in ink: ";—not but that these" ; comma inserted.
83. Preceding three words inserted in pencil.
84. Deleted: "keep up at the same time" ; inserted and deleted in pencil above "up at the" : "clean the" ; inserted in ink: "retain"
85. Deleted in ink: "real" ; inserted in ink: "sexual"
86. Deleted: "anything else" ; inserted in ink: [*del. in ink*] all those [*corrected in pencil from* "these"] pictures and plays,"
87. Deleted in pencil: "quite"
88. Preceding two words inserted in ink; inserted in pencil and deleted in ink: "mere" ; inserted and deleted in ink: "all"
89. Deleted in pencil: "Let me" ; inserted in pencil: "Here"
90. Deleted in pencil: "(for" ; inserted in pencil: "(make or break" ; inserted in ink: "for me"
91. Deleted in pencil: "pourtray" ; inserted in pencil and overwritten in ink: "I sing"
92. Deleted in ink: "full man, owning"
93. Deleted in pencil: "And let [*previously del. in ink*] me I, whatever others do, sing these things, [*previously del. in ink*] sing loud and clear, and without a particle of compromise, as part of *the song of Democracy* [*underlined in pencil*] . . . ." (WW's dots.) About eight lines appear to have been cut off.
94. Black ink. Pasted on a stub; not numbered by WW.
95. Inserted in ink: "[*two words del. in ink*] if personal if all prove propitious"
96. Deleted in pencil: "teeming and applauded" ; inserted and deleted in pencil: "popular"
97. Preceding two words inserted in pencil.
98. Inserted in pencil and erased: "three poets"
99. Deleted in ink: "alone" ; inserted in pencil: "perhaps alone"
1. Inserted in black pencil, deleted in blue pencil: "a book"

to school[2] man[3] in virtues, nor prove anything to the intellect, nor play on the piano[4] nor rhyme, nor sing amours or romances, nor the epics of signal deeds— nor[5] for[6] fashion's coterie-crowds, nor to be trameled with the etiquet of those crowds. but[7] from me to you, whoever you are, we twain[8] alone together[9] a conference, giving up all my private interior [*15;*[10] *14*[11]] musings, yearnings, extasies, and contradictory moods, reserving nothing.[12] A conference[13] amid Nature, and in the spirit of Nature's genesis, and primal sanity.[14] A conference of our two Souls exclusively, as if the rest of the world, with its mocking[15] misconceptions were for a while[16] left[17] and escaped from.[18] . . . . In short, the book will not serve as books serve. But may-be[19] the rude air, the salt sea, the[20] fire, the woods[21] and the rocky ground—sharp, full of danger, full of contradictions and offense. Those[22] elements[23] Silent and old,[24] stand or move,[25] and out of them comes every thing. I too, (though a resident and singer of cities)[26] came from them, and can boast, as I[27] now do, that in their presence, before giving them here[28] I have sternly[29] tried[30] each[31] passage[32] of the following chants. [*16 (back cover) blank*]

2. Deleted in ink: "any"
3. Deleted in pencil: "or woman"
4. Preceding five words inserted.
5. Deleted in pencil: "a song"
6. Deleted: "the" ; inserted: "fashion's"
7. Inserted in pencil: "America I [*del. in ink*] sing in [*del. in pencil*] mode"
8. Preceding two words inserted in ink.
9. Inserted in ink.
10. Black ink. Not numbered by WW.
11. In pencil. "And we conscious of [*ins. and del.*] our rectitude and" . Cf. *n*61 above.
12. Pencilled "*" "tr*" to indicate insertion of next sentence.
13. Deleted: "of you and me"
14. Preceding sentence moved here by an inserted asterisk from original position after the succeeding one.
15. Inserted in ink.
16. Preceding three words inserted in pencil.
17. Deleted in pencil: "behind"
18. Deleted: "(Thence I started, and there I return for my [*del. in ink*] previously? trial" ; inserted in pencil and deleted in ink: "and for final judgement." Deleted: "There all poets, all poems finally return, for theirs."
19. Inserted in ink. Inserted and deleted in ink: "serve rather"
20. Deleted in pencil: "burning"
21. Two preceding words inserted in pencil.
22. Inserted in ink.
23. Inserted in pencil over erased ink insertion. WW neglected to change the upper-case "S" of "Silent" and to alter the period after "old"
24. Deleted in ink: "There they are" ; inserted and deleted in ink: "they"
25. Three words inserted in ink. Inserted and deleted in pencil: "forever"
26. Parenthetical phrase inserted in pencil.
27. Deleted in pencil: "here" ; inserted in pencil: "now"
28. Preceding four words inserted in pencil.
29. Inserted in pencil.
30. Deleted in pencil: "every"
31. Deleted in ink: "every" ; inserted in pencil: "each"
32. Deleted in ink: "passage sentence" ; inserted in ink: "passage"

America (I To Myself.

Manuscript not found. Text from *N&F,* 59 (Pt. 2, #26; *CW,* VI, 11). A variant draft of paragraph two of "Dec 23, 1864" (Introduction No. 1).

America (I to myself have said) demands at any rate one modern, native, all-surrounding song with face like hers turned to the future rather than the present or the past. It should nourish with joy the pride and completion of man in himself. What the mother, our continent, in reference to humanity, finally means (where it centres around the prairies, Missouri, Ohio, the great lakes, and branches away toward the Eastern and Western Seas) is *Individuality* strong and superb, for broadest average use, for man and woman: and that most should such a poem in its own form express. Of such a Poem (I have had that dream) let me initiate the attempt; and bravas to him or to her who, coming after me, triumphs.

Introduction.

Manuscript in NYPL (Lion). Introduction #3. Pasted by WW on second front flyleaf on *LG* (1855, second issue). Homemade notebook of eight leaves of white, wove, unruled paper, $6^5/_{16}''$ x $3\frac{7}{8}''$, self-covered, tied with light blue silk ribbon through holes in a center fold. Inscribed in black ink, brown ink, and black pencil, as noted. The date is approximately May 31, 1861. Furness (256*n*) believes the MS to be an early draft of "Introductory" and hence of "Dec 24, 1864." In Furness, 169–170, with photograph of [3] facing 168. Furness's block paragraphs are not indicated in the MS.

Introduction [1].

[2; [2] 3] [3] is Democracy. The meaning of Democracy is to press on [4] through all failures, ridicules and arguments [5] to put in practice, [6] the idea of the sovereignty, license, [7] sacredness of the individual. This idea [8] isolates [9] for [10] in [11] identity's [12]

    1. Outside cover. Ink.
    2. In black pencil and black ink. May be notes for [3].

[*Pencil*] While courteous to them must be sung from the depths of [*del.*] repe reverence for itself only

[*Black ink*] While courteous to others [*del. in ink*] it must be sung with [*preceding three words del. in ink*] have contented and [*preceding three words ins. in ink*] entire faith in itself only

[*Pencil*] While [*del.*] respecting [*both ins. and del.*] ?the giving courtesy [*alternate ins.*] courteous to others, rest with must [*del.*] stand [*ins.*] be balanced [*preceding three words ins. with no clear indication of their location*] steadily balanced with [*preceding three words ins.*] contented and entire faith [*ins.*] being upon itself only.

[*Pencil*] While courteous to others, must, with contented and entire faith, be steadily balanced only on [*word and punctuation del.*] itself.—itself ["elf" *ins. in ink*] [*both del. in ink*] own balance

    3. A leaf seems to be lacking. Number "3" in the upper right corner in WW's hand.
    4. Preceding three words inserted in pencil.
    5. Preceding six words inserted in ink at top of page and brought down on an arrow.
    6. Inserted and deleted in pencil: "[*del.*] above through all [*del.*] defeats [*written above*] rebuffs [*written below*] failures, ridicule and arguments"
    7. Deleted in ink: "and"
    8. Deleted in ink: "gives" ; inserted in ink: "isolates"
    9. Inserted and deleted in ink: "perfect"
    10. Inserted in pencil, possibly as an alternate to "in"
    11. Inserted in ink.
    12. Possessive added in pencil. Deleted in ink: "isolation" ; inserted and deleted: "and"

and perfect freedom's[13] sake[14] to[15] each separate man and[16] woman human in the world[17]—but while[18] the idea of Love,[19] fuses and combines[20] the whole. The twain are in the following Song. A third idea, also, is, or shall be put, there— namely, Religion—the idea which[21] purifies all other ideas and things, and gives endless meaning and destiny to a man, and in him condenses[22] the drift of all things.

[5; 4[23] blank]. . . . . Prevalent poems[24] cast back only physiognomy. In the following chant, the apparition of the whole form, as of one unclothed before a mirror is[25] cast back.[26] I was aware that the unclothed face is[27] divine,[28] but now I am aware that the unclothed body is diviner still. These Leaves therefore image that divine physiology—not apologizing for it, but taking it to myself[29] but openly[30] exulting[31] in it and[32] myself.[33] . . . . . Of what I am—Of[34] my private musings, yearnings and confessions—Of[35] the vari-phased material[36] esthetic and [7[37]; 6 blank] spiritual animal I am—Of this curious territory, with[38] torrid[39] passions—

13. Preceding two words added in ink. Possessive added in pencil.
14. Inserted in pencil.
15. Inserted in brown ink and deleted in black: "separate" . Redundant "each" here omitted. Inserted in black ink: "each separate man and woman human"
16. Deleted: "every"
17. Preceding three words inserted in brown ink. This very complexly revised passage first read: "This idea gives identity and isolation to every man and woman."
18. Inserted in ink as an alternative to "but"
19. Deleted in ink: "with [del. first in pencil] irresistible [ins.] supreme power"
20. Deleted in pencil: "all" ; inserted in pencil: "the whole"
21. Inserted and deleted in pencil: "exalts and". A vertical pencil slash here. Deleted: "swallows [ins. and del.] exa up and" . Another vertical pencil slash.
22. Inserted: "the drift of"
23. Number "4" in upper right corner, possibly in WW's hand.
24. Deleted in ink: "reflect" ; inserted in ink: "cast"
25. Deleted in ink: "reflected" ; inserted in ink: "cast"
26. Deleted in pencil: "Is the" ; inserted: "I have perceived [preceding two words del.] was aware"
27. Inserted in pencil.
28. Quotation marks inserted in pencil; deleted in pencil: "?" "It is; and" ; inserted in pencil: "but" ; inserted in pencil: "I have perceived [preceding three words del.] that" ; inserted: "now I am aware"
29. Five preceding words inserted in pencil; inserted and deleted in pencil: "specifically" "openly" . WW did not delete inserted "and" which is here omitted.
30. Inserted in pencil.
31. Deleted in pencil: "openly"
32. Inserted and deleted: "representing it" "taking it to"
33. Preceding two words inserted.
34. Deleted in pencil: "all my" ; inserted in pencil: "my"
35. Deleted in ink: "this" ; inserted: "the"
36. Inserted in pencil.
37. Number "5" in upper right in WW's hand.
38. Inserted in pencil and deleted in ink: "its"
39. Deleted in pencil: "and arctic"

with deserts and[40] icy sierras,[41] and productive fields—I seek to[42] draw the outline[43] the map. The joined[44] Body[45] with the Soul I seek. For once[46] any how needs that[47] tantalizing,[48] nonpareil and needs[49] study[50] to go in a poem, not as it might be, or as it is fancied[51] in[52] literature to be[53]—but as it actually is, good and bad, as Nature turns it out.[54] For once the mould[55] need to be set as of a live [9[56]; 8 *blank*] flush, eating and drinking man—and[57] from that,[58] without wincing, I[59] mould the book . . . . I commenced[60] Leaves of Grass in my thirty-sixth year, by publishing their first issue. Twice have I issued them since, with successive[61] increase,[62] the present being the Fourth Issue, with the latest increase.[63] I am to-day (May 31, 1861) just forty-two years old; for I write this Introduction [11[64]; 10[65]] on my birth-day—after having looked over the poem,

40. Deleted in pencil: "rocky" ; inserted and deleted in pencil: "iron" "harsh" ; inserted: "icy"
41. Deleted in ink: "as well as" ; inserted in ink: "and"
42. Deleted in pencil: "make" ; inserted in pencil: "draw"
43. Deleted: plural "s" of "outlines" "of"
44. Inserted in ink.
45. Deleted in pencil: "and" ; inserted in pencil: "with"
46. Deleted in pencil: "let" ; inserted and deleted in pencil: "I say" ; inserted in pencil: "any how needs"
47. Deleted in pencil: "amazing,"
48. Deleted in pencil: "immortal wonder put itself in" ; inserted in pencil: "nonpareil and" ; inserted in brown ink with a broad-nibbed pen: "needs" ; inserted in pencil, deleted in brown ink: "shall to" ; inserted in brown ink, here omitted as redundant: "needs" ; inserted and deleted in pencil: "go to"
49. Inserted in pencil: "[*del.*] needs"
50. Inserted in pencil: "to go in [*del.*] into"
51. Deleted in pencil: "to be"
52. Deleted in pencil: "ostensible"
53. Two words inserted in pencil.
54. Deleted in pencil: "Let a" ; inserted in pencil: "For once the"
55. Deleted in pencil: "be made as from" ; inserted in pencil: "[*del.*] taken" "need to be shall be [*preceding two words del.*] set as of [*del.*] one"
56. Number "6" in upper right corner in WW's hand.
57. Deleted in ink: "in" ; inserted and deleted in ink: "from" ; inserted in ink, deleted in pencil: "by" ; inserted in pencil: "from"
58. Deleted in ink: "mould,"
59. Deleted in ink: "cast" ; inserted in ink: "mould"
60. That is, *LG* was published. Cf. almost identical passage in "I Commenced Leaves of Grass."
61. Inserted in pencil.
62. Deleted in pencil: "d" from "increased." Comma inserted in pencil; deleted in pencil: "matter"
63. Since *LG* (1860) is the third "issue" (if one does not count the second issue of 1855) and had been published in May, 1860, this introduction may be for the unpublished *Banner at Day Break*, which was announced sometime after June, 1860 (Allen, 267). See "Dec 23. 1864".
64. Possibly in WW's hand. Entry as far as "I do not school" on a pasted-over scrap. The backing sheet cannot be read except for a deleted marginal entry: "All as is appropriate to me."
65. Pencil and ink notes for [11]; probably written after the original [11] but before the past-over.

[*Pencil*] The teeming and applauded crowds of poets in literature [*del*] do [*ins.*] perform the service that is appropriate to them. They to their use (which is great)—I alone to mine.

as far as accomplished. So far, so well; but the most and best of it, I perceive, remains to be written—the work of my life ahead, which I will yet do. . . . All as is appropriate to me. Of[66] the teeming and applauded crowds of poets in literature, performing[67] the service appropriate to them—they to their use, (which is great;)—I alone to mine . . . . . I do not[68] school[69] any man or woman in virtues, nor prove anything to the intellect, nor[70] celebrate amours or romances, nor make[71] the mere[72] epics of[73] deeds done,[74]

[13 [75]; 12 blank] In short, the book will not serve as books serve[76]—But[77] as the rude air, the salt sea, the burning fire, and the rocky ground—sharp, full of danger,[78] full of contradictions and offense[79] . . . . . Those silent old[80] suggestions! Can[81] you, perusing them, and never understanding them, yet dwell upon with them with[82] profit and joy? Then try these chants. [14–16 blank]

[Black ink] Of the poets of the world [preceding three words del.] in literature [preceding two words ins. and del.] [ins. and del. in pencil] of [del.] that teeming and [del.] popular applauded [del.] crowd—of poets in literature, they to their need (which is great)—I alone to mine

[Pencil] They a [del.] popular [del.] a teeming and [del.] an applauded crowd) [parentheses in ink] to their work, (which is great)—I alone to mine. [Pencil] [del.] Numberless a [ins. and del.] crowd popular understood, [del.] and prepared for, a crowd, [both ins.] [del.] honored with honors

66. Inserted in pencil; upper case "T" of "the" not reduced, not printed.
67. Originally "have performed" ; "have" was deleted and "ing" was added in pencil although "ed" was not deleted.
68. Deleted in pencil: "propose to"
69. End of paste-over.
70. Deleted in pencil: "sing" ; inserted in pencil: "celebrate"
71. Inserted in pencil.
72. Inserted in ink.
73. Deleted in ink: "land or sea" ; inserted in ink: "deeds done, here or anywhere [preceding three words del. in ink]. "
74. Deleted in pencil: "They to their work" . Inserted and deleted in pencil: "appropriate need [ins.] use [ins. and del.] use (which is great)—I to mine. . . . . ."
75. Number "8" in upper right corner in WW's hand.
76. Period deleted; dash inserted.
77. Inserted in brown ink with a larger pen, deleted in pencil: "perhaps"
78. Deleted in pencil: "and offense and"
79. Preceding two words and dash inserted in pencil; "serve" deleted.
80. Deleted: "-faced" ; inserted and deleted: "always fresh ever new"
81. Inserted in pencil; original "Do" here omitted.
82. Inserted in ink as an alternate.

Introductory.

Manuscript in NYPL (Lion). Introduction #4. Pasted by WW in *LG* (1855, 2nd issue), second front flyleaf. Inscribed in black ink. Emendations were made with a finer-nibbed pen. Homemade self-bound notebook of nine leaves ([*11–12*] cut out) of white wove unruled paper, 6¼" x 4½", tied with white string through center fold. Illegible embossing on lower right of {*1*}. Type of paragraphing varies randomly in MS. Furness (256*n*) believes that this MS is a revision of *"Introduction."* , which is pasted preceding it and that both MS are drafts of "Dec. 23. 1864." It is also related to "I Commenced Leaves." It will be noted however, that WW does not relate it to his birthday as he does "Dec 23. 1864" and "Introduction." First published by Furness, 171–172; cover, {*1*}, reproduced facing 170. The date is probably in the early 1860s.

{*1*}[1] (The best of the two Introductions)[2]

Introductory ion[3]

To the Reader
Advertisement
Notice
Introductory Notice to the Reader[4]

[*3;*[5] *2 blank*] *Introductory*.
America, (I have said to myself,)[6] demands one Song, at any rate, that is bold,[7] modern, and[8] unconfined as she is herself.[9] Its[10] spirit like hers,[11] must have

1. Outside front cover. This leaf is pasted on leaf [*3–4*] at the left edge.
2. More irregular writing in brown ink with a finer-pointed pen at the upper left. Furness (256*n*) believes that this remark refers to the "Introduction" (No. 3) which precedes it, rather than to "Dec 23. 1864" (No. 1), and that "Introduction" (No. 3) was used as a quarry for this one.
3. Written above "ory" with a heavy pen point. Black ink.
4. In black pencil in a column. There is a greater distance between "To the Reader"- and "Advertisement" than between any of the others.
5. Pasted on a stub, which appears to have no conjugate. The heading is centered, but the paragraph is in hanging indentation.
6. Deleted: "must have" ; inserted in ink: "demands"
7. Deleted: "broad" ; inserted and deleted: "spiritual"
8. Inserted and deleted: "deep-founded"
9. Deleted: "Its history and spirit," . A cancelled hanging indentation follows: "As she [*del.*] herself [*ins.*] too, extricating herself (with [*del.*] much tug and [*ins.*] agonistic turmoil from the crustings of the [*preceding three words ins.*] past has reference [*del.*] the [*ins. and del.*] the [*ins.*] great

reference to the[12] future,[13] more than the present or the past[14] Like her,[15] it must extricate itself from the past, and be sung with[16] eye [5;[17] 4 *blank*] fixed on the interminable future.[18] Like her, it must[19] bring[20] to the front,[21] and hold up at[22] every hasard[23] inalienable rights, and the divine pride of[24] man in[25] himself. [7;[26] 6 *blank*]*[27] Long have the geniuses of other nations[28] listened to poems in which[29] man bends[30] himself down,[31] and abdicates[32] himself . . . But[33] the genius of[34] America[35] cannot listen[36] to such poems.[37]

Erect[38] and haughty[39] must[40] the[41] chant be, and then[42] the genius of America will listen,[43] with pleased ears.

future, more than the present or the past [*preceding seven words ins.*] so [*del.*] must this song [*del.*] progressive"

    10. Deleted: "history and"
    11. Inserted and deleted: "extricating itself from the past"
    12. Deleted: "interminable"
    13. Deleted: "and defend"
    14. Deleted: "and extend"
    15. Preceding two words and comma inserted. WW did not reduce "It" to lowercase.
    16. Deleted: "steady"
    17. Pasted on a hinge. Since writing at the left edge is on the hinge, the inscription is later than the notebook.
    18. Deleted: ", which the present prophecies, while it Like her, it must depend on [*del.*] ample time for its history, and not [*del.*] mind trouble itself about [*preceding three words ins. and del.*] the favor or disfavor [*ins.*] of a day"
    19. Deleted: "be founded on [*illeg.*] the divine pride of man in"
    20. Deleted: "out"
    21. Preceding three words inserted.
    22. Deleted: "all" ; inserted: "every"
    23. Final "s" deleted.
    24. Deleted: "humanity" ; inserted: "man."
    25. Deleted: "itself" ; inserted: "himself"
    26. Appears to be pasted to [9–10] at the left edge; written with hanging indentation. Deleted: "My song arrogates the [*preceding two words del.*] to a" "A Man"
    27. The significance of the asterisk is not clear. Deleted: "Long enough have" ; inserted: "Long . . . other"
    28. Deleted: "permitted" ; inserted and deleted: "that the song" ; inserted: "listened to"
    29. Deleted: "man bowed" ; inserted: "[*del.*] a man [*del.*] bow bends"
    30. Inserted and deleted: "down lowly"
    31. Inserted. Deleted: "or" ; inserted: "and"
    32. Originally "abdicated"
    33. Deleted: "not so can"
    34. Preceding three words inserted.
    35. Deleted: "permit"
    36. Two preceding words inserted. Deleted: "poems that song"
    37. Deleted words in hanging indentation: "Whatever is in below the"
    38. Original opening deleted: "Upright" ; inserted and deleted: "Her"
    39. Deleted: [*illeg.*]
    40. Deleted: "be"
    41. Deleted: "song of the permitted by the genius of America" ; inserted: "chant"
    42. Inserted.
    43. Deleted: "with joy"

[9 [44]; 8 *blank*] ? [45] The [46] meaning of America, is Democracy. The meaning of Democracy is to put in practice [47] the idea of the [48] sovereignty, license, sacredness of the individual. This idea gives identity and isolation to [49] every man and woman—but the idea of Love with power fuses and combines all. [50] The twain are in the following Song. [51] A third idea, also, is, or shall be put there, [52] namely, [53] Religion,—the idea [54] which swallows up and purifies all other ideas and [55] things— and gives endless meaning and destiny [56] [*illeg.*] to a man [57] and condenses in him all things [*illeg.*]. [58]

[*13;* [59] *10 blank; 11–12 cut out*] Prevalent poems reflect back only physiognomy. [60] In [61] the following chant, [62] the apparition of [63] the whole form [64] as of one [65] unclothed before [66] a mirror [67] is reflected back. [68] Is the face [69] unclothed face divine? [70] Yes; [71] the unclothed body is [72] more [*illeg.*] divine [73] still. [74]

44. Pasted on stub.
45. Deleted: "For"
46. Deleted: "typ"
47. Preceding four words inserted.
48. Preceding three words inserted.
49. Deleted: "a" ; inserted: "every"
50. This sentence is the result of heavy revision in the course of which WW wrote his revision between the lines of the original emended sentence, salvaging such undeleted words as he could find. The original seems to have been as follows: "It is [*preceding two words del.*] this simple [*preceding two words del.*] Idea is the male [*del.*] to [*ins. and del.*] for [*ins.*] to which the idea of Love is the man — *but the idea of Love* female."
51. Deleted: "chants" . Original reading (see *n*50): "These ideas are in the following song"
52. Deleted: "ascending above all" ; inserted and deleted: "towering high" corrected to "to tower high"
53. Deleted: "the idea of"
54. Dash and two words inserted.
55. Deleted: "all"
56. Two words inserted.
57. Deleted: "[*illeg.*] all things"
58. Preceding six words inserted.
59. Mounted on stub conjugate to [*11–12*] stub. Slight traces of writing on [*12*].
60. The emendations are difficult to follow. There seem to be two earlier attempts at this sentence: "Other poems show the physiognomy only" ; "Hitherto I have perceived poems reflect back the physiognomy only"
61. Deleted: "this" ; inserted: "the following"
62. Deleted: "as"
63. Deleted: "one undraped is"
64. Inserted and deleted: "which stands bef undraped"
65. Inserted and deleted: "standing"
66. Deleted: "the"
67. Preceding seven words inserted.
68. Deleted: "from the mirror" ; inserted: period. Deleted: "This chant therefore shows the the [*three words previously del.*] images the whole physiology also."
69. Preceding two words inserted.
70. Deleted: "Yes" ; inserted: "Yes It is [*preceding two words del.*]"
71. Deleted: "and and but [*preceding two words del.*] then"
72. Deleted: "still"
73. Deleted: "still" ; inserted and deleted: "Yet still" ; inserted: "still"
74. Cancelled sentence: "This chant [*preceding two words del.*] These Leaves [*preceding two words ins.*] of mine [*preceding two words ins. and del.*] therefore image ["s" *del.*] the whole [*preceding two words del.*] that divine [*preceding two words ins.*] physiology [*del.*] also—not apologizing for it, but with exuberance and pride openly and [*preceding six words del.*] exulting [*ins.*] openly in it."

[15;[75] 14 blank][76] Of what I am—Of all my private musings and hopes and dreads—[77]Of[78] this vari-phased[79] animal, esthetic, and spiritual being I am—Of[80] this[81] curious territory, with torrid and arctic passions—[82]with[83] deserts and rocky sierras[84] as well as[85] productive fields—I[86] seek to make[87] a[88] map;[89] or rather[90] give[91] indirect suggestions for the real depths elude us.[92]

[16;[93] 17;[94] 18 blank]

75. Two scraps pasted on a stub.
76. Deleted: "Make a fa"
77. Preceding nine words and dash inserted.
78. Raised from lowercase. Deleted: "my animal" ; inserted and deleted: "all"
79. Inserted.
80. Raised from lowercase.
81. Deleted: "passio spread of"
82. Deleted: "of the"
83. Deleted: "its"
84. Preceding three words inserted.
85. Deleted: "its fields"
86. Deleted: "would outline" ; inserted: "seek to"
87. Deleted: "the" ; inserted: "a"
88. Deleted: "faithful"
89. Inserted and deleted: "as it is"
90. Deleted: "indicate the outlines"
91. Deleted: "by"
92. Inserted: "give . . . elude us." Inserted and deleted: "seek turn him out" . Deleted: "wonder" . End of first scrap.
Cancelled sentence on second scrap: "[del.] wonder   For once let [preceding three words ins.] [del.] this [ins.] the amazing tantalizing, immortal [preceding two words ins.] [del.] fact [ins.] something I represent, put itself in a poem, not as it might be or as it is supposed to be in ostensible literature, but as it [ins.] actually is, good and bad, as Nature turns it out."
93. Two scraps, both with hanging indentation, both cancelled.

Scrap 1. "What a shame it [del.] is would be to America if she whatever others do say [preceding four words del.] from the embryo and [preceding two words ins.] heart of her literature [preceding eight words ins.] did not [del.] say speak[?] the words of perfect faith in the no [preceding three words del.] in the body and Soul of man — whatever [del.] others[?] say speak   gauging herself by eternal the principles of sane, [preceding five words del.] eternal theory [del.] on which underlies the making of
Scrap 2: "abandons the body and dares not assert it, from top to toe [preceding eight words del.] connives with the shame of it [?] [preceding six words ins.] is not the [illeg., scrap trimmed]"

94. Page cancelled.
Not [del.] after to books and conventions [del.] will [illeg.] [del.] I [del.] now have sought to conform my song.

[Hanging indentation] What facts of [preceding two words ins.] organism and impulse I find in myself, I will have scrupulously [ins.] put in my [del.] poem [ins. and del.] book song. Not [illeg.] after books and conventions. For once [preceding two words del.] [Following entries helter-skelter] For it A the [preceding four words del.] A mould there shall be a man it A [preceding two words del.] mould Let a mould poem was has has has been [preceding seven words del.] [del.] shall a book shall [preceding two words deleted] be have have I [preceding two words del.] [ins.] be made as from [del.] from taken the mould of [preceding four words del.] a [del.] living [ins.] live flush, ?not goo [preceding two words del.] eating and drinking [preceding three words ins.] man, for once, naively, of [ins.] from myself, [preceding five words del.] and in that mould, for once [preceding two words ins. and del.] without wincing I [del.] will shall be [preceding two words ins. and del.] shall be let [preceding three words ins. and del.] I [del.] will have have been [preceding three words del.] [preceding nine words ins.] cast [del.] a the book.

To the Reader at the Entrance of Leaves of Grass.

Manuscript in NYPL (Lion). Introduction #2. Inscribed in brown ink and black pencil on white wove paper approx. 7½" x 4½". Vertical brown lines ⅜" apart on [1]. These leaves are mounted on hinges to form a crude notebook, which is mounted in *LG* (1855, 2d issue), on verso, first front flyleaf. Since it is relatively compressed, it is probably not the earliest of the Lion MSS leading to "One's-Self I Sing." The date, however, must be before 1867.

[1] TO THE READER
    At the Entrance of Leaves of Grass.[1]

———

Small is my theme, the theme of the following chant[2] yet the greatest—namely
    One's-self, a simple, separate person. That, for the use of the New World, I
    sing.[3]

You[4], male[5] or female, pour'd into whom all that you read or hear as past,[6] or
    that you see in landscape, heavens and every beast and bird or that *existent is,*[7]
    becomes[8] [2[9]; *3*[10]] so only then, with play and interplay.[11]

    1. Short centered rule.
    2. Preceding seven words inserted on two lines above "my theme . . . yet the" . Redundant "the" not printed.
    3. The following strophe is marked with a line curving around and the word "out" in the left margin.
        One's self—through crowds of epic heroes and events, the usual stock of songs—through
            many a tale of passions, pensive, picturesque, &c., comes pressing straight toward
            me, and will not be denied, my theme.
    4. Strophe written on pasted-on slip. Word either blurred or heavily inked.
    5. Two first words on slip pasted on scrap which is pasted on page. Deleted in black ink: "you
[?], male"
    6. Inserted in pencil: "or that you see in landscape, heavens and every beast and bird" on two
lines above "or hear . . . that"
    7. Two preceding words underlined in pencil; inserted and deleted in pencil above "*existent*" : "in outside heroes" ; deleted in pencil: "in [*ins. above* "heroes"] outside heroes or events, with landscape, heavens and every beast and bird,"
    8. End of large scrap.
    9. In pencil. Entries seem to be notes for [3].
    with all the things of Nature, and all events and her [*a wide space before next entry*]

For what to you or me is this[12] round universe, with all its[13] pageants[14] except as[15] touching you and me?

(What is this universe? Who knows? May-be created *by* us, by winking of our eyes?—[16] preparing us, by giving us identity—[17]the apparent known,[18] important only with reference to[19] the really great unknown.[20]

When[21] As I beheld[22] the universe the things of Nature,[23] the least as well as[24] largest item ever[25] inexplicable, I thought[26] the things of Nature,[27] as in the main suggestive and gymnastic—not[28] great[29] because of objects or events themselves,[30] but great in reference to a human personality[31] and for identity

Nothing in themselves
      and to the soul's identity [*line del.*]
        and
for identity [*two preceding words ins.*]

                                      and [*ins.*] needful exercise

      I thought the universe with all its [*two preceding words del.*] [*ins. above deletion*] every objects, and all events and heroes, as in the main suggestive and symnastic to my Soul

      10. On two scraps.

      11. New strophe on authority of "¶" in pencil.

      12. Deleted in pencil: "this" ; inserted in pencil and erased: "the" ; original deletion erased.

      13. Deleted in pencil: "changing"

      14. Deleted in pencil: "of success and failure"

      15. Deleted in pencil: "feeding" ; inserted above: "touching"

      16. Deleted: "?" ; inserted: dash. Remainder of strophe marked in left margin with pencil line curving around and with the query "? out"; deleted in pencil: "May-be"

      17. Deleted in pencil: "then sailing us with winds, o'er the great seas, [*del.*] through"

      18. Deleted in pencil: "thither into the harbors," ;"inserted in pencil; "important only with reference" above "[*del.*] into the harbors," and "the"

      19. "to" inserted in pencil after the following "the" . Preceded by deleted: "? [*illeg.*]" in left margin.

      20. End of first scrap of [3].

      21. Inserted in pencil. "As" not reduced to lowercase in MS.

      22. Original "o" corrected above in pencil to "e" . Deleted: "with curious eyes" ; inserted: "the universe" above "the things"

      23. Deleted in ink: "and of life"

      24. Deleted in ink: "greatest" ; inserted above in ink: "largest"

      25. Inserted in ink above "in" in "inexplicable"

      26. Inserted in pencil above: "think" ; not deleted, not printed.

      27. Deleted in pencil: "and life itself"

      28. Deleted in ink: "at all"

      29. Deleted in pencil: "in" ; inserted in pencil: "because of" above "eat" in "great" , the deletion, and "obj" in "objects"

      30. Word and comma inserted in ink above "events"

      31. Preceding three words inserted in pencil above "reference to" ; deleted in ink: "an unknown" ; inserted and deleted in ink: "the" above "[*del.*] an" ; deleted in pencil: "future" ; inserted in pencil from left margin: "and for identity and needful exercise." Deleted in ink: [*del.*] "I have [*ins. above* "have"] will not disobey the hint in my songs."

and needful exercise.[32] Such is the hint that[33] coming in whispers[34] to me[35]—
and[36] out of it I chant the following poems.)[4][37]

[5][38] Man's[39] Physiology from top to toe, I[40] sing. Not physiognomy alone, nor
brain alone, is worthy for the muse birth'd in the West.[41] I say the *perfect
form*,[42] received with absolute faith[43] is worthier yet. Let others give the parts
that please them;—I the ensemble seek to give,[44] and actual fibres.[45]

One[46] song at any rate,[47] America demands[48] that breathes her native air alone—
an utterance to invigorate Democracy—(*Democracy*, the destined conqueror, yet
treacherous[49] lip-smiles always luring, and death and infidelity at every step.)[50]
Of such a song, I launch the novice's attempt—and bravas[51] to the bards who,
coming after me, achieve the work complete.[52]

32. Deleted in pencil: "This" ; inserted in pencil: "such"
33. Deleted in pencil: "has" ; "come" emended to "coming"
34. Preceding two words inserted in pencil above "[*del.*] my songs"
35. Deleted in pencil: "night and day at every step"
36. Deleted in pencil: "it underlies these Leaves.)" ; inserted below: "out of it have come
[*preceding two words del.*] I chant [*preceding two words ins. above* "come"] the following [*del.*] these
poems.)"
37. In black pencil. Entry seems to be a note for [3].
*tr back)

As I behold with curious eyes the things of Nature and every circumstance [*preceding two
words del.*] of life, the last as well as well as greatest item inexplicable, I see the things of
Nature and [*pasted over*]"

38. Black ink. Three scraps pasted on backing sheet.
39. Written across first scrap to stub, but first two letters in pencil; probably original letters
in ink were trimmed when scrap was mounted.
40. End of first scrap. Second scrap shows descenders of trimmed letters at top.
41. Preceding four words inserted in pencil above "muse. . . . I"
42. Underlined in pencil.
43. Preceding four words inserted in pencil above "ct" in "perfect" and pencilled deletion
below: "from top to toe,"
44. Deleted in pencil: "with the" ; inserted in pencil: "and" above "a" in "actual"
45. End of second scrap.
46. Deleted in ink: "wholly native"
47. Preceding four words and the deletion in *n*46 inserted in pencil above "[*del.*] A
song" and "America demands" ; deleted in pencil: "A song"
48. Deleted in pencil: "that breathes her native air" ; inserted in ink with a fine-nibbed
pen: "that breathes her native air alone—" above "[*del.*] breathes her native air" and "—an"
49. Spelling corrected in ink.
50. Beginning of new paragraph in pencil deleted in pencil: "You and that"
51. It is not clear whether WW thought he was using Italian or Spanish. In either case he is
ungrammatical.
52. Ascenders of trimmed letters show at bottom of leaf.

[7;[53] 6 *blank*] O friend, whoe'er you are, at last arriving hither, accept from me, as one in waiting for you at this entrance, welcome and hospitality.[54] This is no[55] book[56]—but I myself, in loving flesh and blood. I feel at every leaf,[57] the pressure of your hand, which I return; and thus throughout upon the journey, linked together will we go. [*8 blank*]

53. Scrap pasted on backing-sheet. Hinge reinforced with shreds of newsprint. Trimmed at top.

54. End of scrap.

55. Inserted and deleted in pencil: "you"

56. Blurred or very heavily inked. Deleted in pencil: "alone" ; inserted above: "[*redundant, not printed*] you [*del.*] hold" ; deleted in ink: "tis" ; inserted above in ink: "but"

57. Preceding three words and comma inserted in pencil above "the" and "pre" in "pressure"

Inscription To the Reader.

Manuscript in NYPL (Lion). Introduction #5. Pasted in *Leaves of Grass* (2nd. issue, 1855), first rear flyleaf. Homemade notebook of white wove paper, 8" x 5", except as noted. Unidentifiable embossed stamp. Tied with light blue silk ribbon, between [12–13]. Inscribed in black ink with emendations and preliminary drafts in black ink, black pencil, and occasional blue crayon and red crayon. WW evidently made up a notebook for a fresh version of this particular introduction (see Introductory Note) of probably eighteen pages (including the front cover), as his numbering of certain pages ([1, 9, 11, 13, 15, 17]) indicates. But, as the numbering "8" on [1] (as well as the binding of several leaves) indicates, he did some shifting around of old leaves and inserting of new ones. There is only a stub for [3–4], and [5–6], which is 6¾" x 4¾", is on a stub or hinge with [7–8], seems to be on original paper. Certain pages are also written with a broader-nibbed pen. The order of inscription, however, cannot be determined. Since this MS appears to be somewhere in the middle of the development of this particular introduction, this introduction was written after 1860 and before 1867. First printed by Furness, 131–134. Photograph of [1] faces 130.

[1]¹ Inscription
To² the Reader at the entrance of Leaves of
Grass.³

———

Dear friend, whoe'er⁴ you are, at last⁵ arriving hither, accept from me,⁶ (as one in waiting for you⁷ at this entrance,)⁸ but⁹ a word of living hospitality and¹⁰

1. In upper right corner, "8" in blue crayon. Alternate pencilled title above:"? *or To the Reader* at the entrance of *Leaves of Grass."* See "To the Reader at the Entrance " On word "Inscription" pencilled directions to printer: *"not too large"*
2. On this line, pencilled directions to printer: "middling large"
3. Ornamental rule centered below subtitle. Various squiggles at right and below title as if WW were testing his pen.
4. Originally "whoever" ; changed in pencil.
5. Deleted in pencil: "wandering"
6. Deleted in pencil: "at this entrance"
7. Deleted in pencil: "here" ; inserted in pencil: "at this entrance" above "you" and the deletion.
8. Deleted in pencil: "not a vain ceremony of words" ; inserted and deleted above "[*del.*] ceremony of" in pencil: "rhyming show of" ; inserted in pencil above deletion described in *n*9: "a word of what I have [*preceding three words del. in ink*]"

love. I almost[11] feel the[12] curving hold and pressure of your hand, which I return, and thus throughout[13] upon the journey[14] linked together will we go. Indeed[15] this[16] is no book, but[17] more a man, within whose breast[18] the common heart is[19] throbbing;—no leaves of[20] print are these, but[21] lips[22] for your[23] sake freely speaking.[24] From me[25] to you[26] alone, a conference,[27] to ensue to yield interior[28] yearnings,[29] discords, and all my private egotisms and[30] moods, reserving nothing.[31] Conference, wherein[32] along the robust virgin[33] Western World, abandon we ourselves to Nature's primal[34] mode again, our two exclusive souls, as if[35] the imported society world were left behind, with[36] all[37] polite accumulations of[38] the East. While untried, yet the greatest, is the theme of my recitative.

9. Deleted in pencil: "the salute of" ; inserted in ink: "living [*del.*] breath" above "of" and "hos" in "hospitality"

10. Deleted in pencil: "affection" ; inserted above in pencil: "love"

11. Inserted in pencil above "I feel"

12. Deleted in pencil: "hold" ; inserted in pencil: "curving hold and pressure" on two lines above "[*del.*] hold"

13. Inserted in pencil above "upon"

14. Deleted in pencil: "henceforth" ; inserted above: "linked together"

15. Inserted in pencil above "This" ; uppercase "T" in "This" not reduced, not printed here.

16. Inserted and deleted: "indeed" above "is no"

17. Inserted in pencil: "[*del.*] indeed more" above "but"

18. Deleted in ink: "one in whom a throbbing" ; inserted in ink above deletion and in left margin inserted: "one within whose breast the common"

19. Deleted in pencil: "beating" ; inserted above in pencil: "throbbing"

20. Deleted in pencil: "paper" ; inserted and deleted above in pencil: "prove" "will" ; inserted in ink, deleted in pencil: "must" above "these" ; inserted and deleted in pencil: "prove" above "but" ; inserted in pencil: "print are" above deleted "moving" (*n*21).

21. Deleted in ink: "moving"

22. Deleted in pencil: "that" ; inserted above in pencil: "for" ; deleted in ink: "for" ; inserted in ink, deleted in pencil: "to" above "[*del.*] for"

23. "r" added in pencil; deleted in pencil: "open and" ; inserted above in pencil: "freely"

24. "ing" added in pencil.

25. Deleted in pencil: "to" ; inserted in pencil: "to"

26. Comma deleted in pencil.

27. Deleted in pencil: "yielding up" ; inserted above in pencil: "to ensue to yield"

28. Deleted by smearing: "musing"

29. Comma inserted in pencil; deleted in pencil: "and"

30. Preceding two words inserted in pencil above "ate" in "private" and "moods"

31. Deleted: "unwonted" ; "conference" capitalized.

32. "in" added in pencil; deleted in ink on next line: "walking" ; inserted above in pencil: "along" ; deleted in ink: "through"

33. Preceding two words inserted in pencil above "the . . . Western"

34. Deleted in pencil: "sanity" ; inserted above: "mode again,"

35. Deleted in ink: "the" ; deleted in pencil: "world" ; deleted in ink: "in rooms" ; inserted and deleted above "[*del.*] in" : "of" ; inserted in pencil on two lines: "the imported society world" above the deletions.

36. Inserted and deleted: [*illeg.*] above "with"

37. Deleted in pencil: "its" ; inserted and deleted: "its" ; inserted in pencil in margin: "polite [*del.*] piled accumulations" ; deleted in pencil: "masking misconceptions" ; inserted above in ink: "the blind obedience from [*preceding three words del. in pencil*] [*ins. in pencil*] of the East."

38. Deleted in ink: "talk, my"

{5; 2; [39] 3 and 4 cut out}[40] For, main and spine of[41] this,[42] my talk—leaving[43] all outside heroes and events, the stock of previous[44] bards,—up through such epic movements,[45] masses, history, war, the rise and fall of[46] lands, with the[47] rich rich turmoil of their[48] ascent and[49] precipitation, comes ever[50] surely rising,

39. Apparently notes for [5] or missing [3, 4]. In black pencil. The asterisks do not seem to indicate connections or transpositions.

*It is this that [del. illeg.] has moved me [following two words del.] what prophecies [ins.] means where it [following five words del.] establishes as its greatest fruit ?[the question mark is above "fruit"

{Del.} The What the [preceding two words ins. above the deletion] New World centering [del.] around [ins.] centres [ins.] itself in the prairies, the Missouri, and the great lakes, and branches thence east and west [preceding six words ins. above "lakes" and "[del.] charts in living"] and south [preceding two words ins. and del.] chants in living objects the song of [preceding seven words del.] is to the seas is [preceding five words ins. above "INDIVIDUALITY"] INDIVIDUALITY for the pr broadest [preceding four words del.] the broadest [preceding two words ins. above "[del.] broadest" and "average"] average use for man and woman.— [preceding four words and punctuation ins. on two lines above and to the right of "use"] and I of the same [preceding three words ins. above "[del.]will"] will chant the chant. This demands [preceding eleven words del.]. to be the [following three words del.] spine of hearts [ins. above the del. "hearts"] vital impulse of [del. illeg.] a poem."

{Following three words del.} The principle of [following eight words including deletions ins.] *Dear friend! I [del.] do [ins. and del. above "do"] make [ins. above "not"] put not [illeg. del.] in these Leaves is not to make perfect [preceding five words del.] melodious narratives or [preceding three words ins. above "[del.] "to make perfect" and "pict" in "pictures"] pictures or narratives, but and present them to [preceding seven words del.] [ins. above "[del.] to"] for you, to examine them [preceding two words del.] [ins. above "ex" in "examine"] con read of [preceding two words ins. and del. deleted "examine"] at [del.] your leisure [del.] as for [ins. above deleted "as"] [del.] beautiful bright [ins. above "utiful" in deleted "beautiful"] creations all [ins. above "ou" in "outside"] outside [del.] of yourself—[del.] but Not [del.] so—but of SUGGESTIVENESS to you alone [preceding three words ins. above "ESTIVENESS" in "SUGGESTIVENESS"] this is [del.] the [ins.] the song [comma del.] —[del.] nothing [ins. above the deletion] naught made and finished for you but all invited to be made [preceding three words ins. above "from"] by you and [preceding two words ins. in ink above "you"] [ins.] indeed from you. I have not done the work and cannot do it—[preceding four words and redundant dash (not printed) ins.] but you must do the work to really [ins. above "ma" in "make"] make what is [preceding two words ins. above "the"] the following [del.] poems sing ["poems" ins. above deleted] Which if you [del.] truly do I promise you return and satisfaction more than ever book [ins. above "has"] before has given you

40. In ink with emendations in ink and black pencil. First twenty-four words on a pasted-down slip.

41. Deleted: "all"

42. Deleted in pencil: "chant" ; inserted above in pencil: ", my talk"

43. Deleted in pencil: "those" ; inserted: "all" above wordspace between "[del.] those" and "outside"

44. Deleted in pencil: "poems" ; inserted in pencil: "bards" above "[del.] ms" in "poems—"

45. End of paste-over.

46. Deleted in ink: "nations" ; inserted in ink: "lands" above "s" in "nation-s" and "w" in "with"

47. Deleted in pencil: "splendid hub-bub" ; inserted above in pencil: "rich [illeg. del.] rich turmoil"

48. Deleted in pencil: "heroes" ; inserted and deleted above in pencil: "forming" ; inserted below line in pencil: "ascent"

49. Deleted in pencil: "disruption" [previously reduced to singular]; inserted in pencil: "pre-

advancing towards[51] me, when[52] times are still again,[53] [*illeg.*] that audience claims[54] more close and deep than all those powerful themes; namely, ONE'S-SELF,—[55]that wondrous thing, a Person. *2[56] That,[57] I—alone among[58] bards, and carrying in the following chants sing.

One's self—you, whoever you are, pour'd into whom[59] all that you read and hear and[60] what existent is in heroes or events, with[61] landscape,[62] heavens, and[63] every beast and bird, becomes so,[64] only then, with play and interplay. For what[65] to you or me[66] is this[67] round[68] universe,[69] (with all its changing pageants[70] of success and failure,)[71] except as[72] feeding[73] you and me? May-be

cipitation" above "d" in "and" and "disrup" in "[*del.*] disruption" ; deleted in ink: "the powerful themes of poets,"

50. Deleted in pencil: "unfailingly" ; inserted in pencil: "surely" above "unfai" in "[*del.*] unfailing" ; deleted in ink: "up and" ; deleted in pencil: "forward" ; inserted in ink: "rising, advancing" above the deletions.

51. "wards" added in pencil.

52. Deleted in pencil: "the hours" ; inserted in pencil: "times" above wordspace between the deletions.

53. Deleted in pencil: "something" Furness, 131, reads "something," which is common sense, but without MS authority. Inserted above in pencil: [*illeg.*]; deleted in pencil: "that" ; inserted in pencil: "[*del.*] which that" above "th" in "[*del.*] that" ; inserted in ink: "audience" above "t" in "[*del.*] that" and "claims" .

54. Deleted in ink: "of me audience, closer and deeper" , inserted in ink: "more close and deep" above "ser" in "[*del.*] closer" and "[*del.*] and the" and "than"

55. Dash inserted; deleted in pencil: "a joined [*illeg. transferred from margin on an arrow*]" ; deleted in ink: "body and spirit, an eternal individuality" ; inserted and deleted in ink: "spirit and forms" above "[*del.*] body and spirit" ; inserted in ink: "that wondrous thing, a Person." above "[*del.*] an eternal individuality."

56. Probably refers to [2]. See *n*39. In pencil. Inserted in pencil deleted in ink: "carrying it to its climax"

57. "This" corrected to "That" in pencil.

58. Deleted in pencil: "poets" ; inserted in pencil: "bards, and carrying" to the left before the deletion, above and over "in" ; inserted in pencil and deleted: "it to its climax"

59. Deleted in ink: "that there [?] exists in wondrous in" [*redundant* "all" *before* "that" *not deleted, not printed*]; inserted in pencil: "all that you read and hear and" above "m" in "whom"

60. Inserted in left margin in pencil and deleted: "all that" ; inserted in ink in left margin and above "per" in "persons" : "what existent is in" ; deleted in pencil: "persons" ; inserted above in pencil: "heroes"

61. Deleted in pencil: "the"

62. Deleted in pencil: "the"

63. Deleted in ink: "all animals, only there" ; inserted above in ink: "every beast and bird"

64. Inserted in ink: "only" above "s" in "becomes" and "s" in "so" ; inserted in pencil: "then," above "wi" in "with"

65. Inserted in pencil above "to"

66. Deleted in pencil: "what" ; inserted and deleted in pencil: "truly" above "is"

67. "the" changed to "this" in pencil.

68. Inserted in pencil above "univ" in "universal"

69. Deleted: "(*may be in itself little or nothing," . No connecting passage has been noted.

70. Deleted in pencil: "ry" in "pageantry" ; added in pencil: "s"

71. Deleted in pencil: "only" ; inserted above in pencil: "except"

72. Deleted in pencil: "if" ; inserted and deleted above in pencil: "it"

73. Added in ink: "ing" ; deleted in pencil: "and developes"

indeed,[74] it is[75] created by us, in[76] winking of our eyes. Or may-be[77] for pre-paring us, by giving us[78] identity—then[79] sailing us, with winds,[80] o'er the great[81] seas, the apparent known, steadily[82] to the harbors of the really[83] great unknown.

[7; 6[84]][85] Dear Friend! I put not in[86] the following Leaves melodious narratives or pictures, for you to con at leisure as bright creations finished all outside yourself.[87] With such[88] the world is well enough supplied.[89] But of SUGGES-TIVENESS alone, with steady reference to the life to come[90] this is the song— For[91] from this book[92] Yourself before unknown shall now[93] rise up and be revealed. out of the things around us,[94] naught made by me for you, but[95] only

74. Inserted from margin and deleted in black pencil: "with all its changing pageants of success and failure" ; inserted and deleted in pencil: "The whole universe by us" above deletions described in n75 below.

75. Deleted in pencil: "but continually" ; inserted in ink and deleted: "but" above "ally" in "continually"

76. Deleted in pencil: "the"

77. Deleted in pencil: "it is" ; inserted and deleted above in pencil: "but"

78. Preceding two words inserted in pencil in left margin and above "id" in "identity"

79. Inserted and deleted in ink: "for" above wordspace between "then sailing"

80. Deleted in pencil: "over seas, through" ; inserted above "[del.] over" in pencil: "o'er"

81. Inserted in pencil: "seas, the apparent" above "the great" and "know" in "known"

82. Deleted in pencil: "onward"

83. Inserted in pencil above "great"

84. In pencil. Emendations in pencil except as noted. First entry about a third of the way down the leaf; the second at the bottom. Probably notes for [7].

From [del.] me this book [preceding two words ins. above the deletion and "shall"] shall [del.] appear yourself, before unknown, rise up and be revealed.

*—the [illeg. ins. in pencil, del. in ink] men of [preceding two words del. in ink] the a mighty new race [preceding five words ins. and del. in ink above [del.]"men of" and "America"] America and all its mighty masses of men [preceding seven words ins. in ink on five short lines above and to the right of [del.] "in their"] in their workshops, [preceding three words del. in ink] and the men of steamships and engines [preceding seven words ins. and del. above the line] amid [del.] the [ins. above de-leted "the"] our turbulent friendly free cities and the [illeg. del. in ink] masses every where, [pre-ceding nine words del.] and [del. in ink] the [ins. and del. in ink above deleted "the"] the [ins. in pencil, del. in ink] our [ins. in ink above "new"] a new and grand race of women will appear.— [ink entries were made with a very broad-nibbed pen].

85. In black ink with a very broad-nibbed pen.

86. Deleted in pencil: "these" ; inserted in pencil: "the following" above the deletion and "Leaves"

87. Deleted in ink: "Not so."

88. Preceding two words inserted above "self" in pencil. "T" of "The" not reduced, not printed.

89. Preceding six words inserted in ink above "[del.] Not so." and "But of" ; deleted in pencil: "with them." This was inserted following inserted "supplied" and above "SUGGES" in "SUGGESTIVENESS" . Period inserted.

90. Preceding eight words inserted in pencil above "this is the song—naught"

91. Inserted in ink. "F" of "From" not reduced, not printed.

92. Deleted in ink: "shall"

93. Preceding two words inserted in ink.

94. Preceding twenty words in pencil inserted from end of strophe on arrow. At top of leaf in ink deleted in pencil, brought down on arrow: "and to the miracles of our day"

95. Deleted in pencil: "all invited" ; inserted above in pencil: "all hinted"

hinted to be made by yourself. Indeed I[96] have not done the work, and cannot do it. But you must do the work to really make what is within the following song—which, if you do, I promise you more satisfaction, earned by yourself far[97] more than ever book before has given you.

This[98] book shall hint the poem of America and[99] its mighty masses of men, and a new and grand race of women.

[9; 8[1]][2] Man's[3] PHYSIOLOGY complete[4] I sing[5].—[6] Not[7] physiognomy alone is

96. Deleted in ink: "cannot do" ; inserted above: "have not done"
97. Preceding comma and four words inserted in pencil above "tion" in "satisfaction" and "more than"
98. Original opening deleted: "From" ; uppercase "T" written over "t"
99. Deleted in ink: "all"
1. In black ink, at bottom of leaf. Notes for [9]. Emendations in ink except as noted.

I think* [*preceding two words and asterisk del.*] [*Ins.*] And as [*original uppercase "A" on "as" not reduced, not printed*] for me whatever others do I will seek [*preceding two words del.*] will the [*preceding two words ins. above "seek"*] ensemble [*illeg. del.*] seek and [*del.*] with [*del.*] the actual fibres [*preceding five words ins. above "ensemble . . . I"*]. I will [*del.*] seek adhere, beyond all delicatesse and art, [*preceding nine words del.*] in Man I avow, [*ins. above "n" in "nude"*] him, nude and abysmal man,—and if there were to be [*preceding six words del.*] as for [*preceding two words ins. above the deleted "if there"*] delicatesse and art, they are indifferent as [*preceding three words ins. above "they" and "[del.] shall"*] [*del.*] shall [*ins. above "fo" in "follow"*] may follow him,—but— [*dashes and word ins.*] [*del.*] not [*ins. above deleted "not"*] never he them. He shall [*preceding two words del.*]

2. Black ink. Numbered "2" in upper right corner in blue crayon. The following strophe is deleted with a vertical stroke. All emendations in pencil except as noted.

America, (I have said to myself,) demands one song, at any rate, that is [*del.*] bold [*ins. above*] radical, modern, and all-surrounding as she is herself. Its aim, like hers, must have reference to [*preceding four words del.*] [*ins. and del. above "st" in deleted "must"*] has should mirror [*preceding two words ins. above deleted "ve" in "have" and "referen" in "reference"*] the future more than [*preceding two words del.*] [*ins. and del. before deleted "not"*] not [*ins.*] more the present or the [*preceding three words del.*] past. Like her it [*del.*] must [*ins. above the deletion*] should rise confident [*preceding two words del.*] [*ins. above deleted "rise"*] follow in [*del.*] its [*ins. above deleted "its"*] this own native genius—(not that of foreign lands):— [*preceding dashes, colon and five words ins. in ink above "own native genius" ; parentheses in pencil*] [*del.*] exclusively [*ins. above "excl" in "exclusively"*] alone and [*ins. above "nour" in "nourish"*] should nourish of its own and [*preceding four words ins. above "with joy"*] with joy the pride of man in himself. [*illeg.*] It must be the [*del.*] song [*ins.*] poem of the utterance of democratic life [*preceding thirteen words ins. above "of man in himself. Of "*] Of such a [*del.*] song [*ins. above*], poem (I have had that dream,) let me initiate the attempt and bravas to him or her who comes after me, and succeeds.

Deleted in ink at beginning of next strophe: "The" ; deleted in pencil: "entire"
3. Inserted in ink: "Man's" above "[*del.*] entire"
4. Inserted in ink above "LOGY" in "PHYSIOLOGY" and "I"
5. Period inserted in pencil.
6. Deleted in pencil: "not the [*ins. in ink, not del.*] the physiognomy only."
7. Deleted in ink: "only the face, a portion" ; inserted in pencil: "physiognomy alone" above "[*del.*] portion" and "is"

worthy[8] for the muse—I say[9] the perfect form,[?], with all that[10] with it goes,[11] is[12] only fully worthy. I[13] think the[14] human[15] form the epitome of all the universal emblem.[16]

[11;[17] 10 [18]] Therefore so thus[19] it comes, our New World chords in diapason gathering.[20] I chant, with reference[21] to the original, the flush and strength of

8. Inserted and deleted in pencil: "fitting for" above "worthy"
9. Deleted in pencil: "the perfect" above "l say" ; deleted in red crayon: "body" ; deleted in pencil: "the entirety" ; inserted in ink: "the perfect" ; inserted in pencil: "form [?]" ; inserted and deleted in pencil: "nothing less than the entire [ink]"
10. Deleted in ink: "goes"
11. Inserted in ink. Period deleted.
12. Deleted in pencil: "worthier still" ; inserted in ink: "only" ; inserted in pencil: "fully worthy." All inserts above the deletion.
13. Deleted in ink: "believe" ; inserted above in ink: "think"
14. Inserted and deleted in pencil: "perfect"   ; inserted in pencil, deleted in ink: "entire" above "an"
15. Deleted in ink: "body is the" ; inserted above in ink: "form the"
16. A line drawn from this point to the left margin, thence to the foot of the page, and a deletion sign in the left margin indicate that WW wished to omit the following two sentences between asterisks. Emendations in black pencil, except as noted.

I [del. in ink] believe [ins. in ink above "lieve" in "believe"] thinke in literature or what not, we [ins. and del. in ink above   "e"   in   "we"   and   "r"   in   "roam"   ] shall [ins. in ink above "oam" in "roam"] will roam lost without redemption, [preceding three words del.] unsystematic and barbarous, [preceding three words ins. above the deletion] except we keep up the idea of the [preceding six words del.] [ins. above "p" in deleted "keep" and deleted "up"] seek ensemble, through it, [preceding two words and comma ins. above "and"] and let sprout [preceding two words del.] [ins. above deleted "spr" in "sprout"] honor the actual fibre of things whatever they may be.—[preceding three words and punctuation ins. above "ngs" in "things" and "[del.] steadily" ; redundant dash not printed] [del.] steadily acknowledging supreme among delicatesse and art, even the best, [preceding three words del.] man, nude and abysmal, and indifferent to mere delicatesse and art.

17. In black ink. At upper right in blue crayon: "4" . At top of page the following in pencil, all deleted: "*Chant from the point of view and in the spirit of my own land and in the spirit of my own race [preceding seven words ins.]. [del.] and [ins.] and not [del.] of other [del.] lands [ins. above "lands"] races—"
18. In black pencil and black ink as noted. Cancelled with slanting strokes in black ink. Since the hinge covers a few letters, the leaf was evidently pasted in after inscription. The text is related to [7] rather than facing [11].

[Pencil] For
¶
Then [ins. above "the man" ; above, a hand pointing down] undisguised the main and [del.] marrow [ins. above] spine of my chant [preceding two words ins. above and following "of"] [ins. in blue crayon following the insert above] with *Leaving [del.] the [ins. and del.] those old theories that [preceding three words del.] [ins.] all of the [preceding two words ins. and del.] outside events and [preceding two words del.] heroes, and events, [preceding two words ins.] [del.] outside [ins.] the present [ins. and del.] as themes for poems,

[Pencil]* We think events and records [del.] records [ins. and del. above "great"] romances [ins. in blue crayon above two preceding words] Leaves great outside as themes for poems [preceding four words ins. above "side" in "outside" and "but"]—but there is something else, [illeg. del.] greater than they.

tastes[22], things—[23]such here, engermed in myself and the following leaves,[24] with new centripetal reference, offering[25] to you, dear friend, for[26] vista,[27] for curious road with me[28] to travel.[29]

Advance[30] therein, nor be too soon discouraged. Much will not appear that other poets, guiding you pleasant and safe, sing, and sweetly pass the time away. But

[Pencil] *2 That something vast and great [preceding three words ins. in blue crayon above "thing" in "something" and "[del.] which" and "I"] [del.] which, I see in you as man or woman to me no fraction of the universe, but curiously absorbing all, as if all made for you, and [del.] you to yourself, you more than all outside yourself, however vast and great [preceding four words ins. above "yourself,—that"]—that is the main and spine of these./ [Rule across leaf in ink]

[Ink] For main and spine of all this chant leaving those outside heroes and events the stock and fr [preceding two words del.] of previous poems—up through such epic movements

19. Preceding two words inserted in pencil above "everfore" in "Therefore" , possibly as alternates to "Therefore"

20. Inserted and deleted in pencil: "with reference always to the future" above "gathering"

21. Preceding two words inserted in pencil above "ant" in "chant" and "the" ; inserted and deleted in pencil: "always to the future" above "flush and" ; inserted in pencil: "to the original" above, "ength" in "strength" , and "of tastes"

22. Inserted in ink; [illeg.] in pencil over or under "tastes"

23. Line in black ink across page separates passage cancelled in black ink. Marked in pencil in left margin: "see back)" . There is another topographical survey on [2] (see n39 above).

Chant materials emanating spirituality—and the human form surcharged the same, with [preceding three words del.] [ins. above "e," in "same," and "wi" in "with"] through all its passions and senses [preceding three words del.] [ins.] veins the same:—Chant [ins. above "Ch" in deleted "Chant"] chant Manhattan [preceding two words del.] [illeg. del.] My states and [illeg. del.] [preceding five words ins. above the deletions] my well-loved city—and forget not the flowing Missouri [ins. above "uri" in "Missouri"] Ohio Mississippi [preceding four words del.] [ins. above "ssissi" in deleted "Mississippi"], rivers the Great Lakes [preceding two words del.] ranges of mountains, and put in my pages [preceding eight words ins. above deleted "Lakes" and "the" and the deleted "prairies and"] the prairies and [previous two words del.] southern savannahs and the shores of the western sea [preceding six words del.] pure-air'd California [del.] on and all [preceding five words ins. in pencil above "and" and the deleted "the shores of the"] and all the sights and facts thereof—Rejoicing.

Rejoicing in all, accepting, proud, myself [ins. in pencil above "myself"] the a part [preceding two words del.] [ins. and del. in pencil above deleted "a"] the [ins. in pencil above deleted "part" and "of"] pourtrayer of all—part of their full-beating pulses of life; them, with their full-beating pulses and the [preceding fourteen words del. in pencil] pourtrayer of cities and modern machines and farmers and farms—[preceding ten words ins. in pencil above the deleted "part of their . . . them, with"] world, and all its [preceding three words del.] both [illeg.] the [preceding two words del. in pencil] present and [preceding four words ins. in pencil above "world . . . its"] with poems, histories, war, and [ins. above wordspace between "war, peace"] peace— [line across page] [Del.] What [del.] that [del.] such

24. Deleted in pencil: "I" ; inserted in pencil: "with new centripetal reference" above the deletion and "offer . . . dear"

25. "ing" added in pencil.

26. Deleted in ink: "a"

27. Deleted in ink: "a" ; inserted in pencil above the deletion and "road" : "for curious"

28. Preceding two words inserted in pencil above "travel"

29. Cf. "Thus wise it comes," [1].

30. Deleted in pencil: "resolute"

traveling with me[31] the rude air, woods and salt sea, fire and the rocky [*13* [32]; *12* [33]] ground, Thoughts arriving there will appear[34] the growth of the soil of America.[35] will appear—genuine,[36] sharp, full of danger, full of contradictions and offense.[37]

Those[38]—and from where it lurks, ever[39] timidly peering, but seldom,[40] ah so seldom really showing itself, that something also[41] may appear, before your very feet and under them[42]—BELIEF,—that fuses past and[43] present, and to come in one, and never doubts them more.[44] This, O friend, perfuming strange the hour that bathes you, the spot you stand on, the work you work at, and every drop of blood that courses through your veins, may[45] prove this journey's gift.

Faith—[46] worth all the lore and[47] riches of the world—[48] may somewhere[49] by the path I lead you,[50] among these leaves, an odorous[51] glistening blossom appear and become yours. [*15–18 blank* [52]]

31. Inserted in ink, deleted in red pencil above "with me . . . woods and" :"America will appear [*preceding two words ins. above* "and"] and all its might array of men, and new race of women," . "T" of "The" reduced to lowercase.
32. Black ink. In upper right corner "5" in blue crayon. WW began to write at left margin but cancelled it by smearing.
33. In pencil.

*From these, as from mirrors [*all del.*]
We will interrogate these curious silent objects. We [*del.*] will too for [*ins. above deletion and* "too"] will no matter how many have gone before us [*preceding eight words ins. on an arrow from below*] will arouse the original echoes.

34. Deleted: "not" ; inserted above: "the"
35. Preceding sentence inserted in pencil at top of the leaf on two lines above "ground, . . . full"
36. Inserted above "sharp"
37. Pencil, erased: "*The thoughts fit for America will appear."
38. Original first word of strophe "Such" deleted in pencil; inserted in pencil above: "Those—"
39. Inserted in ink above "ti" in "timidly"
40. Deleted in pencil: "O" ; inserted in pencil above and before: "ah"
41. Inserted in pencil above "m" in "may"
42. Comma deleted and dash inserted in pencil.
43. Inserted in ink above wordspace between "past present"
44. Deleted in pencil: "Such" ; inserted in pencil above: "This"
45. Deleted: "be my" ; inserted: "prove [*del.*] our [*ins. in the wordspace between deleted* "our" *and* "journey's"] this journey's" above "may . . . gift"
46. Deleted in ink: "a little thing, yet shining brighter than the sun"
47. Preceding two words inserted in ink above "riches"
48. Deleted: "may" ; inserted above in pencil: "may"
49. Deleted: "along" ; inserted above: "by [*del.*] through by [*illeg., del. in pencil*]"
50. Deleted in pencil: "lowly"
51. Deleted: "glittering flower," ; inserted above: "glistening blossom," ; inserted in ink, deleted in pencil: "may" above "a" in "appear"
52. Numbered "6" "7" in upper right corners in blue crayon.

Thus Wise It Comes.

Manuscript in NYPL (Lion). Introduction #6. Pasted in *LG* (1855, 2d issue), second back flyleaf verso. Inscribed in brownish ink, with corrections in black pencil except as noted. The first and third leaves have been trimmed. First printed by Furness, 174, as the conclusion of "Inscription at the Entrance," which is not authorized by the present mounting of the MS, nor by the paper and ink. Since the text is close to "Inscription to the Reader," the date is probably before 1867.

[*1*][1] Thus wise it comes, our New World chords in diapason gathering, chanting the flush and strength of things—[2] I and them engermed in myself[3] I[4] the following leaves offer ? then to[5] you,[6] dear friend, for vista, for curious road with me to travel.

Advance therein—nor be too soon discouraged. Much will not there[7] appear that other poets, guiding you pleasant,[8] sing, and sweetly pass the time away.[9]

But the strong wind shall touch[10] you from the North, and the salt sea. Such virtue as there is in[11] Fire and the rocky ground[12], genuine, sharp, full of danger, full of contradictions and offense.[13]

1. 4⅜″ x 5″. Deleted: "Therefore" ; inserted above "it comes" : "Thus wise"
2. Inserted and deleted: "with new centripetal reference" ; deleted: "chanting the modern" ; inserted and deleted: "and the democracies" ; deleted: "such" ; inserted and deleted: "those such" ; inserted: "I and them"
3. Deleted: "and the following" ; inserted and deleted: "and a few" ; deleted: "leaves with new centripetal reference."
4. Inserted: "[*del.*] in the following leaves"
5. Preceding question mark and two words inserted.
6. Inserted and deleted: "through the following leaves"
7. Inserted.
8. Deleted: "and safe,"
9. Originally the following strophe was part of the present one. It is separated on the authority of "¶?" in the MS.
10. Deleted in ink: "us" ; inserted in ink: "you"
11. Preceding six words inserted.
12. Deleted: "are to appear"
13. Cancelled passage. Question mark and single parenthesis on passage in left margin. "We are to [*preceding two words del.*] [*ins. and del.*] will interrogate [*del.*] silent [*del. in ink*] antique objects. We too are to [*preceding three words del. in ink*] too, as every one must in his turn [*preceding eight words ins. in ink*] [*del.*] arouse will summon [*preceding two words ins.*] the antique echoes."

[3 [14]; 2 [15]] Arouse [16] O friend! for of SUGGESTIVENESS I bring [17] you recitative out of the miracles around you—[18] naught made [19] by me for you, but plainly [20] hinted to be made by you yourself [21] by robust exercise. The pages of the lesson having filled, to train myself [22]—to you I [23] now resign them, with all their blots, to image back the process for your use.

[5 [24]; 4 *blank*] Indeed, this is no book, but more a man, within whose breast the common heart is throbbing so much. [25] These are [26] no printed leaves [27], but human [28] lips O friend [29] for your sake freely speaking. [30] [6 *blank*]

14. 3″ x 5″. Black ink with pencil emendations
15. Pencil: "*(for every apparition in this world is but to [*del.*] start [*ins. and del.*] rouse [*ins.*] rout in you [*preceding two words del.*] the real [*ins. and del.*] unseen object [*del.*] in [*ins.*] up there within [*preceding two words ins. and del.*] from sleeping in [*preceding three words ins.*] yourself)" No related asterisked passage has been noted.
16. Deleted: "! Arouse, dear" ; inserted: "O"
17. Deleted: "the song" ; inserted: "you recitative"
18. Deleted in ink: "every day" ; deleted in pencil: "not" ; inserted in pencil: "naught"
19. Inserted in ink, deleted in pencil: "so much"
20. Inserted.
21. Inserted.
22. Colon deleted; dash inserted.
23. Deleted: "here" ; inserted in ink: "now"
24. 3″ x 5″. Brown ink. Top trimmed.
25. Preceding two words inserted in pencil. Deleted: "You" ; inserted and deleted: "I give" ; deleted: "hear" ; inserted and deleted: "have in there" ; deleted: "not"
26. Preceding two words inserted; inserted and deleted: "no" ; inserted in black ink, deleted in pencil: "Look not for" ; inserted in margin: "no printed"
27. Deleted: "of print, O friend"
28. Inserted.
29. Preceding two words inserted.
30. In ink, cancelled in pencil. Emendations in ink except as noted. "From me to you, alone, a conference to ensue, to yield interior yearnings, discords, and all my private egotisms and moods, reserving nothing. Conference wherein, along [*del.*] this [*ins.*] the Western World, abandon we [*del. and restored in pencil*] ourselves you and [*ins. in pencil and erased*] me to Natures primal sanity again, [*to end of the entry cancelled separately in pencil*] our two exclusive souls and [*preceding four words del. in pencil*] [*del.*] meantime leave behind [*ins. and del.*] us take not for our law [*preceding eight words del. in pencil*] [*del. in pencil*] one for this [*preceding two words ins. and del.*] hour at any rate [*preceding three words ins. and del. in pencil*] [*del.*] or [*del.*] two at least [*preceding two words ins. and del.*] society's conventions [*preceding two words del.*]. While untried, yet, the greatest [*del.*] in the theme of my this [*preceding two words ins. and del. in pencil*] [*del.*] my [*del.*] this [*ins. in pencil*] the [*ins. and del. in pencil*] this [*illeg. ins. in pencil*] recitative."

Inscription. at the Entrance.

Manuscript in NYPL (Lion). Introduction #8. Pasted on *LG* (1855, 2d issue), second back flyleaf, recto. Inscribed in black ink and black pencil on white wove paper: [*1–2, 3–4*] 7⅜" x 4¼"; [*5–6*] 8" x 5". On verso of [*3*] is pasted "Meantime, plans failing." The cleanness of the copy and brevity of the text suggest a late stage in the development of "One's-Self I Sing (1867)." First printed by Furness, 173–174, photograph of [*1*] facing 172.

[*1*]*INSCRIPTION.*[1]
at the entrance of Leaves of Grass

––––––––

Small is the theme of the following chant, yet the greatest—namely, *One's-self,*[2] a simple, separate person. That, for the use of the New World, I sing.

As Nature is not great[3] with reference to itself, but great with reference to a human personality—As all the objects of the universe, and all events and heroes, are in the main suggestive and gymnastic, and only thus to you or me of any service—out of that formule do I sing.[4]

Man's physiology, from top to toe, I sing. Not physiognomy alone, nor brain alone, is worthy for the muse,[5] that makes her home upon the western [*3; 2 blank*] prairies. I say the perfect form, received with absolute faith, is only fully worthy.

One song[6] America demands that breathes her native air[7]—an utterance to invigorate Democracy—[8] (*Democracy*, the destined conqueror, yet treacherous lip-

1. Title printed in pencil.
2. In larger and thicker letters.
3. Deleted in ink: "to me"
4. The entire strophe is marked with a pencilled brace at left and the query: " ? out" . There are also some squiggles in ink at the left and between strophes.
5. Deleted in pencil: "walking" ; inserted above in pencil: "that [*del.*] walks" ; inserted below deleted "walking" and "the western" in pencil: "makes her home upon"
6. Deleted in pencil: "at any rate" . See Traubel, II, 57, for a version of this strophe identical except that it is a block paragraph and "novice's attempt" is in small capitals. See also "I Commenced Leaves of Grass" [*4*].
7. Deleted in pencil: "alone"
8. Following sentence before single parenthesis and "Of" marked in pencil by a brace and " ? out" in the left margin.

smiles always luring[9], and death and infidelity at every step.) Of such a song I launch the novice's attempt—and bravas to the bard who, coming after me, achieves the work[10] triumphant.[11]

For you, O friend, whoe'er you are, journeying[12] at last arriving hither, accept from me, as one in waiting for you at this entrance, welcome and hospitality.[13] I feel at every leaf the pressure of your hand, which I return.—[14] And thus throughout upon the journey linked together will we go.

[5; *4 blank*] Such—and from where it lurks,[15] (but[16] indeed within yourself ah![17] for every apparition[18] in this world is but to rout the real object up from sleeping[19] in yourself, that something[20] to remind you may appear, before your very feet, or under them—[21] that fuses past and present and to-come in One, and never doubts them more.

A little lowly thing, yet shining brighter than the sun, perfuming strange the hour that bathes you, the spot you stand on, the work you work at, and every drop of blood that courses through your veins,*[22] namely—BELIEF IMPLICIT, COMPREHENDING ALL— may prove[23] our journey's gift.

9. Preceding two words over smeared-out "always here" ; inserted and deleted in pencil: "here" above "luring"

10. Deleted in pencil: "complete" ; inserted above in pencil: "[*del.*] in triumphant."

11. At beginning of next strophe, deleted in pencil: *"Friend"* ; inserted and deleted in pencil: "D" in left margin; inserted in pencil: *"For you,* O friend" above "[*del.*] Friend" and "whoever"

12. Inserted in pencil above "are at"

13. Deleted in pencil: "This is no [*ins. and del. above deleted* "book" *in pencil*] mere book, [*ins. and del. in pencil above deleted* "but I"] but merely"

14. Semicolon smeared out; period and dash inserted in ink.

15. Deleted in pencil: "ever timidly waiting"

16. Deleted in ink: "seldom" ; inserted in pencil: "indeed within yourself" above the deletion and "ah!" and "[*del.*] so" following.

17. Deleted in pencil: "so seldom" ; deleted in ink and pencil: "showing itself" ; inserted in ink, deleted in pencil above deleted "showing": "[*not del. by mistake? above deleted* "itself"] clearly gain'd" ; following eighteen words brought up on asterisk, "up" and pointing hand from bottom of leaf.

18. Written over beginning of [*illeg.*]

19. Written over erasure.

20. Inserted in pencil: "[*del.*] also to remind you" above "may appear"

21. Deleted in pencil: "BELIEF" ; deleted in ink: dash.

22. Inserted in pencil: "namely" above "your" ; inserted and deleted in pencil above "veins.* may" : "BELIEF IMPLICIT" ; brought up from bottom of leaf on asterisk: "—BELIEF IMPLICIT, COMPREHENDING ALL—"

23. Deleted in pencil: "this" ; inserted above in pencil: "our"

Sweet[24] FAITH,[25] beyond all lore and riches[26] in the world, may somewhere somehow[27] by the path I lead you, among these leaves, an odorous glistening blossom, appear,[28] O friend, and[29] become[30] yours. [6 *blank*]

24. Inserted in pencil above "F" in "FAITH"

25. Deleted in pencil: "worth all the" ; inserted in pencil: "beyond all" above deleted "th" in "worth" and "all"

26. Deleted in pencil: "of" ; inserted in pencil above and before: "in"

27. Inserted in pencil above "ewhere" in "somewhere"

28. Inserted and deleted in pencil: "burst from {*del.*} its the inward folds" above "pear" in "appear" and "O friend, and become"

29. Inserted and deleted in pencil above and before "yours" : "? indeed"

30. In pencil, deleted, below text at right, but above insertions: "in living"

Meantime, Plans Failing.

Manuscript in NYPL (Lion). Introduction #9. Inscribed in black pencil on white wove scrap, approx. 3¾" x 4¼". Vertical blue rules on recto, ⅜" apart. Pasted by the top edge to the bottom of *"Inscription. at the Entrance"* to which it has no other connection. Cf. the reference to WW's works as *"Whisperings"* in "I commenced Leaves of Grass."

Meantime, plans failing—[1]the true supply of[2] well-form'd whispers lacking — I leave to you, whoee'r you are, to form & breathe them for yourself in,

1. Deleted in pencil: "my full" ; inserted above: "the true"
2. Deleted in pencil: "wh"

The Epos of a Life.

Manuscript in NYPL (Lion). Introduction #10. Inscribed in black pencil on light tan proof? paper, 4¾" x 5½". Cancelled with a vertical stroke. Pasted to *"INSCRIPTION. at the Entrance"* and "Meantime, plans failing." The reference to "crimson" war indicates this was written after 1865. The latest possible date is 1871. First published Furness, 174, as part of *"INSCRIPTION. at the Entrance."*

The epos of a Life;—the road you tread to-day,—the[1] workman's shop or farm-
er's field—the city's hum, or woods or trackless[2] wild—oe'r river, lake or sea—
(with shows I knew of crimson war,)—along the single thread, so interspersed.
Him of the Lands, (perhaps yourself,)[3] identical, I sing.

1. Deleted: "work"
2. Inserted above.
3. Parenthetical statement inserted.

(Some Good Points).

Manuscript in NYPL (Lion). Introduction #7. White folded sheet of notepaper, 8″ x 5″, pasted in *LG* (1855, 2d issue), second rear flyleaf, verso. Blue rules ⁵/₁₆″ apart. Printed as part of "I commenced Leaves of Grass" by Furness, 136. There is no authority for this procedure for, if WW mounted them, the manuscripts are quite distinct. See, however, "I commenced Leaves of Grass." This was written in the early 1860s.

[*1*] (Some good points)

The theory of the poem involves the expression[1] both of[2] boldest wildest[3] passion & bravest, sturdiest[4] character[5] not however illustrated after[6] any of the well known types[7] identities of the great bards, old or modern.[8] Nor Prometheus, nor Agamemnon,[9] nor Æneas, nor Hamlet, nor Iago, nor Antony, nor any of Dantes scenes or person's,[10] nor ballad of lord or lady, nor Lucretian[11] philosophy, nor any [*3; 2*[12]] special system of philosophy[13] nor any tale with   nor any striking lyric achievement[14] nor Childe Harold, nor any[15] epic tale, with begin-

1. Preceding two words inserted.
2. Deleted: "the highest"
3. Preceding three words inserted.
4. Preceding two words inserted.
5. Deleted: "but presented" ; inserted above deletion: "not however illustrated" ; inserted and deleted in left margin: "all" "all" ; deleted: "after none of the types hitherto of any of the great and accepted and great [*preceding four words ins. above* "great bards Nor"] bards Nor Prometheus"
6. Deleted: "none of the well known" ; inserted above "after" : "any of" ; inserted and deleted above "[*del.*] none" : "no" ; inserted: "the well known"
7. "Types" emended to singular then to plural. Deleted: "the" ; inserted and deleted: "the [*illeg.*]"
8. Preceding two words inserted. Deleted: "The illustrious epic & biographic is here,"
9. Deleted: "No"
10. Deleted: "nor any epic of events"
11. Originally "Lucretius' " ; deleted before "philosophy" : "lof"
12. Written sideways: "Only They are the negative suggestions and here is the positive." Probably meant as last sentence.
13. Deleted: "old or new," ; inserted and deleted: "nor any particular lyric [*illeg.*]" ; deleted: "nor any tale with"
14. Deleted: "accomplishment" ; inserted: "nor Childe Harold,"
15. Deleted: "poetic"

ning, climax, and termination.[16] yet something of perhaps similar purport,[17] very definite, compact, very simple, even[18] and applying directly to the reader and[19] curiously digesting & including all the list we have just named[20] is the resultant of this book, namely, to suggest,[21] the substance & form of a large, sane, perfect Human Being or Character, for an American[22] man and for woman. While other things are in the book, studies, digressions of various sorts, this is undoubtedly its essential purpose & its key.*[23]

16. Deleted: "So"

17. Preceding four words inserted.

18. Deleted: "at first hand"

19. Inserted and deleted: "after"

20. Preceding twelve words inserted; inserted and deleted: "at first hand" ; deleted: "Car[?] applying for main purpose" ; inserted: "is the resultant"

21. Inserted and deleted: "for general use"

22. Preceding two words inserted.

23. No matching passage found, but the reference may be to the entry on [2] (see *n*12 above).

I Commenced Leaves of Grass.

Manuscript in NYPL (Lion). Introduction #11. Inscribed in various media on ten leaves of various paper as described in the notes. The discontinuity of the text and the variety of handwriting, media, and paper suggest that WW gathered together perhaps as many as five drafts or fragments of drafts written at various times and pasted them together or to hinges at the left edge. Pinned by WW to *LG* (1855, 2d issue), second back flyleaf verso. He probably worked on it after pasting it together, for on [4] and [14] the writing runs from the leaf on to a hinge. One should note the possible new title, "Whisperings" [9]. Some of it is as late as 1870, but it is probable that most of the material was written in 1861 or slightly later. Printed in Furness, 135–137. Facsimile of [1] facing 134.

[1][1] I commenced[2] Leaves of Grass my thirty-sixth year,[3] by publishing their first issue.[4]—Twice have I[5] issued[6] them since, with increased[7] matter—[8]the present one making the fourth issue, with[9] the latest increase. I am to-day, (May 31, 1861,) just forty-two years old—for I[10] write this[11] introduction on my birthday—after having[12] looked over what I have accomplished.[13] So far so well, but[14]

1. White wove paper, 6¼" x 4", pasted to [3], both pasted to a stub, but now separated from remainder of MS. Black ink; all emendations in ink. Deleted: "I am to-day (May 31, 1861), just forty-two years of age—for I thought I would write [*del.*] this the [*ins. above the deletion*] present paragraph on my birthday."
2. Deleted: "the book in" ; inserted above and to right: "[*del.*] these Leaves of Grass"
3. Deleted: "and" ; probably inserted: "by" ; "ing" inserted over "ed" in "published"
4. Deleted: "Since then [*ins. and del. above* "n" *in deleted* "then"] then it has t"; inserted: "Twice have" above "[*del.*] it has t"
5. Deleted: "have"
6. Deleted: "it" ; inserted: "them" above "ued" in "issued" ; inserted and deleted: "again and again" above "it" and "[*del.*] each time" ; inserted and deleted: "each time" above "with" and under "[*del.*] and" and "a" in "[*del.*] again" ; inserted: "since" above "[*del.*] again"
7. "d" added to "increase" ; deleted: "of"
8. Deleted: "this [*ins. above* "is" *in* "[*del.*] this"] one being" ; inserted above: "the present one making"
9. Deleted: "additional" ; inserted above: "the latest"
10. Deleted: "thought I would"
11. Deleted: "paragraph" ; inserted above: "introduction"
12. Inserted above "——after having"
13. Inserted above "birth-day" : "—after . . . accomplished." Since the insertion is written with a fine pen three lines deep between lines of the MS, with a balloon insert and emended, it is almost indecipherable even twice photomagnified.
14. Preceding five words inserted; capital "S" written over lowercase; earlier opening words deleted: "But" , "Though" . WW neglected to reduce the capital "T" of "The" and to remove a comma after "best" not printed here.

the most and the best,[15] of the Poem I perceive remains unwritten,[16] and is the work of my life, yet to be done.

[*3; 2 blank*][17] I do not[18] purpose to school[19] any person in virtues, nor prove anything[20] to the intellect, nor sing[21] amours[22] or romances, nor[23] the epics of land or sea.[24] They to their work, (which is[25] great)[26]—mine to[27] mine.[28]

[*5;*[29] *4*[30]] I commenced Leaves of Grass in my thirty-sixth year, by my publishing their first issue.[31] Four times have I issued them since, each time with successive increase; this being the[32] fifth issue. I am to-day, (May 31, 1870[33])[34] fifty-one[35] years old; for I write

15. Deleted: "have yet to be" ; inserted: "of [*ins. and del. above* "ha" *in* "have"] [*del.*] my the Poem [*preceding two words ins.*] [*del.*] has I perceive [*preceding two words ins. above deleted* "has" *and* "remains"] remains; deleted: "yet to be"

16. Inserted: "un" on "written," ; deleted: "I consider [*ins. and del. above deleted* "it"] to-day it as" ; inserted: "and is"

17. Deleted: "men, which stands forever This is my way, and this is my way, and this is America's" . Deleted beginning of new paragraph: "All the"

18. Inserted: "seek [*ins. above* "to"] here to" ; deleted: "seek" ; inserted and deleted above "[*del.*] seek" : "here," ; inserted below "[*del.*] seek" : "purpose"

19. Deleted: "you" ; inserted and deleted above: "any one" ; inserted above "[*del.*] you" and "in" : "[*illeg.*] person" ; deleted: [*illeg.*]; inserted: "any" above "[*del.*] you"

20. Deleted: "to you" ; inserted: "to the intellect" above the deletion and "nor"

21. Apparently deleted: "any loves" ; inserted above preceding deletion : "any amours" ; deleted: "any" ; inserted with finer-nibbed pen above preceding deletion: "any"

22. Deleted: "and" ; inserted above: "or"

23. Deleted: "the" ; inserted and deleted above: "any various" ; inserted with finer-nibbed pen above "nor" : "the" ; inserted: "nor the" above "epics" . A redundant undeleted "nor" following "romances" is not printed here.

24. Deleted: "Those" ; inserted above: "They"

25. Deleted: "good" ; inserted above: "great"

26. Parenthetical remark inserted above "their work"

27. Deleted: "mine" ; inserted and deleted above: "I"; inserted: "mine" above "[*del.*] I"

28. Deleted passage: "As [*del.*] the [*ins. above the deletion*] one undraped, [*del.*] sees shows back an apparition [*preceding two words ins. above* "back from"] from [*del.*] the [*ins. above*] a mirror shows not the face merely, but the whole form from top to"

29. White wove scrap, 2⅜″ x 4¼″, black ink, glued on [7–8] at left edge. Paper trimmed at left before it was pasted in.

30. At bottom of leaf, cancelled by two diagonal strokes: "Do you, perusing them,—dwell upon them with pleasure and profit? Then try these chants" Part of "dwell" is written on the stub to which the leaf is attached, indicating that the entry was made after the leaves were bound up.

31. Deleted: "Twice" ; inserted after "issue" inserted: "[*del.*] three times" above "have" ; [*del.*] three" inserted: "Four" above before "times" . The fourth edition of *LG* appeared in 1871, but on December 9, 1869, WW wrote William Michael Rossetti to thank him for transmitting Mrs. Gilchrist's ardent words of praise and announced that he hoped for a new edition in "the coming spring." (*Corr.,* II, 92.)

32. Deleted: "fourth" ; inserted above: "fifth"

33. "70" is written over "61"

34. Deleted: "just"

35. Deleted: "forty-two" ; inserted above: "fifty-one"

[7; [36] 6 *blank*] The paths to the house are[37] made—but where is the house itself? At most,[38] only indicated or touched.

Nevertheless, as while we live some dream will play its part, I keep it in my plan of work ahead to yet fill up these *Whisperings,*[39] (if I live, and have luck,) somehow proportionate to their original design.[40] If it should turn out[41] otherwise, (which is most likely, dear Reader,)[42] I hereby bequeath to you—& that, no doubt, is much[43] the best—[44] to form & breathe[45] Whisperings[42] for yourself, in heart-felt[47] meditations fitter far than words. Or, rather, let me say, O friend, unless such meditations come, at reading any page or pages of our Chant, no matter which, the Chant, the Book, is really not for you, & has not done its office. [9; [48] 8 *blank*] Need we to mark,[49] in this, the only true communion with our Book, which we have made, purposed,[50] indeed, unlike all others, & not we finally confess[51] for literary satisfactions, ends, or ornaments;—made, first, to be the Chant, the Book of Universal Life, and of the Body,—and then, and just as much, to be the Chant of Universal Death, and of the Soul.[52]

36. Black ink on white laid letter paper, approx. 7″ x 4″, embossed capitol (probably Platner and Porter manufacture) upper left of original sheet. Vertical blue rules ⅜″ apart. Some emendations in pencil. The writing is more regular than elsewhere in this notebook. Corrections in black pencil and brown crayon. Number "486" in WW's hand in red-brown crayon at top right. One cannot think of a long prose work of which this and the following leaf might have been a part.

37. Deleted in pencil: "all"

38. Deleted in pencil: "it is"

39. Cf. "whispers" in "Meantime, plans failing." Parenthetical statement inserted in pencil above "somehow proportionate"

40. Deleted in pencil: "If I live, [*previously del. in ink*] then & have luck, they may then additionally appear."

41. Preceding four words inserted in pencil above "If otherwise," and "(w" in "(which"

42. Deleted in pencil: "and if this Notice prove, from me to you, our final interview, (though, as to that who shall dare undertake to tell?)"

43. Deleted in pencil: "for" ; inserted in pencil: "much" above the deletion and "the"

44. Preceding eight words inserted in pencil above "th" in "bequeath" and "to you . . . breathe"

45. Deleted: "such"

46. Lowercase "w" made uppercase in ink.

47. Inserted in pencil above "medi" in "meditations"

48. Paper and writing material identical to [7]. Numbered "487" at top right in WW's hand in red/brown crayon. The writing, like that of [7], is very smooth and regular as compared to elsewhere.

49. Inserted and deleted in pencil: "finally" above "mark,"

50. Inserted and deleted in pencil: "we finally confess" above "indeed unlike"

51. Preceding three words inserted in pencil above "not for literary"

52. Following cancelled after "Soul." with a diagonal pencil stroke:

"And now, with a remaining page or two, Wherein we would pourtray, at least in pale reflection, the passionate flush'd heart—visage of one that, having offer'd Salutation ["S" *raised from lowercase*], & join'd & journey'd on awhile in close companionship—has now to resign you, Dearest Reader, and, with mingled cheer and sadness, bid Farewell.

W.W."

Furness (136) inserts, without authority, "(Some good points)" which, since WW mounted the MSS in this book, is to be taken as a distinct MS. See, however, n53.

{*11;*[53] *10 blank*} So that[54] in the[55] poems, taken as a[56] whole, unquestionably[57] appears a great Person,[58] entirely modern, at least as great as any[59] thing in the[60] Homeric or Shakesperian characters,[61] Person with[62] the[63] free courage of Achilles,[64] the craft of Ulysses, the attributes even[65] of[66] the Greek deities, majesty[67] passion,[68] temper, amativeness, Romeo, Lear, Antony, immense[69] self-esteem, but after democratic forms, measureless love, the old eternal elements of first-class humanity

Yet[70] worked over, cast[71] in a new mould,[72] and here chanted or any how[73] put down & stated with invariable reference[74] to the United States & the occasions of to-day & the future [75]

{*13;*[76] *12 blank*}[77] Dear friend![78]—not here for you melodious narratives[79] —no pictures, here[80] for you to con at leisure, as bright creations all outside your-

53. Very heavy white laid paper, 8″ x 5″, with blue rules 5/16″ apart. Inscription and emendations entirely in black pencil, somewhat loose and giving the impression of haste (or illness?), as compared to the previous leaves, especially {7, 9}. The paper and writing are very like those of "(Some good points)"

54. Preceding two words inserted above "In the" . WW did not reduce capital "I" of "In" ; not printed here.

55. Deleted: "work" ; inserted above: "poems"

56. Deleted: "p" {?}

57. Inserted above "appears"

58. Lowercase "p" raised to uppercase.

59. Deleted: "portra"

60. Deleted: "antique" ; inserted above: "Homeric"

61. Inserted and deleted: "a" ; inserted: "Person" above "with"

62. Deleted: "all"

63. Deleted: "pride" ; inserted: "free courage"

64. Deleted: "all"

65. Inserted above "of"

66. Deleted: "Homer's" ; inserted above: "the Greek"

67. Inserted above "ties" in "deities"

68. The end of the line falls somewhat short of the other line endings. Possibly WW intended to insert another attribute. Deleted at the beginning of the following line: "mystery"

69. Deleted: "pride" ; inserted above: "self-esteem"

70. Deleted: "in a"

71. Inserted above "in"

72. Deleted: "in" ; inserted above: "and"

73. Written over the beginning of another word.

74. Preceding three words inserted above "stated" and "{*del.*} for the"

75. The preceding words are the result of a sequence of emendations. The original entry, following the just noted insertion, seems to have read: "for the service of America now & henceforth" . This was emended between the lines to "for applicability to the United States & the occasions of to-day & the future." ; "for applicability" then deleted.

76. White wove paper, unruled, 8″ x 5″. Numbered "4" by WW in upper right corner. Hanging indentation. Inscribed with broad-nibbed pen in dark brown ink. Emendations in brown ink and black pencil. The ink is almost unique to these Introductions, but see Bowers (xxvii) who mentions the use of light brown ink in the Valentine MSS of the late 1850s. Comparison of the two inks was not feasible. The use of the broad-nibbed pen changes the character of WW's writing somewhat, but despite its blockiness it is his hand of the decade of 1860 to 1870 rather than the smaller hand of the 1850s or the irregular hand after 1870. Nothing in the content indicates any

self.[81] But of SUGGESTIVENESS,[82] out of the miracles[83] of every day, with new centripetal reference[84] this is the song—[85]naught[86] made by me for you, but only[87] hinted, to be made by you[88] by robust exercise.[89] I have not[90] done the work, and cannot do it. But you must do the work to[91] and make what[92] is within the following song—[93]

date, except that lack of reference to newer and more spiritual poems or to the family of states suggests that this was written no later than 1870. Furness (132) prints as part of "INSCRIPTION." The handwriting is the same.

77. Inserted and deleted in pencil: "Therefore" in the upper left of the leaf above "Dear"

78. Deleted in pencil: "put not in the following book" ; opening "I" not deleted by accident, not printed here; at one point "this book" was inserted and deleted in pencil above "the following" ; inserted in pencil: "—not here for you" above "I" and "put not in the"

79. Deleted in pencil: "or" ; inserted above in pencil: "—no"

80. Inserted in pencil, deleted in pencil: "for" ; deleted in ink: "bright creations you" ; inserted and deleted in pencil: "finished" above "ations" in "[del.] creations" ; inserted in pencil: "for you" above "[del.] you" and "to"

81. Deleted in pencil: "With such, the world is well enough supplied."

82. Deleted in pencil: "alone,"

83. Deleted in pencil: "around us" ; inserted: "[in pencil] of [in ink] every day"

84. Preceding four words inserted in pencil above the preceding line, above "[del.] alone, out of" and brought down here on an arrow.

85. Inserted and deleted in pencil: "not" above "naught"

86. Inserted and deleted in pencil: "complete" above "made by"

87. Deleted in pencil: "offered" ; inserted above in pencil: "hinted"

88. Deleted in pencil: "yourself" ; inserted above in pencil: "by robust exercise"

89. An indistinct pencil line carries up to a deleted pencil passage inserted at the top of the page, above the ink text: "Which here I [ins. above "I"] seek give, and not the usual finished book"

90. Inserted and deleted in pencil: "therefore" above "not done"

91. Deleted in pencil: "really" ; inserted above in pencil: "and" . WW forgot to correct "to" to "too" or to delete it.

92. Inserted and deleted in pencil: "for you" above "is" and "with" in "within"

93. [Passage deleted in pencil]: "which if you do by robust exercise [three words ins. in pencil above deleted "you . . . promise"] I promise you return and satisfaction more than ever [del. in pencil] book [two words ins. and del. in pencil above deleted "book" and "be" in "before"] printed leaves [ins. in pencil below deleted "book"] print before has [ins. in pencil above "has"] have given you." [Deleted in ink] "For from this book your own soul*before [ins. in pencil above "be" in "before"] I [ins. in pencil and del. following "b"] give unknown, shall be revealed, and give encouraging answer ? call you to [query and three words ins. in pencil above "answer" . An arrow leads from the asterisk off the left edge of the leaf, possibly to one of the asterisked entries on [14]. Following passage cancelled with an oblique pencil slash. Opposite the last eleven words, in pencil at left: "?out altogether" supported by a pencil line to the left of the entire passage. Inside the vertical pencil line is "X2" in a circle.]" This book shall [three words del. in pencil] preceding [del. in ink]mirror I fain [ins. in pencil above "This book shall"] would [ins. in ink, del. in pencil above "shall] would [del. in pencil] back. Yourself that fathomless, that unaccountable, [preceding four words ins. in pencil above "an equal soul"] an equal soul and body joined. [The next sentence is emended beyond clear transcription.] "Then [illeg.] I fain Besides would ["also" del.] besides hint the [three words ins. in ink] all-surrounding modern song [del.] poem [del. of America demands. [four words inserted above in ink]—the utterance of Democracy." [Then:] "Let me ([ins. in ink] for I have had that dream) initiate the attempt—and [del. in pencil] bravas [ins. and del. in pencil] bravo [ins. in pencil] hail him or her, [three words ins. in pencil above "her . . . who,"] as yet unknown, [three words del. in ink] and succeeds—triumphs achieves [del. in pencil] it the work [del. in pencil] indeed in triumph" [last five words ins. in pencil] on two lines at the foot of the leaf. Cf. [14]n4 below.

[*14*][94] to celebrate the modern, the working man[?][95]
Not for[96]
One[97]*[98]* song[99] at any rate America demands   *   expanding large[1] that breathes her native air alone the[2] Chant of Democracy—the INDIVIDUAL's chant.[3]

*[4]Let me,[5] (for [6]I have had that dream,) initiate of that song[7] the[8]—and bravas to[9] the one who, coming after me, achieves the[10] work in triumph.[11]

Therefore it comes our New World chords in diapason gathering[12] I sound and spread them[13] forth,[14] dear friend,[15] for vista, for curious road[16] to travel.

[*15*][17] The pages of the lesson having writ to train myself—to you I bring them here, and now resign[18] with all their blots, to image back the[19] process for your use.

94. In black pencil. This verso seems not to be notes for the facing recto. Deleted: "and"

95. End of word on stub to which leaf is pasted suggests that these notes were scrawled after binding. Deleted: "and [*dash not del.*] and the utterance of D"

96. A gap sufficient for two or three lines follows. Below "Not for" but at right of page is deleted: "Should no one dare that"

97. Entry with hanging indentation. Cf. "Inscription at the entrance."

98. There are two asterisks, one in pencil, one in black ink. From the latter a curving line loops across the page above the text. The former seems keyed to the following cancelled line: "*One song, at any rate, America [*ink over pencil*] demands, [*two words del.*] from and that breathes her native air alone." See *n*11 below.

99. Deleted: "at any rate" ; inserted and deleted in light pencil: "I say" ; inserted in light pencil below line: "at any rate" below ["*del.* at any rate"].

1. Preceding two words inserted above "that" and "br" in "breathes" . A marginal asterisk floats to the left of this phrase.

2. Deleted: "song"

3. Preceding seven words inserted in a balloon written above "[*del.*] Shall no one dare that," . See *n*96 above. A much-emended but totally cancelled sentence follows of which the following is one possible reading: "Fain would I hint the modern all-surrounding song America demands—the utterance or DEMOCRACY." See *n*93 above.

4. Possibly refers to "(X2)" on [*13*]. Cf. *n*93.

5. Inserted and deleted: "at any rate" above "me"

6. Inserted above "I"

7. Preceding three words inserted above "the" and into the margin.

8. Deleted: "attempt"

9. Deleted: "him or her" ; inserted: "the one" above "[*del.*] him or"

10. Deleted: "work in triumph" ; inserted and deleted above: "bardic work complete" ; deleted: "meantime"

11. Deleted line "*One song, at any rate, America [*following word ink over pencil*] demands, [*following two words del.*] from and that breathes her native air alone." See *n*98 above.

12. Inserted in light pencil on two lines: "our New World chords in diapason gathering" above "I" and "[*del.*] have" ; deleted: "have" [*preceding redundant* "I" *not deleted, not printed here*]; inserted: "I sound and" to left of "spread" and "and" above "spre" in "spread"

13. Inserted above wordspace between "spread forth"

14. Deleted: "for you"

15. Deleted: "the ensuing,"

16. Inserted and deleted: "for you" above "to"

17. White wove scrap, 2¾" x 3¾", pasted to left edge of [*17*] at bottom. Black pencil. First nine words lightly marked by vertical line at left.

18. Preceding three words inserted above "here with all"

19. Over [*illeg.*]

[17; 16 blank][20] *To the Reader.*
As[21] a traveler,[22] journey resuming[23]
Delays till he[24] find a memo

[19;[25] *18 blank]* Clipt by life's shortness with no[26] time to complete
    elaborate   finish[27]
Hurried, I bring
[20 blank]

20. Folded sheet, 9″ x 10½″, of white foolscap pasted in at fold. Right edges torn roughly. Blue rules, here vertical, ⁷⁄₁₆″ apart, red-blue-red (horizontal margin 1¼″ from bottom.
    21. Deleted: "one"
    22. Deleted: "his" above wordspace between "traveller, journey"
    23. Cancelled lines or fragments of lines: "Wishes" above "[*del.*] Hunts" "Hunts for a little gift" "Stays" [*ins. above* "[*del.*] Turns"] "Turns him making [*del. above* "making"] offering a little gift a certain " "Turns" "Stays" inserted on two lines above "Stays" "Stays till he leave" "Turns" "de"
    24. Deleted: "make" ; inserted and deleted above: [*illeg.*] ; inserted: "find"
    25. Probably a continuation of the verses on [*17*].
    26. Preceding word "Hurried" deleted.
    27. Preceding three words in a column.

Criticism.

Manuscript in LC (Feinberg). Inscribed in black pencil and black ink on white wove paper as noted. Handwriting and paper both indicate a date after July, 1865, when WW was appointed to a post in the Attorney General's office. The order of pages follows that of the first published edition, Carteret Book Club (Newark, NJ, 1913). Published in fac-simile in *The Literary Review* (Autumn, 1960), 49–59.

{*1*}[1] *Criticism*

Margaret Fuller[2] began her essay on American Literature with the dry[3] re-mark that[4] persons[5] might perhaps at the very outset, object to reading an essay on[6] something that had no earthly existence. So I[6a] may say I am going to write a chapter on something that does not exist—namely Criticism.

{*3; 2 blank*}[7] The lecturers have[8] a stereotyped saying[9] that only[10] on the decline of a superior Literature comes Criticism. It may be historically true in the past; but it does not need to be so[11] for our[12] day or for the future. I can fancy how the right kind of Criticism—the Pen indeed in the hands of men entirely great—[13] might arrest, hold up to scorn & in due time[14] thoroughly exterminate,

1. Inscribed in black pencil on white wove paper, 5½" x 7⅝". Embossed upper left "Congress [view of Capitol] P & P". Blue rules ½" apart. Ascenders from trimmed-off words show at bottom of leaf.
2. Deleted: "once" . "American Literature" first appeared in Fuller's *Papers on Literature and Art*, II (NY, 1846). The paraphrased statement is on p. 127.
3. Deleted: "criticism" ; inserted: "remark"
4. Deleted: "acute"
5. Deleted: "would doubtless" ; inserted: "might perhaps [*del.*] probably at the very out-set," on a line above "persons object to"
6. Deleted: "a ma" ; inserted: "something" above "[*del.*] ma"
6a. Deleted: "a"
7. Inscribed in black pencil on white wove paper, 9¾" x 7¾". Blue rules ½" apart. On verso, Attorney General's letterhead "186—"
8. Deleted: "it"
9. Inserted above "ped" in "stereotyped"
10. Deleted: "in" ; inserted above: "on"
11. Deleted: dash.
12. Deleted: "purposes" ; inserted above: "day or"
13. Deleted: "may" ; inserted above: "might"
14. Deleted: "destroy" ; inserted: "thoroughly exterminate" on a line above "due time" and "[*del.*] destroy"

a false & vicious school of current[15] writers,[16] & might prepare for,[17] beget, & bring[18] forward to maturity,[19] crops[20] of[21] noble writers & even poets, instead. But[22] this is supposing a[23] stature of [5; 4 *blank*][24] Critics & Criticism—not higher than I think possible, nor perhaps probable, some day—but for higher than British, or European literature has ever yet[25] afforded.

Few[26] are they whose[27] scale can measure[28] the unspeakable value, to man,[29] of Literature. Yet over it all is Criticism. [7; 6 *blank*][30] For criticism, carried to the height worthy of it,[31] is[32] a majestic[33] office, perhaps an Art, perhaps even a Church,[34] necessitating in its ministry[35] all the elements, all the acquirements— having central principles, comprehending the universal, the all,[36] yet with[37] keen eye to detail,[38] and with quick ear, well[39] aware of[40] Passions & emotions, intuitive, intellectual, yet far more than merely intellectual, [9; 8 *blank*][41]—[42]possesses the wisdom of the experienced father,[43] & the wisdom of the mother,[44] possesses the[45] most fervent love of country,[46] is equipt of course[47] from the libraries, has

15. Inserted above "of" and "wr" in "writers"
16. Deleted: "however popular they were at the outset"
17. Preceding two words and comma inserted above "ght" in "might" and "beget"
18. Deleted: "to" , "out" ; inserted above: "forward"
19. Deleted: "[*illeg.*] a"
20. "s" added to "crop"
21. Deleted: "to[?]"
22. Deleted: "[*ins.*] this is giving criticism the judicial"
23. Deleted: "for"
24. Inscribed in black pencil on paper identical with [*1*].
25. Deleted: "approached."
26. Deleted false start of paragraph: "fe"
27. Deleted: "space" ; inserted and deleted above: "estimate" ; inserted: "scale" above [*del.*] estimate"
28. Deleted: "that" ; inserted above: "the"
29. Deleted: "or nati"
30. Inscribed in pencil with black ink emendations on white laid paper, 4¼" x 7¾", trimmed at top.
31. Preceding seven words and comma inserted in black ink above "cism" of "criticism" and "m" of "majestic"
32. Deleted: "itself"
33. Deleted: "Art"
34. Preceding four words and comma inserted in black pencil above "perhaps an Art"
35. Preceding three words inserted in black pencil above "necessitating"
36. Preceding two words and comma inserted above "sal" of "universal" and wordspace.
37. Deleted in black ink: "the"
38. Preceding two words and comma inserted above "keen eye" ; deleted in black ink: "the" ; inserted in black ink above deleted "the" and "quick": "and with,"
39. Inserted above "a" of "aware"
40. Deleted in black ink: "all the"
41. Inscribed in pencil and black ink emendations on white laid paper, 9¾" x 7¾", as in [*1*].
42. Deleted: "has" ; inserted above deletion and "the": "possesses"
43. Deleted: "has" ; inserted above: "&"
44. Deleted: "loves" "has" ; inserted above "has" : "possesses"
45. Deleted: "lovedec"
46. Deleted: "has of course" ; inserted above deleted "has of" and deleted: "include the" ; deleted in black ink: "is" ; inserted in black ink above deleted "is" : "is"
47. Deleted: "with" ; inserted above: "from"

indeed at command[48] the whole[49] arsenal[50] of books, and[51] must perhaps[52] contain the special instinct of the love of books.[53] These, with other traits, go to form the Critic. Then, as the breath of life to the fore-mentioned,[54] or subtle coloring through which it all appears, a distinct perception & recognition, of[55] the wonders, Humanity and Nature,[56] as before[57] all books; and of[58] the latter,[59] while[60] nothing in themselves,[61] yet of the utmost importance as endeavoring to provide some argument or suggestive explanation[62] on those tremendous wonders.[63]

{*11; 10 blank*}[64] Above all, he must be Religious. Not the[65] melted butter[66] of[67] that deference[68] we see in[69] every "respectable" volume[70] & magazine article[71]; but the devout realising,—which comes from the[72] amplest knowledge[73] as strange to say, it also comes from extremest simplicity—that man & the universe have a[74] fitting purpose, & that Soul *is*.[75]

Such,[76] it behoves to understand is the[77] outline of a Critic,[78] appropriate

48. Deleted: "all"
49. Inserted above "ars" in "arsenal"
50. Changed to singular.
51. Inserted in black ink above wordspace. Deleted: "may" ; inserted above deleted "may" : "must"
52. Deleted in black ink: "be idiocratically? ["?" *over* "idiocratically"] a lover" ; inserted in black ink: "[*del.*] have [*ins.* above] the special [*ins.* above "inst" of "instinct"] instinct of the love"
53. Period inserted over comma.
54. Deleted: "must be [*ins. and del.*] possess" ; inserted: "or . . . all appears," above "fore-mentioned" and deleted "must be"
55. Inserted: "[*black ink, del. in pencil*] the [*pencil, del. in pencil*] the [*pencil*] the [*black ink*] wonders" above "of humanity"
56. Deleted: "as" ; inserted above: "as"
57. Deleted: "and"
58. Inserted in black ink above wordspace.
59. Inserted in black ink above wordspace, deleted in pencil: [*illeg.*]
60. Inserted above "nothing"
61. Deleted: "but" ; inserted above: "yet"
62. Preceding three words inserted above "ument" in "argument" and "on those" and "tre" in "tremendous"
63. Inserted in pencil, deleted in black ink: "topics"
64. Identical with [9].
65. Deleted: "soft gause meted"
66. Deleted: comma
67. Deleted: "such" ; inserted above: "that"
68. Deleted: "& politeness as"
69. Deleted: "all" ; inserted above: "every"
70. Changed to singular.
71. Changed to singular.
72. Deleted: "vastest" ; inserted above: "amplest"
73. Deleted: ", or" ; inserted: "[*del.*] —strange to say, [*ins. in black ink*] it also [*ins. in black ink above* "from"] comes from" above "[*del.*] , or" and "extremist" and "sim" in "simplicity"
74. Deleted: "proportionate" ; inserted: "fitting" above "tionate" in "proportionate"
75. Deleted: "an" ; inserted: "the"
76. Deleted false start: "This," ; "Such," inserted above
77. Deleted: "an" ; inserted above: "the"
78. Deleted: "prof"

to[79] the charge of the great thing, Literature any where,[80] and especially[81] to its office & regulation for the splendid new[82] era and inauguration of it, on the vast bases, & unprecedented faith & directness, of the New World.

[*13; 12 blank*][83] Such & no less, is[84] the[85] kind of[86] planter, waterer overseer & pruning-master[87] in the dearest[88] of the gardens of civilisation demanded by our land & time.[89] Such the style that America, from her very geography, of unparallelled spread & variety, and from the nature of her race of many races, & from her crowning[90] theory of[91] seeking the strong & full & perfect[92] individual man,[93] provides for & presupposes.

[*15; 14 blank*][94] What[95] Criticism also needs to-day[96] is[97] something fresh from the mountains,[98]—some[99] pure gales of[1] Huron—something well oxygenated, from the[2] snow & ice of the North. As[3] it stands,[4] it is helplessly listless, impotent,[5] mangy, beyond[6] toleration, and[7] bids fair,[8] to[9] soon become[10] a surface

79. Deleted: "this" ; inserted: "the charge of" above "to" and "[*del.*] this" and "great"
80. Deleted: comma; inserted: "any where" above "ure" in "literature" and "and"
81. Deleted: "for" ; inserted in black ink: "to its [*above deleted* "for" *and* "the" ; "s" *del.*] office & regulation for [*three words ins. in black ink* above "ce" in "office" and in two lines in right margin]"
82. Inserted above "e" in "era"
83. Identical with [9]. Deleted: "This & no less, not a grain less" ; inserted: "Such" above "[*del.*] This" and "& no less," above "[*del.*] less, not a"
84. Inserted and deleted in black ink: "are"
85. Deleted: "sort" ; inserted and deleted above: "Now" ; inserted: "kind" above "of"
86. Deleted: "chooser[?]"
87. Preceding three words inserted in black ink above "seer" in "overseer" and "in the"
88. Inserted in pencil, deleted in black ink: "section" above "of"
89. Deleted in black ink: "This" ; inserted in black ink: "Such the style [*del. in black ink*] of [*illeg. del. in black ink*] that [*del. in black ink*] our" above "[*del.*] This" and "America, from her"
90. Inserted above "theo" in "theory"
91. Deleted in black ink: "perfecting & making" ; inserted in black ink: "seeking the" above "[*del.*] making" ; deleted: "large" ; inserted above: "strong"
92. Preceding two words inserted in black ink; deleted: "the"
93. Deleted in black ink: "and from all that is here" ; deleted: "prepa" ; inserted above: "provides"
94. Inscribed in pencil with black ink emendations on white wove paper, 9¾" x 7⅝". Blue rules ½" apart.
95. Deleted in black ink: "Literature & Criticism" ; inserted in black ink: "Criticism also" above "ature" in [*del.*] "Literature" and "Cri" in [*del.*] "Criticism"
96. Deleted: "above all things [*comma not deleted, not printed*]"
97. Deleted: "surely"
98. Deleted: "with the strong wind"
99. Deleted: "strong"
1. Deleted: "Erie & Michi"
2. Inserted in black ink above wordspace between "from snow"
3. Deleted: "they" ; inserted above: "it"
4. "s" added; deleted: "they are" ; inserted above: "it is helplessly"
5. Deleted: "rotten" ; inserted after: "mangy," ; deleted: "I [*del.*] wil not intend to trust myself" . Following brought up to "mangy," on an arrow.
6. Deleted: "all"
7. Deleted: "is rapidly"
8. Deleted in black ink: "indeed" [*comma not deleted, not printed*]
9. Deleted: "became rotten"
10. Deleted: "little not much a mass" ; inserted: "a surface" above "a mass"

of sour bubbles covering a mass of putrefaction. Here is the Hercules' task of all. A resolute & original theory is indispensable.

[*17; 16 blank*][11] Has it never occurred to any one[12] that[13] the real tests applicable to a book entirely outside of[14] literary tests; and that,[15] any truly[16] original & grand[17] production[18] has little or nothing to do with the rules &[19] calibres now in mode.

[Note: Montaigne's ¶][20] I have fancied the ocean & the daylight, the mountain & the forest, putting their spirit in an utterance—& that utterance a judgment on our books, & especially on the current poetry of this country & Europe. I have fancied some lofty &[21] disembodied human soul giving its judgment; & fancied emotional[22] Humanity, in some single representative, giving its.

Perhaps the thought of[23] this[24] is the pre-requisite to[25] an eminent literature, & to[26] the beginning of[27] any thing like good criticism. Yet certainly it is[28] unthought of[29] & unbreathed among all[30] this European reviewers; as I certainly know of no Poetic theory or practise, except that of *Leaves of Grass,*[31] holding it steadily in view.

11. Inscribed in black ink with black pencil emendation on two pasted-together white wove scraps, 10⁹/₁₈″ x 7¾″ overall. Arrow leads from opening line to trimmed off words at top.

12. Deleted in black ink: "to" .Preceding seven words inserted above.

13. Deleted in black ink: "there are standards of merit" ; inserted in black ink above: "the real tests applicable to [*del.*] for a book"

14. Deleted in black ink: "literature" [*semicolon not deleted, not printed*]; inserted above: "literary tests,"

15. Deleted in black ink: "of a [*ins. above deleted* "a"] the grand ["est" *ins.*] production, the last of"

16. Inserted in black ink above wordspace between "any original"

17. Deleted in black ink: "est"

18. Deleted in black ink: "it is"

19. Deleted in black ink: "limits of" ; inserted in black ink: "calibres now in mode" above "[*del.*] limits of . . . these 'book notices'" ; deleted in pencil: "these amusing 'book notices' & 'reviews' & the airy gentlemen that make them." Inserted and deleted: "prevalent writers'-' above "[*del.*] of these amusing

20. Pencil. WW's square brackets. End of first scrap, which is irregular. The paragraph from Montaigne has not been located.

21. Deleted in pencil: "disentangled" ; inserted above in black ink: "disembodied"

22. Inserted above "cied" in "fancied" and "Hu" in "Human"

23. Preceding three words inserted in black ink above "Perhaps"

24. Deleted in black ink: "indispensible" ; inserted above: "is the pre-requisite"

25. Deleted in black ink: "any thing like good critic good" ; inserted in black ink above: "the prevalence of [*preceding three words del. in black ink*] an eminent"

26. Deleted in black ink: "even"

27. Deleted in black ink: "founding"

28. Deleted in black ink: "unknown in [*ins. above deleted* "in"] yet"

29. Deleted in black ink: "as yet, in" ; inserted above in black ink: "& unbreathed among"

30. Deleted in pencil: "American & English" ; deleted in black ink: "criticism" ; inserted in pencil: "this European" above "[*del.*] American & English" ; inserted in black ink; "reviewers" above "[*del.*] criticism"

31. Deleted in pencil: "bearing" ; inserted above: "holding" ; deleted in black ink: "all that" ; inserted: "it" above the wordspace between "[*del.*] all that"

Coming To Discuss.

Manuscript in the collection of Mr. Richard G. Coker. Inscribed in black ink on thick white paper, "neither laid nor wove," 10" x 7½". Blue rules on verso approx. ½" apart. The writing and content suggest that it is a draft for the "Orbic Literature" section of *Democratic Vistas,* that is about 1869 or 1870. The theme, however, was a favorite one. Cf. the Introductions of the late 1860s (pp. 1445–1490). Description from Mr. Coker.

Coming to discuss[1] the question of the Literature of a country, from high points of view, with wide sweep, we[2] first inquire all about that country itself,[3] & fully satisfy ourselves of its special & general character,[4] geograhy, politics, race-stock, purpose,[5] of (to use a modern phrase) the philosophy of it,[6] of[7] the develoopement of Humanity in its[8] history? Of the features, & below the features,[9] of its[10] physiognomy, & physiology?[11]—using those words in a[12] moral, social[13] & political,[14] just as much as material sense.[15]—After fully[16] getting & stating the answers to such questions, we proceed to ask of[17] the literature of that country, as the main matter, what does it propose, or what has it[18] achieved, in the

1. Deleted: "In considering" ; three preceding words inserted above "[*del.*] considering" and "the" and "qu" of "question"
2. Deleted: "are to ask inevitably to ask of &" ; inserted: "first inquire all"
3. Inserted above "country" ; deleted: "What" ; inserted: "& fully satisfy ourselves"
4. Following four words inserted above "[*del.*] What" and "and of its special"
5. Deleted: "— & the" ; inserted and deleted: "what the"; inserted: "of (to use a modern phrase) the"
6. Deleted: "in the"
7. Deleted: "long dep history &"
8. Inserted above wordspace.
9. Deleted: "What" ; inserted above "[*del.*] What" and "of physiognomy" : "Of . . . features,"
10. Deleted: "own"
11. Question mark inserted.
12. Phrase inserted after "physiology"
13. Comma deleted.
14. Deleted: "[*illeg.*] as"
15. Question mark deleted.
16. Deleted: "answering &" ; inserted above: "getting &"
17. Deleted: "its" ; inserted above: "the"
18. Preceding three words inserted above "or" and "achie" in "achieved"

Introduction to the London Edition.

Manuscript in Morgan (MA 1056). Inscribed in black ink with emendations in black ink, black pencil, and brown and blue crayon on white laid paper, 7^{11}/$_{16}$" x 4¾". Blue rules vertically ⅜" apart on rectos only of 1–4, 13, 14, on rectos and versos of 5–12. Foliation in WW's hand at center top. No watermarks. Embossed stamp of Capitol building with "Congress" above and "P & P" (Platner and Porter) below on 1–8. Evidently large sheets were folded horizontally and torn as shown by edges. Page 1 has one cluster of pinholes, whereas 2–14 have two, suggesting a rewriting of 1. In upper left of 1 blue crayon in WW's hand: "*Copy.*" Probably at one time with envelope now in LC (#79, item #743) inscribed by WW: "seems to come down to 1871 before my paralysis copy of the London "Introduction" in Mr. Conway's possession."

It is clear that this MS is the draft "original" of an "Introduction," purportedly by W. D. O'Connor and (presumably) in his hand, which was sent to Moncure Daniel Conway, with a copy of *LG* (1867) on July 24, 1867 (*Corr.,* I, 332–333). The circumstances surrounding the writing of this introduction are discussed in Furness, 141–149, Allen, 382–387, Bodgett, 22–27. To this information may be added the fact that on November 10, undaunted by the decision to publish only selections, but *before* Rossetti's thought of a somewhat more complete, but expurgated, edition (November 17, 1867), WW had O'Connor send another letter purportedly of his own composition to Conway which developed "two or three points" that WW obviously wanted Rossetti to make in his preface (probably those in Traubel, I, 383–384). Rossetti tactfully replied, as if in passing, that the printing was too far advanced.

WW, however, had later hopes of a complete English edition for which he might use this introduction, for he amended his statement that *LG* had been published "three times" to "five" and later "six" times. Similarly, he originally said he was in his "49th year," later changed to "53rd" and "62d." The statement that *LG* had been published three times is strange, for the fourth edition had appeared in November, 1866, but he was similarly confused in the MS "Introductions" he was also writing in the 1860s. His forty-ninth year is, of course, May, 1867–May, 1868. The other dates and ages refer to 1872 and 1881. Furness points out (147–148) that in both years there were possibilities of a London edition. In 1876 WW had also tried to promote a London edition for which he wrote a different preface ("Personal."). By 1888 WW no longer cared, for English editions were appearing from American sheets (Traubel, III, 420).

First printed in Furness, 150–154, with facsimile of MS p. 1 facing 150. Facsimile of p. 1 also in Anderson Galleries Catalogue, #2198 (1927) in Francis, Gloria, and Artem Loyzinsky, *Walt Whitman at Auction, 1899–1912,* 131.

Introduction to the
London Edition.[1]

America—that new world in so many respects besides its geography—has perhaps afforded nothing even in the astonishing products of the fields of its politics, its mechanical invention, material growth, & the like, more original, more autochthonic, than its late contribution in the field of literature, the Poem, or poetic writings, named[2] LEAVES OF GRASS, which in the following pages, we present to the British public.

2 At the first sight, the form of these versus, not only without rhyme, but wholly regardless of the customary[3] verbal melody & regularity so much labored after by modern poets, will strike the reader with incredulous amazement. Then the perusal of[4] the book will open to his view other & still profounder innovations. The absolute & unqualified acceptance of Nature; the unprecedently candid treatment of the human body, & in all its parts, without the exclusion 3 of any; the absence, ostensibly at least, of any thing like plot, or definite point or purpose in the poems; their boundless outcroppage of arrogant animal muscle & brawn, closely tracked everywhere by an equal outcroppage of the most refined transcendentalism, & loftiest spirituality;—these, expressed through[5] phraseology[6] of never-surpassed earnestness & determination, make indeed a book whose presence & pages, & the action between them & their reader, resemble the struggles of[7] of the gymnastic arena, more than the usual orderly entertainment given by authors.

4 Taken as a unity, LEAVES OF GRASS, true to its American origin, is a song of "the great pride of man in himself." It assumes to bring the materials & outline the architecture of a[8] more complete, more advanced, idiocratic, masterful, Western personality—the combination & model of a new Man. It does not dwell on the past, & celebrates in no way the superb old feudal world, or its gorgeous reminiscences; it is built forward in the demesnes of the future, and it would seem as if, somehow, a[9] great coming & regnant Democracy—the dream of poets from the time of Plato, & before him, & since, too—had[10] & here given genesis to every[11] line.—5 It possesses, more than any other known book, the magnetism of

1. At upper left: *"Copy"* diagonally in blue crayon in WW's hand. At upper right circled number 12, not in WW's hand. Below and to right of title, in another hand, black pencil, '["Leaves of Grass"] 1881' . Circular stain as of bottom of wet glass on title.
2. Deleted: "of" ; inserted above: "named"
3. Inserted above "verbal"
4. Deleted: [*illeg.*] ; inserted above [*illeg.*]: "the"
5. Deleted: "a"
6. Deleted: "which is plainly [*del. in pencil*] but the echoing [*originally* "echo"] of a" ; inserted above deleted "a" : "of"
7. Deleted: "the" ; inserted and deleted above: "a" ; inserted above: "the"
8. Inserted above wordspace.
9. Deleted: "the" ; inserted above wordspace: "a"
10. Deleted in blue crayon: "advanced" ; deleted in black ink: "sufficiently" ; inserted in black ink and deleted in blue crayon above "sufficiently" : "already"
11. Deleted: "page &"

living flesh & blood,[12] sitting near the reader, & looking & talking. It is marvellously cosmopolitan. Always manly friendship, the ties of nations & cities, & their common sympathies & common brotherhood—never their jealousies, vaunts, special glories,[13] or any thought or thing calculated to keep them apart—are encouraged & persistently upheld. The book may be further described as a genuine confession & conference of one single representative humanity with & to another single humanity; a free, yet ardently intensified *tete-a-tete*.[14] The crowded parlor or a promiscuous audience is not 6 its sphere. It is the most emotional & yearning of poems, & really unfolds itself only in the presence of YOU, the reader, with no third person near.

Like the world itself, it is not without passages that will puzzle, cause hesitation, & even shock[15] the conventional, well-meaning student & beholder. But its fervent & powerful efflux evidently flows from a devout soul, & its writer as evidently writes from deep plan & science, & with an elaborated, ethic intention, born of & designed to justify, the Democratic[16] theory of his country, & carry it out far beyond the merely political beginning already made.

7 If indeed the various parts of LEAVES OF GRASS demanded a single word to sum up & characterise them, it would seem to be the word Democracy that was wanted. But it would mean a Democracy not confined to politics; that would describe but a portion only. It would need the application of the word[17] extended to all departments of civilization & humanity, & include especially the moral, esthetic, & philosophic departments.

(a blank line here[18]

In giving the preceding introduction we have not had so much in view to advocate or praise the book,[19] as to prepare 8 the reader, by a few general hints, for its novel form, & more novel & most free, sturdy, & all-tolerating spirit.

—(a blank line here[20]

And as there has perhaps never been a book so resolvable into the personality that composed it, & so knitted with, & faithfully reflecting that personality, we will add to the hasty synopsis of LEAVES OF GRASS, just given, a brief memorandum of the author, WALT WHITMAN. He was born on his father's farm, not far from the sea, in New York state, May 31, 1819. His descent is from Dutch and 9 English ancestry, dating back,[21] both in[22] father's & mother's lines, to the first colonization[23]

---

12. Deleted: "man,"
13. Preceding two words inserted above "vaunts, are"
14. Preceding six words seem to have been inserted later in small writing between lines.
15. Deleted and inserted above "k" in "shock" : "the"
16. Inserted above: "the theory"
17. Deleted: "to be"
18. In brown crayon.
19. Deleted: "or to commend it,"
20. In brown crayon.
21. Deleted: "in"
22. Inserted above wordspace.
23. Originally: "colonizing"

of that part of the country; and is thus of the fullest & purest stock[24] which America affords,[25] bred of her own soil. He grew up,[26] healthy & strong, alternating his life equally between the country-farm & New York city. He has since lived in the south, explored the west, & sailed the Mississippi, the Gulf of Mexico, & the great Canadian lakes. He has been a farmer, builder of houses, & printer & editor of newspapers. He first issued Leaves of Grass in 1855.—10 The book has since been printed, with successive enlargements & readjustments,[27] six times. As given in this volume, it was[28] put forth by the author within the last year, & includes the poems & songs of DRUM-TAPS, written during, & at the close of the[29] civil war of 1861–'5.[30]

For Walt Whitman was in the midst of the war, throughout. A volunteer caretaker of the wounded & sick, he joined the army early in the contest & steadily remained[31] at active work, in camp, or the battlefield, or in some or other[32] of the huge Military hospitals, ministering 11 to southerner as well as northerner,[33] till Richmond fell, & Lee capitulated.[34]

The Poet[35] is now in his[36] 62d year, & is pourtrayed by one who knows him intimately, as tall in stature, with shapely limbs, slow of movement, florid & clear face, bearded & gray-blue eyes, an expression of great equanimity, of decided presence 12 & singular personal magnetism, very little of a talker,[37] generally undemonstrative, yet capable[38] on emergencies, of the strongest emotions, resolution, & even[39] hauteur.

By report of an English gentleman & traveler,[40] a believing reader of Walt

24. Deleted: "that" ; inserted above: "with"
25. Deleted: "grown" ; inserted above: "bred"
26. Deleted: "large" ; inserted above: "healthy"
27. Deleted: "three" ; inserted above and deleted: "five" ; inserted above "t" in "times" : "six"
28. Deleted: "finished" ; inserted above: "put forth"
29. Deleted successively: "war" "late"
30. Preceding phrase inserted above "war [del.] also" ; deleted in blue crayon: "also PASSAGE TO INDIA—and indeed all his poems down to the present time."
31. Deleted: "as an amateur"
32. Preceding two words inserted above "some of"
33. Deleted in blue crayon: "not only"
34. Deleted: "he lingers even yet, as we hear, regularly visiting the collections of maimed & broken-down men, the sad legacy bequeathed by those vast armies, long campaigns, & sanguinary battles."
35. Preceding two words inserted above "[del. He" and "is" ; deleted: "He"
36. Deleted: "49th" "53d"
37. Deleted: "always compassionate"
38. Inserted in pencil above "of emotions" : "when on due emergencies," ; "when" deleted in black pencil; "due" deleted in black ink.
39. Inserted above wordspace.
40. The existence of this "English gentleman & traveller" may be doubted. WW did, however, send to Moncure D. Conway, in England, a copy of LG (1867) "prepared with care for the printers" with this MS introduction in care of a Mr. Philp. Philp is conjecturally identified with James B. Philp, a lithographer and engraver of NYC, or Franklin Philp, of Philp & Solomon, Washington booksellers (Corr., I, 332–333). The latter identification seems more likely, for WW occasionally used paper manufactured or sold by this firm. See, for example, "Review—," which has their em-

Whitman, who sought & found him out in America, we have our latest direct account of the poet. He was, in[41] September 1871, residing at Washington city, the capital of the United States, & held a small, but pleasant & honorable post in the Attorney General's office there. Our informant 13 had several interviews with[42] him, & besides confirming the main parts of the foregoing account, adds one item, with which we may conclude our record. It is on a point that[43] gives the[44] final test to human character. He considers Walt Whitman the most thoroughly *religious* being that in the course of much travel, & long & varied contact with the world, he has ever encountered. The interior & foundation quality of the man is Hebraic, Biblical, mystic. This exhibited & fused through a full & passionate physiology, a complete animal body, and 14 joined with the most thorough-going realization & cordial acceptance of his country, & belief in its mission,[45] and with a mind[46] fully awake to the sacred practical[47] obligations of each person as citizen, neighbor & friend—deferentially[48] absorbing modern science, yet with[49] the distinct acknowledgment that science, grand as it is, stands[50] baffled before the impenetrable miracle of the least law of the universe, & even the least leaf or insect,— All this, we say, or something like this, gives the best clue both to the personal character & life, & to the poetic utterance, of this new, powerful, and we think we must say, most typical American.

bossed stamp at the upper left. Philp had also been a member of Conway's church in Washington and the firm sold *LG*. WW made calculations about Philp's departure from the United States and his arrival in England ("Ad*dr*esses").

41. Deleted: "August, 1867" ; inserted: "September, 1871" above deletion.

42. Deleted: "Walt Whitman"

43. Deleted in black pencil: "[*illeg.*] has" ; inserted in pencil above deletion: "gives"

44. Deleted in ink: "main" ; deleted in black pencil: "bearing on" ; inserted in ink above "main" : "final" ; inserted in pencil above "bearing on" : "test to"

45. Deleted: "with a similar belief of the"

46. Preceding three words inserted above "d" in "and" and "fully"

47. Inserted above "cred" in "sacred" and "obli" in "obligations"

48. Deleted: "accepting"

49. Deleted: "a" ; inserted above: "the"

50. Deleted: "at last utterly"

Of William Blake.

Manuscript in Duke (47, #28). Inscribed in black ink with emendations in black ink or blue pencil as noted on two sheets of laid white paper. The first is 9⅝″ x 7½″. Blue rules ½″ apart with Attorney General's letterhead for "186—" on verso. The second is white laid paper, 8⅛″ x 7½″ Blue lines ⅜″ apart and red-blue-red margin at the left. The date is obviously contemporary with Algernon C. Swinburne, *William Blake* (London, 1868), 300–303, a comparison of WW and Blake, which WW had received from John Camden Hotten, the publisher, in February or March, 1868. John Swinton also noticed a resemblance in September, but WW remained unconvinced. O'Connor was scornful. See *Corr.,* III, 48–49. First published *FC&I,* 53.

Of William Blake & Walt Whitman[1] Both are mystics, extatics[2] but[3] the[4] difference between them is this—and a vast difference it is: Blake's visions grow to be the rule,[5] displace the normal condition, fill the field,[6] spurn[7] this visible,[8] objective life, & place the subjective spirit on an absolute throne, wilful &[9] uncontrolled.[10] But Whitman, though he occasionaly[11] prances off or takes flight with an abandon & capriciousness of step or[12] wing,[13] and a rapidity & whirling power, which quite[14] dizzy the reader in his first attempts to follow, always holds the mastery[15] over himself, &,[16] even in[17] his most intoxicated[18] lunges or pirouettes, never

1. Preceding six words in small letters inserted above before "Both" on a caret.
2. Inserted above "but"
3. Deleted in blue pencil: "a great" ; inserted following in blue: "the"
4. Deleted in blue pencil: "The" , which opened a paragraph.
5. Deleted in blue pencil: "usurp" ; inserted above in blue: "displace"
6. Deleted: "and"
7. Deleted: "the" ; inserted: "this" above and before "[*del.*] the" ; inserted and deleted: "our" following "this" and above "[*del.*] the"
8. Two [*illeg.*] words deleted.
9. Inserted: "wilful &" above "one" in "throne" and "un" in "uncontrolled" . An [*illeg. del.*] follows "un" in "uncontrolled" , possibly a "t" for "untrammelled".
10. Deleted in blue pencil: "despot"
11. Inserted and deleted: "dances" above "takes" ; inserted above the deletion: "prances" ; inserted: "off or" following deleted "dances"
12. Preceding two words inserted in blue above "of wing"
13. Deleted in blue: "whose rapidy"
14. Inserted above wordspace between "which dizzy"
15. Deleted: "of"
16. Deleted: "never"
17. Inserted above wordspace between "even his"
18. Deleted: [*illeg.*]

once[19] loses[20] control[21], or even equilibrium. To the perfect[22] sense, it is evident that he[23] goes off[24] because he "permits"[25] himself to do so,[26] [*illeg.*] [2] while ever[27] the director,[28] or directing[29] principle sits coolly at hand, able to stop the[30] wild teetotum & reduce it[31] to order,[32] at any a moment. In Walt Whitman, escapades of this sort are the exceptions.[33] The main character of[34] his poettry is the normal, the universal, the simple, the eternal platform of the best[35] manly & womanly qualities.

19. Inserted above "er" in "never"
20. Deleted: [*illeg.*]; inserted and deleted in blue: "that" above "co" in "control"
21. Deleted in blue: "&" ; inserted above in blue: "or even"
22. Corner of sheet damaged. Deleted: "sen"
23. Inserted above "g" in "goes"
24. Deleted: "in" ; corner of sheet damaged.
25. A fragment of a word in black ink remained below after the sheet was trimmed.
26. Deleted: "&"
27. Preceding two words inserted in blue before and above "the"
28. Deleted: "stands"
29. Deleted: [*illeg.*]
30. Deleted in blue: "dance" ; inserted above in blue: "wild teetotum"
31. Inserted in blue in the left margin before "to"
32. Deleted in blue: "in" ; inserted above: "at any"
33. Sentence inserted above on a brace between "moment" and "the"
34. Deleted: "Walt Whitman's" ; inserted: "his" above "wh" in "Whitman"
35. Inserted above wordspace between "the manly"

Then Whitman Himself.

Manuscript in Virginia (Barrett). Inscribed in black pencil on faded white laid paper, approx. 6″ x 7⅝″. Vertical blue rules ⁵/₁₆″ apart. Paper identical with "Whitman, democrat" with which it is bound. The manuscripts are not related. The writing suggests a date of the late 1860s or early 1870s.

Then Whitman himself has more than once spoken to me[1] of his poetry as[2] largely the result of[3] a resolute determination to[4] put his own[5] individuality[6] & his own esthetic moral, social and political[7] idiosyncrasies in a statement—[8] an unparalleled wilfulness,[9] self-set, and arrogant,[10] to[11] give expression to himself,[12] in defiance of precedent[13]

1. Preceding two words inserted above "of"
2. Deleted: "mainly" ; inserted above: "largely"
3. Deleted: "his own wilfulness his" "deter" ; inserted: "a" above "d" in "[del.] deter"
4. Deleted: "express"
5. Deleted: "own"
6. Deleted: "traits," ; inserted: "& his own" above "viduality" in "individuality"
7. Deleted: "traits" ; inserted: "idiosyncracies" above "[del.] traits" and "in a"
8. Deleted: "his" ; inserted following: "an" ; deleted: "—he himself spoke of [del.] his it as his [del.] own obstinate determination (substantially his own words) [parentheses ins.]" ; redundant "an" after deletion not printed here.
9. Deleted: "and a"
10. Deleted: "determ"
11. Deleted: "put"
12. Preceding two words inserted above "ion" in "expression,"
13. A line seems to have been erased. Centered between lines: "2" . The following is deleted with slanting stroke: "Health, Democracy, Comradeship, America, are his [illeg. del.] [del.] great [ins.] visible themes, with a hundred little ones affording—his pages abound with them—lines or short bits of inimitable"

Mr. Burroughs.

Manuscript in Yale. Inscribed in black ink on white wove scraps, approx. [1] 2″ x 5¾″ and [2] 4¾″ x 5¾″. Both leaves cancelled. The reference to John Burroughs are to *Notes on Walt Whitman as Poet and Person* (New York: American News Co., 1867) or the revised edition of 1871. On verso notes for "With Husky-Haughty Lips, O Sea!" which are probably unrelated and much later. The date is probably the late 1860s or early 1870s.

Mr. Burroughs[1] modestly avows[2] in[3] his Notes, that "the literary hints in them are experimental, & will show the student of Nature more than the student of books."[4] [2] It is in this quiet way he introduces[5] some of the boldest doctrines[6] ever propounded[7] on the laws of poetry. For instance,[8] he says:[9]

Then in another place, the following pregnant sentence:[10] "The highest art is not to express[11] art, but to communicate life [*illeg.*]"[12]—a maxim well [*illeg.*] all

1. Deleted: [*illeg.*]
2. Inserted above "ly" in "modestly" and "in"
3. Deleted: "the preface of to the" ; inserted: "his" above "[*del.*] the"
4. The quotation is from Burroughs (1867), 4. Deleted: "With this [*ins. and del.*] Notwithstanding quiet hint But the veteran in literature" . Paper cut through the last seven words. Descenders appear on [2]. Deleted on [2]: "[*illeg.*] all the love of the libraries in letters will find" . Space follows. Succeeding text attached by arrow to last uncancelled sentence. Inserted: "It is" above "in" ; WW did not reduce "In" to lowercase.
5. Inserted and deleted: "what are in fact so" on a line above "uces" in "introduces" and "some of"
6. Deleted: "yet" ; inserted: "ever"
7. Deleted: "as the [*illeg.*] by any critic." Inserted: "on the laws of [*del.*] poetry poetry." above "ounded" in "propounded" and "as the"
8. Preceding two words and comma inserted above "[*del.*] critic" ; WW did not reduce "He" to lowercase.
9. Space of four or five lines left blank. About two-thirds of the way across the leaf is a curved line with a "¶" at the top right connecting preceding text with that succeeding. Deleted: "He has this" ; inserted: "Then [*del.*] here in another [*preceding two words ins. above* "here in"] place the following" above the deleted "has this" and "pregnant sentence"
10. Deleted: "which it were will for all our [*del.*] poets, [*two words ins. above deleted* "poets"] actual or would-be poets, painters, sculptors, & musicians, to stamp indelibly upon their brains" . WW did not delete a terminal colon.
11. Deleted: "a"
12. Succeeding words almost entirely trimmed off. Inserted: "a [*del.*] sentence maxim" . The quotation is from Burroughs (1867), 45: "The highest art is not to express art, but to express life and communicate power."

He Has Not.

Manuscript in Virginia. Inscribed in black pencil on white wove paper, 6¹³/₁₆″ x 7¾″. Vertical blue rules ⁵/₁₆″ apart. The MS does not appear to be part of the other leaves—"Whitman, democrat"—bound with it. The reference to Kant suggests this was written in the 1860s and the writing is probably earlier than 1873.

He has not[1] cared to make sweet things or polished or graceful conventional[2] things, but to give[3] full swing and utterance to[4] power, often inexplicable, in the universe and in[5] man—the microcosm and macrocosm. Immanual Kant said that of the manifold wonders[6] pressing upon his receptivity the play of law in the outside world[7] and the other play of[8] passion and spirit in the human[9] Soul most excited his awe and admiration. And[10] these[11] are the centripetal[12] and centrifugal[13] motives of all Walt Whitman's pages.

1. Deleted: "sought" ; inserted above: "cared"
2. Inserted above "ceful" in "graceful" and "thin" in "things"
3. Deleted: "fl"
4. Deleted: "the the powers of nature, as" ; inserted: "power, often inexplicable," above "[del.] the powers of"
5. Deleted: "the"
6. Deleted: "that" ; "pressed" emended to "pressing"
7. Centered between lines: "3"
8. Written over [illeg.] ; deleted: "human"
9. Preceding two words inserted above "spirit . . . Soul"
10. Inserted above "T" in "These" . "These" is uppercase in MS.
11. Deleted: "two"
12. "petal" written above deleted "fugal" in "centrifugal"
13. Deleted: "impetus" ; inserted above: "motives"

"Don't Read My Books."

Manuscript in Boston Public Library. Inscribed in black ink on white wove paper, 10" x 8". Blue rules ½" apart. On verso is letterhead of Attorney General's Office with printed date filled in "April 16, [18]69." Emendations in black ink and a few in soft black pencil. At top of the page, in blue pencil, "2" in WW's hand. The brackets are in the MS. This is probably, as the brackets and number suggest, part of a larger Ms. First printed in *N&F,* 69–70 (Pl. II, #57; *CW,* IX, 33–34).

["Don't read my books,"[1] I heard Walt Whitman[2] good-naturedly, yet emphatically, say[3] one day, to an intelligent but [4]conventional questioner whom he personally liked:[5] "You want something good in the usual sense,[6] a plot, a love-story—something based on[7] the accepted principles,[8] and on etiquette,[9] & precedent. You dont want something to wrestle with you, & puzzle you, you want one of the good English poets' books—or the good & pleasing Longfellow's—or such.[10] I have written no such books[10a] I have[11] attempted to construct a poem[12] on the open principles of Nature,[13] as comprehended in[14] not only in[15] the material worlds

1. Corrected from singular: "books" . Deleted in black pencil: "he said" ; inserted in black pencil above: "I heard" ; inserted and deleted in black pencil: "say" at the right.
2. Name inserted in black pencil above "good" and "-nat" in "-naturedly"
3. Inserted in black pencil above "day" . Deleted in black pencil: "the other" ; inserted in black pencil: "one" above "[*del.*] other"
4. Deleted in black pencil: "very"
5. Preceding four words inserted in black ink above "er" in "questioner" and "You want"
6. Deleted in black ink: "of [*illeg.*] something founded" ; inserted above in black ink: "a plot, a love-story—something based" above "[*del.*] something founded"
7. Deleted in black ink: "the orthodox" ; inserted above: "the accepted"
8. Deleted in black ink: "of poetry, on precedents & conforming to precedents and [*preceding two words inserted and deleted above the deleted* "to the"] to the"
9. Deleted in black ink: "of parlors" following "etiquette, "; inserted above in black ink: "& precedents"
10. Preceding sentence inserted from top margin; "dont" above "w" in "want" ; "that" deleted after "want" ; "one of" inserted above "nt" in "want" and "the" ; sentence preceded by asterisk in red pencil, point of insertion marked by asterisks in red pencil and black ink.
10a. "s" inserted.
11. Deleted in black ink: "constructed, or"
12. Inserted in black ink and deleted in pencil: "as it were" above "em" in "poem" and "you"
13. Deleted in black pencil: "not only"
14. Preceding two words inserted in black ink; "as" following the deletion and "comprehended" written above.
15. Preceding three words inserted in black pencil above "the material"

of astronomy,[16] with the earth and[17] sea, but as[18] in all[19] the movements of history &[20] civilization, wars, the shows of[21] cities and in[22] man,[23] with all his attributes animal,[24] moral & spiritual.[25] The whole drift[26] of my books is to form a new race of fuller & athletic yet unknown characters, men & women, for the United States to come. I do not write to amuse or furnish fine poetry, so- called; and will surely repel at first those who have been used to sweets, & the jingle of rhymes. Every page of my book emanates[27] Democracy, absolute, unintermitted[28] without the slightest compromise,[29] & the sense of the New World[30] in its future, a thoroughly[31] revolutionary[32] formation[33] to be exhibited less in politics, and more in theology, literature and manners; all of which, at present, while interested in and discussing many things,[34] America[35] curious as it may appear, knows[36] of, and in[37] fact,[38] amid all[39] her knowledge,[40] knows[41] almost nothing of[42] her[43] real destination & life. But all will come along in proper time."]

16. Inserted and deleted in black ink: "and of" above "the" (before "earth") ; inserted in black ink: "with" below "[del.] and"
17. Inserted in black ink at end of line following "earth"
18. Inserted in black ink above wordspace between "but in"
19. Inserted in black ink above "the"
20. Preceding two words inserted in black ink above "of" ; inserted and deleted in black pencil before "history" : "human"
21. Deleted: [illeg.]
22. Deleted in black ink: "the full-grown & proportioned man"
23. Deleted in black ink: "physical" ; inserted in black ink: "with all his attributes animal," above "tioned" in "proportioned" and "man" and "[del.] physical"
24. Deleted in black pencil: "intellectual" ; inserted above in black pencil: "moral"
25. Deleted in black ink: "My book is [emended to: "books are"] [four words inserted above deleted "books are"] intended to be new American & the" . Inserted in black ink: "The" above "wh" in "whole"
26. The emendations piled upon emendations in what appear to be two kinds of black ink and two kinds of black pencil in this and the following sentence are unrecordable in any practicable form.
27. Preceding four words inserted in black ink, after several illegible trials.
28. Inserted in black ink above "absolute"
29. Preceding four words inserted in black ink above "& the sense of the New"
30. Deleted: "of the" ; inserted above in black pencil: "in its"
31. Inserted in black pencil above "revo" in "revolutionary"
32. Inserted and deleted in black pencil: "unwelcomed" above "utionary"
33. Inserted in black ink and deleted in black pencil: "as" above "m" in "formation" and insert following; inserted in ink: "to be exhibited" above "ation" in "formation" and "less"
34. Deleted in black ink: "& knowing largely of other then,"
35. Deleted in black ink: "yet" ; inserted in black ink: "curious as it may appear" above "erica" in "America" , the deletion, and "knows"
36. Deleted in black ink: "nothing [illeg.] the"
37. Deleted in black ink: "fact"
38. Deleted in black ink: "knows"
39. Deleted in black ink: [illeg.]
40. Deleted in black ink: "knows least [two words ins. and del. in black ink] almost of herself, her own theory [del. illeg.] & that which concerns her deepest." The remainder of the sentence and the last sentence are added below without observing the left margin.
41. Deleted in black ink: "little or" ; inserted in black ink: "almost" above "[del.] or"
42. Deleted in black pencil: "her real [inserted and deleted above "real"] her self or"
43. Deleted in black ink: "real true" ; inserted in black ink: "real" above "[del.] true"

Seems to Me.

Manuscript in Yale. Inscribed in black ink with emendations in black pencil and blue crayon on two scraps of white wove paper pasted on backing, the whole measuring 5¼" x 7½". Blue rules on larger scrap ⅝" apart. The "preceding Notes" referred to in the sentence cancelled at the end have not been identified. The writing is similar to that of the NYPL "Introductions (pp. 1445–1490)." WW probably wrote this in 1871, after the publication of *Democratic Vistas*.

seems[1] to me not too much to say, that as[2] the Idea of Nature[3] eludes us, except as formulated in the[4] physical[5] concrete of the Universe, and is only to be[6] explained thence,[7] so, in a sense,[8] the pages of Leaves of Grass & Democratic Vistas[9] are not[10] most in themselves,[11] but[12] in their author, as a Person, a Body.[13]

1. Original first word, "It" , deleted in blue crayon; inserted and deleted in blue crayon: "and I would [*illeg.*]" above "seems"
2. End of first scrap.
3. Deleted: "is" ; inserted in black ink: "nothing to [*both words del. above* "ure" *in* "Nature" *and del.* "is"] [*ins. in black pencil above* [*del.*] "nothing to"] "eludes"
4. Inserted above wordspace between "in physical"
5. Deleted: "form in" ; inserted above: "concrete of"
6. Preceding two words inserted in black pencil above "y" in "only" and "e" in "explained"
7. Preceding seven words inserted in black pencil above "Universe"
8. Deleted: "Walt Whit" ; inserted above: "the pages of"
9. Preceding three words inserted above "Grass are"
10. Inserted and deleted in black ink: "[*illeg.*] so much"; inserted above "in" below deletion: "most"
11. Deleted in black ink: "or their so great" . Comma not deleted, not shown.
12. Deleted: "a great"
13. Deleted: "[*del.*] For [*ins. above deleted* "For"] From these convictions I have sought [*ins. and del. above* "have"] however insufficiently in the preceding [*del.*] pages [*ins. above deleted* "pages"] Notes to pourtray [*del.*] the visible, [*ins. above* "ible" *in* "visible" *and* "Walt"] corporeal Walt Whitman [*three words del.*] but have not—and [*del.*] here [*ins. and del. above* "a" *in* "added"] here added ["-ed" *del.*], [*three words ins.*] toward that end a few excerpts in the present supplement."

Note A* While.

Manuscript in LC (#63, sheet #307). Inscribed in black ink, black pencil, and blue crayon on gray brown wove scrap. Cf. paper of "Light" and "the intellectual and emotional." The writing and paper suggest a date well after 1860. Because of the condition of the MS the exact placement of the emendations is uncertain.

Note

Note A*[1] While I am about it I should like[2] to put on record[3] here my[4] devout acknowledgment not only of the great masterpieces of the past,[5] but of the supreme benefit of *all* poets, past and present,[6] and *all*[7] poetic utterances—in its entirety[8] the dominant[9] moral factor of humanity's progress[10]

1. Asterisk and "Note" in heading and upper right in blue crayon. Pencilled words at top deleted in pencil: "say I should be illy understood [*two words ins.*] not only if [*ins.*] it I did not"
2. Preceding two words inserted.
3. Inserted and deleted: "beyond possible misunderstanding"
4. Inserted.
5. Preceding nine words inserted.
6. Preceding two words inserted.
7. Deleted: "poetry" ; inserted: "poetic utterance"
8. Preceding three words inserted in blue crayon.
9. Deleted: "spiritual" ; inserted: "moral"
10. Text trimmed off.

Carlyle Vol 1.

Manuscript in Texas. Inscribed in black ink on white laid paper with red-blue-red rule in margin 1⅜″ from left, blue rules ½″ apart. The page references have been located in *Critical and Miscellaneous Essays. Collected and Republished by Thomas Carlyle.* Popular Edition. Four Volumes in Two (Boston: Houghton-Mifflin, 188?). This appears to be a cheap reissue either of a four volume *Critical and Miscellaneous Essays* published by Houghton-Mifflin in Boston in 1860 or of a four-volume edition published by Hurd and Houghton in 1864. WW could have used either. The passages WW refers to are more conveniently found in the Centenary Edition (London, 1896–1899): *German Romance,* II, 127–128; *Wilhelm Meister's Apprenticeship and Travels,* I, 33. The former is too long to quote; the later concludes: ". . . I may be allowed to remind my readers that the existence or non-existence of a new Poet for the world in our own time, of a new Instructor and Preacher of Truth to all men, is already a question of more importance to us than many that are agitated with far greater noise."

Six examples of paper with wide left margins (not all identical in width) marked by a red-blue-red rule have been found, but no conclusions as to date can be formed. The firm writing seems to be that of the late 1860s or early 1870s. First printed by Emory Holloway, "Notes from a Whitman Student's Scrapbook," *Am Schol,* 21 (May, 1933), 277.

Carlyle vol 1, pp 450–51, Carlyle's sort of summing-up of the genius of[1] Richter is singularly applicable to W.W.—see also last sentence on p. 468 vol.1.

---

1. Preceding three words inserted above "of Richter"

There Will Never.

Manuscript in Brown. Inscribed in black pencil and red ink on verso of lower half of a single sheet of the statement of the Public Debt as of January 31, 1871 signed by Geo. S. Boutwell, Secretary of the Treasury. I am indebted to John Hay Library, Brown University for the description. The date must be 1871 or later.

There will never come a time when Eschylus shall not[1] express human will, more terrible than storms, unshakable by suffering or by fate, and the old Saturnian democracy[2] the Psalms of David shall not sing[3] the rapt devotee[4] his extasy nor the Book of Job echo to him who is eligible,[5] the sense of[6] the mystery of[7] life's good & evil, nor—never a time when[8] Shakespeare shall[9] cease to be the poet of[10] kingly presence, & the stormy passions, & of the presence[11] of love. (? shall I bring in Tennyson)[12]

I too have dreamed of great[13] future America Democratic bards true to America

But I know[14] all will turn back to those venerable[15]

1. Deleted: "reign"
2. Preceding twenty-one words written in top and right margins and inserted on an asterisk.
3. Deleted: "to" ; inserted and deleted: "what moves" above the deleted "to" and "the"
4. Deleted at end of word: "s" ; deleted: "to" ; inserted above: "his"
5. Preceding five words and deleted {*illeg.*} inserted above "echo the" and "sen" in "sense"
6. Deleted: "an the" ; inserted: "the" above deleted "the"
7. Deleted: "good"
8. Preceding four words and dash inserted above "nor Shakespeare"
9. Inserted above "ce" in "cease"
10. Deleted: "the"
11. Alternate: "errors"
12. Parenthetical entry written in red ink on separate line above "too have dreamed"
13. Inserted above "fu" in "future"
14. Deleted: "well w"
15. In hanging indentation.

Is Walt Whitman's Poetry Poetical?

Manuscript in Virginia (Barrett). Inscribed in black ink with additions and emendations in blue crayon and in black ink with a finer-nibbed pen as noted on half-sheets of white wove paper, 10″ x 8″. Torn on right edges. Page numbers in blue crayon in WW's hand. WW composed this reply to an attack on his poetry in the *Nation,* 448 (January 29, 1874), pp. 77–78, in a review of Joaquin Miller's *Songs of the Sunlands,"* and sent it to John Burroughs to be published over the latter's name (*Corr.,* II, 278); cf. *"Introduction to the London Edition,"* and letters to R. J. Hinton (*Corr.,* V, 295). He had already collaborated anonymously with Burroughs in *Notes on Walt Whitman as Poet and Person* (1867) and would significantly rewrite Bucke's *Walt Whitman.* Either Burroughs declined or the *Nation* refused it, for no publication has been found. The omission of reference to probably the most significant event in the development of his transatlantic reputation, William Michael Rossetti's *Poems by Walt Whitman* (London, 1868) is striking. First published in Barrus, 107–111.

IS WALT WHITMAN'S POETRY POETICAL?

MIDDLETOWN, N.Y. Feb. 17,
1874[1]

To the Editor of the Nation: [2]

As I suppose—or rather, know—that your paper is open to statements & views, even opposed to your own, if duly[3] put, I would like to take up your[4] review—that part of it devoted to analyzing Walt Whitman,[5] which appears to be the main part of the notice—[6] of[7] Mr. Miller's last volume of poems, given in the *Nation* of Jan. 29,—[8]and offer something[9] on the other side. Your idea of the *ad captandum* character of Whitman's verse is quite[10] certainly the reverse of well-

---

1. Written with a finer-nibbed pen and possibly inserted later above "[*del.*] you" (*n2*) and into the margin at the right.
2. Deleted: "I take issue with you" squeezed in above *"To the Editor . . . :"*
3. Deleted: "p"
4. Deleted: "notice mostly" ; inserted above: "review—that part of it"
5. Dash deleted.
6. Preceding three words and dash inserted above "part—"
7. Quotation mark deleted.
8. Preceding seven words and punctuation inserted on a line above "ume" in "volume" and "s" in "something"
9. Deleted: "further, and"
10. Inserted with finer-nibbed pen above "is" and "cer" in "certainly"

founded;[11] the almost[12] universal testimony is,[13] that,[14] at first harsh & offensive, "Leaves of Grass" needs study, & more than one perusal, to give up its meaning, & confer pleasure. The author's theory from the outset,[15] has evidently been based upon[16] the[17] deep axiom, "it is[18] reserved for first rate poems[19] never immediately to[20] gratify." Whitman does not lap in sweets or graces, but[21] is eminently[22] an exercise, a stimulus, an inexhaustable suggestion. An Italian critic complains that there is something cold & severe behind every piece[23] He nourishes, if at all, by removes & indirections, & by a sort of harshness,[24] He is not sugar or cake, or any cosseting,[25] or ornament, or a warm bath,[26] or any spiced liquor or special cookery, for a banquet. He is not even, (at least apparently,) art, or beauty, or 2 melody, as those[27] are technically[28] construed. He construes them differently, and forms his verse thereon. To carry out the figure, he[29] gives homely beef and bread and fruit, and water to[30] quench thirst. His theory is that the prettinesses and artificial[31] graces & *concetti* of verse have been exhausted—have indeed become over-plentiful &[32] nauseating;[33] and that, for modern & popular[34] purposes, here in America, &[35] to express[36] the Democratic spirit, the simple, the natural, the perennial, the

11. Deleted: "it is"

12. Inserted above "univ" in "universal"

13. Inserted above "y" in "testimony"

14. Deleted: "it" ; inserted: "at first harsh and offensive, "Leaves of Grass" above "[del.] it . . . & more" . The last three words are written with a finer-nibbed pen.

15. Preceding three words inserted above "theory . . . evi" in "evidently" ; inserted and deleted: "first" under "ou" in "ouset" ; inserted: "outset" . Written with a finer-nibbed pen.

16. Preceding two words inserted with a finer-nibbed pen above "the" and "f" in "[del.] famous"

17. Deleted: "famous"

18. Deleted: "always"

19. Deleted: "not to" ; inserted above: "never"

20. Inserted above wordspace between "immediately gratify"

21. Preceding eight words inserted above "man" in "Whitman" and "an"

22. Deleted and reinserted above: "an"

23. Entire sentence inserted with a finer-nibbed pen. Redundant "&" not shown. The Italian critic is perhaps a close relation of the English gentleman of "Introduction to the London Edition," for the earliest known Italian notice of WW is Enrico Nencioni: "Walt Whitman," *Fanfulla della Domenico* (December 7, 1879).

24. Preceding six words inserted above "and indirections,"

25. Preceding three words inserted above "r" in "sugar" and "or cake,"

26. Preceding four words inserted above "ament" in "ornament" and "or any"

27. Deleted: [*illeg.*]

28. Inserted above "are" and "cons" in "construed"

29. Deleted: "is" ; inserted above: "gives"

30. Deleted: "d"

31. Inserted above "and" and "gra" in "graces"

32. Preceding two words inserted with finer-nibbed pen above "come" in "become" and "naus" in "nauseating"

33. Deleted: "—but" ; inserted above: "and"

34. Preceding two words inserted above "ern" in "modern" and "purp" in "purposes"

35. Deleted: "to"

36. Deleted: "Science and"

familiar[37] and the practical,[38] (henceforth ignoring the mythologies,[39] all the lyrical[40] lay-figures, and the diamonds, feathers, silk[41] and the[42] fine gentlemen and ladies of[43] the saloons,)[44] must be permanently returned to, & called upon & used; and these he[45] merges[46] in his pages. He is never a garden with[47] regular beds,[48] and walks, and a marble fountain; but frequently[49] the stretching landscape and distant sky,[50] the rushing river, or[51] briny sea,—or perhaps[52] the common and general road.[53]

3 I grant you also[54] that the so-called intellectual elements of poetry,[55] are not prominent in Walt Whitman's verse.[56] yet it is singularly emotional; probably no one has so daringly & freely carried "manly attachment" into expression[57] as this author. The "rapture in being," and in the physical existence of things is also vehement, beyond example. Cheerfulness overarches all, like a sky. Out of[58] his apparent materialism,[59] an unerring spirituality[60] always & certainly[61] emerges. A distinguished scientist,[62] in Washington, told me not long since, that,[63] in its tally

37. Preceding two words inserted with a finer-nibbed pen above "nial" in "perennial," and "and"

38. Deleted: "(quite altogether" ; inserted: "(henceforth" above "[del.] altogether"

39. Deleted: "and" ; inserted above: "all" with finer-nibbed pen.

40. Inserted with finer point above "the" and "l" in "lay"

41. Preceding five words inserted with finer-nibbed pen above "-figures . . . fine" ; deleted before "silk" : "&"

42. Deleted: [illeg.]

43. Deleted: "feudalism" ; inserted: "the saloons" with a finer-nibbed pen.

44. Deleted: "are to" ; inserted: "must . . . to, &" with a finer-nibbed pen above "[del.] are to" and "called upon &"

45. Preceding two words inserted with a finer-nibbed pen above "and" and "mer" in "merged"

46. Changed from past to present tense.

47. Deleted: "flowers in"

48. Deleted: "never" ; inserted: "and walks, and" above "[del.] never" and "a mar" (in "marble")

49. Inserted at a diagonal above "but"

50. Deleted: "or a" inserted above "the"

51. Deleted: "the"

52. Inserted above "the"

53. Preceding two sentences with a finer-nibbed pen, as if inserted later. Lower third of the leaf blank.

54. Inserted above "u" in "you"

55. Deleted: "& perhaps even its specially esthetic forms,"

56. Deleted: "It" ; inserted above: "yet it"

57. Deleted: "so [illeg.] far"

58. Deleted: "this" ; inserted: "his" above and following "[del.] this"

59. Deleted: "of its pages"

60. Deleted: "is"[?] ; inserted: "always &" with a finer-nibbed pen above "lity" in "spirituality" and the deletion.

61. "ly" added to "certain" ; deleted: "to" ; inserted and deleted: "and always" above "[del.] ap" in "appear"; "s" added to "appear" , whole word deleted; inserted: "emerges" with a finer-nibbed pen above "[del.] pears" in "appears"

62. Another "Italian critic"?

63. Deleted: "while beneath the surface, &"

& spirit,[64] Whitman's was the only poetry he could mention that is thoroughly consistent with modern science & philosophy, & that[65] does not infringe[66] upon them[67] in a single line.

4[68] During some ten years, formerly[69] the principal[70] charge against Leaves of Grass was[71] its[72] offensively outspoken amativeness. The Danish critic,& admirer,[73] Rudolf Schmidt,[74] speaks of this as "like the roar of a wild beast in rutting time"—yet considers it[75] not disproportioned to the magnified and vehement possession, by the ideal subject of these poems, of all the passions. But of late years, since the author's plan has[76] expanded, & his edifice has been carried out to fuller and fuller proportions, that particular section of it has[77] become less conspicuous, or perhaps has been seen to form,[78] in Whitman's[79] scheme,[80] an honest and integral part of it.[81] That[82] point of attack has therefore[83] been abandoned; and I notice you do not mention it in your[84] analysis of the 29th.

5 I am not sure but now[85] the principal trouble is in the "*shirt*[86] *sleeves.*" Our poets each & all seem[87] conventionally determined, (like an Englishman in Jamaica or Ceylon,) to wear the[88] cloth coat of society,[89] and stiff stock & hat, if they die for it; but Whitman, roaming the fields or cities[90] in July or August, or whenever[91] he has[92] active work to do, is pretty sure to throw off his superficial

64. Deleted: "it" ; inserted: "Whitman's" above the deletion and "war"
65. Deleted: "they are" ; inserted: "does" above the deleted "are"
66. Deleted: final "d"
67. Inserted above "n" in "upon" and "in"
68. Deleted: "For a while and for" ; inserted: "During" above "[del.] for" and "So" in "Some" . The entire page seems to be written with a finer-nibbed pen.
69. Inserted above "s" in "years," and "the"
70. Deleted: "outcry" ; inserted above: "charge"
71. Deleted: "for"
72. Deleted: "of[?] outsp"
73. Preceding two words inserted above "critic" and "R" in "Rudolf"
74. "Walt Whitman, det amerikanske Demokratis Digter," *For Idé og Virkelighed,* I (1872), 152–216. See p. 6 below and "WALT WHITMAN travels."
75. Deleted: "certainly"
76. Deleted: "been"[?]
77. Deleted: "fallen into a" ; inserted: "become" above "[del.] into a"
78. Deleted: "from" ; inserted above: "in"
79. Deleted: "plan" ; inserted above: "scheme"
80. Inserted and deleted: "at any rate" above "an" and "ho" in "honest"
81. Deleted: "I At any rate," ; "that" capitalized.
82. Inserted and deleted: "particular" above "t" in "that" and "poin" in "point"
83. Inserted above "has been"
84. Deleted: "notice"
85. Preceding six words inserted above "the principal trouble" ; capital "T" on "The" not reduced. Paragraph symbol at left of insertion.
86. Deleted: "sleeves" before "sleeves." on line following.
87. Deleted: "All The poets are" ; preceding six words inserted above "[del.] The poets are" and "conven" in "conventionally"
88. Deleted: "tight"
89. Preceding two words inserted above "coat"
90. Preceding four words inserted above "ing" in "roaming" and "in July or"
91. Inserted: "ever" above "n" in "when"
92. Deleted: "some"

broadcloth, &[93] unloosen his[94] neck-buttons. It cannot be denied that this unfits him for the dress circle of the opera, or a[95] Saratoga ball room, or a State dinner at the White house. But for my part, I feel refreshed by an imaginative literature which escapes from all[96] merely genteel associations, & their standards. I think such escape, (with something to make up for it,) is what we all now most want, in poetical[97] composition.

6 The foreign recognition of Walt Whitman's poems is by no[98] means the mere flash in the pan inferred by[99] your criticism. The long & very searching article[1] some months since in the *Westminster Review*[2] entitled "the Poetry of Democracy—Walt Whitman," by Prof. Dowden, of Trinity College;[3] the article on[4] "Leaves of Grass" in the *Revue des Deux*[5] Mondes, by M. Barthon,[6] pronouncing[7] "Drums Taps," unapproached in its vivid pictures[8] of American campaigning, & as modern[9] war poetry; the splendid euloqiums of Freilegrath[10] in his German[11] translations of the[12] "*Leaves,*"[13] and life of[14] their author;[15] the reproduction in Denmark, in the *Ide*[16] *og Virkelighed,* (the Copenhagen magazine, "the Idea and Reality,") of these poems with great enthusiasm;[17] their rendering[18] in Hungarian, at Pesth-Buda,[19] & reception[20] with equal enthusiasm;[21] with sev-

93. Deleted: "toss aside his ne"
94. Deleted: "s"
95. Deleted: "Long Branch" ; inserted above: "Saratoga"
96. Deleted: "those" ; inserted: "merely genteel" with a finer-nibbed pen above the and deletion and "associa" in "association"
97. Deleted: "literature" ; inserted following: "composition." with a finer-nibbed pen.
98. Inserted above wordspace between "by means"
99. Deleted: "the article" ; inserted: "your" above "artic" in "article"
1. Deleted: "a few" ; inserted above: "some"
2. Preceding six words inserted above "acy" in "Democracy" and "the"
3. July, 1871. See "Jeff Mary Han."
4. Deleted: "Mr. Whitman" ; inserted and deleted: "him" above "[*del.*] Mr." ; deleted: "W." ; inserted: " "Leaves of Grass" " above "in the *R*" in "*Revue*"
5. "Deux" raised from lower to uppercase.
6. Preceding three words inserted above "*des*" in "*Mondes,*" and "pron" in "pronouncing" . WW meant Thérèse Bentzon (Mme. Blanc), "Un Poète Américain Walt Whitman," June 1, 1872. In "D.W. Wilder" he has the name and sex correct.
7. Deleted: "his"
8. Deleted "and" following "pictures" ; inserted: "of American campaigning, &" above "its . . . [*del.*] and"
9. Inserted above "war"
10. Ferdinand Freiligrath, "Walt Whitman," *Allgemeine Zeitung* (May 10, 1868). See "Addresses."
11. Inserted above "his" and "tran" in "translations"
12. Inserted above "of" and "L" in "*Leaves*"
13. Deleted: "of *Grass*"
14. Deleted: "its"
15. Deleted: "in Germany"
16. Deleted: "of"
17. See *n*74, above.
18. Inserted and deleted: "& reception" above "ering" in "rendering" and "in"
19. William Sloane Kennedy, *The Fight of a Book for the World* (West Yarmouth, Mass., 1926), 45, refers to *Fővárosilapok* (May 14, 1872). See "D. W. Wilder" for other Hungarian connections.
20. Preceding two words inserted above "with" and "e" in "equal"
21. Deleted: "the" ; inserted: "with several" above the deletion and "lectures"

eral lectures on the[22] new American,[23] by poets, scholars, and divines, in Great
Britain, & on the continent; these, I submit,[24] are signs[25] & accumulating proofs,
steadily enlarging & deepening, of Whitman's *permanent*[26] reception in Europe

7   Then a serious principle, far beyond the merits or demerits of this indi-
vidual writer is involved.[27] The question is not whether Walt Whitman, tried by
the technical and ostensible literary[28] standards, is a poet—as Tennyson, Long-
fellow, Poe, and[29] even N.P. Willis,[30] undoubtedly are. The real question is, of a
new theory and standard,[31] discarding[32] the old, restricted selection of the beau-
tiful—discarding exact metre and rhyme, (not[33] rhythm,) and[34] branching out for
themes[35] into all quarters,[36] including the modern practical & industrial ones,[37]
idealizing democracy,[38] and finding, as Whitman[39] himself puts[40] it, that

"—not[41] face alone, not brain alone, is worthy for the Muse;
    The Form complete is worthier far."[42]

By[43] those ostensible, until lately current[44] standards, tightly drawn,[45] it is[46]
probably doubtful, whether indeed[47] he is a poet. The question remains, &[48] must
remain[49] for the future to settle, whether in him & by him[50] are not planted the

---

22. Deleted: "new" ; inserted above: "new"
23. Inserted and deleted: "poet," above deleted "not" ; deleted: "not seldom" ; inserted: "by
poets, scholars, and divines," above "[*del.*] not seldom" and "in Great"
24. Preceding two words inserted above "are" and "si" in "signs"
25. Deleted: "& proofs"
26. Inserted above "an's" in "Whitman's" and "rece" in "receptions"
27. Sentence inserted on two lines above "The question is not"
28. Inserted on at angle at the left above "stan" in "standards"
29. Deleted: "G" ; inserted above: "even"
30. Deleted: "certainly" ; inserted above: "undoubtedly"
31. Deleted: "s"
32. Deleted: "met" ; inserted and deleted above "discarding" : "the old idea" ; inserted:
"the old . . . discarding" above "[*del.*] met" and "exact metre and rhyme, (not"
33. Inserted and deleted: "discarding" above "[*del.*] rhythm" ; deleted: "rhythm at all"
34. Inserted above wordspace between "rhythm,)" and "branching"
35. Preceding two words inserted above "out into"
36. Deleted: "as" ; inserted: "including" above the deletion and "the"
37. Deleted: "d"
38. Deleted: "phys"
39. Deleted: "has"
40. Deleted: "has" ; inserted above: "puts"
41. Deleted: "head" ; inserted above: "face alone" . "alone" is above a blank space.
42. Cf. "One's Self I Sing" (1867), l. 4. This text differs from all versions published by WW.
The first line is marked by a ¶ in black ink, both lines are bracketed at the left with the word
"smaller" in purple crayon.
43. Paragraph sign in left margin in blue crayon. Deleted: "the" ; inserted above: "those"
44. Preceding three words inserted above "ostensible" and "stand" in "standards"
45. Preceding two words and punctuation inserted above "ds" in "standards" and "it is"
46. Deleted: "indeed" ; inserted above: "probably"
47. Inserted above wordspace between "whether he"
48. Deleted: "probably"
49. Deleted: ", whether for a long time for a long time"
50. Preceding three words inserted above "him" ; deleted: "is" ; inserted above: "are"

hardy germs of a new & grander[51] stock[52] and a new & freer form, for poetry—certainly not less than the old, any more than our Science and Philosophy are—but necessitated by our vaster[53] conditions[54] of Democracy & expressing them.[55] In the[56] cultus of our race, every really new, original first class exemplification[57] in poetry, (as in religion, politics, or any thing) is a battle, a campaign, a fury, a parturition[58] throe of bitterness & revolt.[59]

    8   [60]Finally, I would ask, on the great subject of Poetry, do we not need the introduction of the new vein which has been[61] opened by modern thought[62] for the treatment of[63] Language, Religion,[64] History, and so on—what is called the Comparative Method—into this subject also?[65] In fact, is it not becoming[66] indispensable,[67] in order to get beyond narrow & sectarian[68] views? Suppose the comparative method applied to such[69] a theory & practice of poetry as Walt Whitman's, and[70] floods of light are forthwith[71] thrown on what would otherwise be puzzling & dark. Largely considered, great & true[72] poetic expression is a growth (& a signifying portrait also,)[73] of clime, age, cultus, race,—even of species & crises[74] & politics. The[75] immortal Hebraic poems—Homer's, Virgil's, and Juvenal's compositions—Dante's, Shakspere's and even Tennyson's—from the highest point of

51. Preceding two words inserted above "new" and "st" in "stock"

52. Deleted: "revolutionary & modern" ; inserted and deleted: "and seed" above "[*del.*] revolut" in "revolutionary" ; inserted: "and a new and freer [*two preceding words inserted*] form" above "nary" in "[*del.*] revolutionary" and "& modern"

53. Inserted above "cond" in "conditions"

54. Inserted: "[*illeg., del.*] of Democracy [*illeg., del.*]." above "tions" in "conditions" and "& expressing"

55. Sentence beginning deleted: "Every original &" ; following ten words inserted above the deletion and "first class exemplification"

56. Deleted: "mythos" before "culture"

57. "fi" inserted in "exemplification"

58. Deleted: "p" ; inserted above: "throe"

59. Preceding four words written on last line of leaf at right. What appears to be a cancelled period after "bitterness" suggests that "& revolt." was an afterthought.

60. "8" written over illegible figure, possibly "7" . Original opening cancelled:"Do [*illeg.*]"; following eleven words inserted above the deletion and "we need not the introduction" . Last seven words written with a finer-nibbed pen or a lighter touch may have been inserted later.

61. Preceding three words inserted above "opened by"

62. Deleted: "upon" "into" ; inserted: "for" above "[*del.*] upon"

63. Deleted: "the great subjects of"

64. Deleted: "Politics" ; inserted above: "History"

65. Inserted above "ct" in "subject?"

66. Inserted above "ot" in "not" and "in" in "indispensible"

67. Deleted: "to getting be"

68. Preceding two words inserted above "row" in "narrow" and into the right margin.

69. Deleted: "an order" ; inserted: "a theory & practice" above the deletion and "of"

70. Deleted: "a new"

71. Inserted above "thr" in "thrown"

72. Deleted: "poetry" ; inserted: "poetic expression" above the deletion and "is a"

73. Parenthetical phrase inserted with a finer-nibbed pen, suggesting a later addition, above "wth" in "growth" and "of clime"

74. Preceding two words inserted above "es" in "species" and "&"

75. Deleted: "divine and" ; inserted above: "immortal"

view[76] are all and each, such characteristic yet generic[77] growths. Walt Whitman's is the same in my opinion. The physiognomy of a race—of each race in the past[78]—of our American race in the present—[79] has the same old generic[80] type[81] & yet is[82] markedly different, and is characteristic only[83] of itself.[84] John Burroughs[85]

76. Preceding six words and punctuation inserted, apparently with a finer-nibbed pen above "n's" in "Tennyson's" and "all are and"

77. Preceding three words inserted with a finer-nibbed pen above "ch" in "each" and "such growths."

78. Preceding six words and punctuation inserted above "race of our" and "A" in "American"

79. Preceding three words and punctuation inserted above "—has the"

80. Inserted above "type"

81. Deleted: "of"

82. Deleted: "characteristic"

83. Inserted above "of"

84. Preceding six words centered on leaf.

85. In blue crayon slightly below and at the right.

No One of the Themes.

Manuscript in Duke (47, #27). Inscribed in black ink and black pencil on nine scraps of white paper as noted. It was probably pinned together originally. Bucke prints a final paragraph not now with the MS. With the MS is a note by W. S. Kennedy, who must have been given the MS by Bucke, which dates it to Washington in the summer of 1871. Bucke's addition confirms this date. First printed N&F, 63 (Pt. II, #38; CW, IX, 20–22).

[*1*][1] No one of the[2] Themes[3] generally considered[4] fit for stock or *motif*[5] for poetry[6] is taken by W. W. for his foundation[7]. No romantic[8] occurence nor legend, nor plot of mystery, [2][9] nor[10] sentimentalism nor[11] historic[12] personage or event, nor any[13] woven tale of[14] love, ambition, or[15] jealousy,[16] is in his work.

1. Two white laid scraps, approx. 6⅞″ x 4″. Blue rules ⅜″ apart on recto. Black pencil with some black ink emendations. Deleted: "None" "Not one" ; inserted above a blank space: "No one"
2. Deleted: "The" "that which has"
3. Deleted: "long is"
4. Deleted: "as the" ; inserted above "[*del.*] the" and "stock" : "fit for"
5. Preceding two words inserted above "ck" in "stock" and into the right margin. Deleted: "of" ; inserted and deleted above: "fit" ; inserted: "for" above "p" in "poetry"
6. Deleted: "& poet are" ; inserted: "is" [*redundant, not printed*] ; inserted above and deleted in black ink: "er" ; deleted in black ink: "are here" ; inserted and deleted above "re" in deleted "here" : "in" ; deleted in black ink: "tre the" ; inserted and deleted on the line in black ink: "sole" ; inserted in black ink above deleted "tre the sole" and "foun" in "foundations" ; "is taken by W. W. for his"
7. Final "s" deleted. Inserted and deleted in black ink: "sole" above "[*del.*] the book" "the book" . Inserted in black ink, redundant but not deleted, not shown here: "it." "of L of G" . Irrelevant waved line not shown.
8. Deleted: "take, nor epic series nor loves of hero and heroine" ; inserted: "occurrence" above "[*del.*] nor epic"
9. White laid scrap, approx. 5⅛″ x 4″. Blue rules ⅜″ apart. Black pencil with some black ink emendations.
10. Inserted: "nor sentimentalism" above "nor [*del.*] any historic" . Redundant "nor" not printed.
11. Deleted: "any"
12. Deleted: "in"
13. Deleted: "tale or"
14. Deleted: {*illeg.*}
15. Inserted in black ink above wordspace between "ambition" and "jealousy"
16. Deleted: "such as" ; inserted in pencil: "is [*del. in black ink*] here" ; inserted in black ink: "in [*del.*] it his work."

The[17] usual dominant requirements Beauty, art, hero & heroine[18] form, metre, rhyme, regularity—[19] have not only not been the laws of[20] its creation,[21] but might almost seem at first glance[22] to have[23] never been suspected by the author {3} [24]Thus compared with the rich ornamentation[25] of the plots & passions of the[26] best other poems the wine-like quality, the palace-hall, the velvet, the banquet, the masterpieces of paintings & statues, the costly vessels & furnishings,[27] the melody, the multitudinous wealth of conceit, trope,[28] incident, florid & dulcet versification and all the[29] much-[30]elaborated beauty of the accepted poets, there is something in[31] Leaves of Grass that seems singularly simple and bare. {4}[32] Instead of[33] any such appetizing richness[34] you[35] are vouchsafed merely a spring, or springs, of[36] plain water, bubbling & cold.[37] You[38] stand in a cluster of silent[39] trees, at sunrise,[40] or walk a zig-zag[41] path through the fields, or pace the barren

17. Deleted: "conventional and literary Beaut" ; inserted above "[black ink] usual & dominant requirements"
18. Preceding two words inserted above "art" ; deleted: "the esthetic"
19. Deleted: "as at any [preceding two words ins. and del.] rate as hitherto and now accepted"
20. Deleted: "their" ; inserted in black ink and deleted: "this" above "their" ; inserted in black ink: "its" above "cr" in "creation"
21. Deleted in black ink: "of Leaves of Grass"
22. Preceding three words inserted above "seem"
23. Deleted: "have" ; inserted in pencil and deleted in black ink above deleted "have" : "remained" ; deleted in black ink: "unknown to the" ; inserted in pencil: "never been [both in black ink; deleted "have" and "unknown"] suspected by its [del.] the [preceding three words in black ink]"
24. White laid paper with unfinished surface, approx. 5" x 4⅛". Black ink with some pencil emendations. Deleted in black ink: "Thus many things are severely bare and simple with in this poetry"; inserted: "Thus" above "etry" in "[del.] poetry"
25. Inserted in black ink above the line: "[first two words del.] and p of the plots and passions of the best other poems"
26. Deleted in black ink: "sumptuous ornament" ; inserted above deleted "Ornament" and "the" : "wine-like quality"
27. Preceding seventeen words written at top of leaf and brought down on asterisks. "costly" inserted above "ve" in "vessels" ; deleted "of gold &"
28. Inserted and deleted: "passion"
29. Preceding two words inserted in pencil above "and"
30. Inserted above "elab" in "elaborated"
31. Deleted: "Walt Whitman" ; inserted: "Leaves of Grass" above "man" in "Whitman" and "that seems"
32. Paper identical with {3}, approx. 5⅛" x 4¼". Black ink with some black pencil emendations. Deleted: "His"
33. Inserted on four lines at right above "of" and "[del.] these": "[in pencil] any such appetizing [two words del.] all that richness [three words del.] & architectural elaboration"
34. Deleted: "those his analogues" ; inserted: "you" above "he"
35. Deleted: "he has" ; inserted: "[del. above deleted "has"] see [ins. above deleted "see are"] vouchsafed [del.] only merely"
36. Deleted: "cold clear" ; inserted: "plain" above "ear" in "clear"
37. Deleted: "Your"
38. Deleted: "are in under" ; inserted above: "stand in"
39. Inserted in space at end of line: "silent" ; deleted: "old"
40. Preceding comma and two words inserted above "es" in "trees" and "or" . Deleted: "in a grass"
41. Inserted above "a" and "p" in "path"

sea-beach and look out on nothing but solitary[42] sky or sand,[43] hear only the monotonous[44] surging of the waves.

yet the book also with[45] active human life, the stir [5][46] and hum of cities, the[47] noise & show of trades,[48] factories, ships locomotives,[49] fill page after page with you move all the[50] practical activity—of our[51] aroused[?] land & time.[52] These occupy half the book or more.[53] Again you meet of[54] domestic and other[55] transactions common to your and every one's personal[56] life,[57] and again many a secret thought, wish, and memory, supposed unknown. Through these, and through the whole[58] world[59] of visible shows employments[60] and of thought, you are continually[61] hurried along, while[62] a dim form, a friendly face, accompanies and guides[63] you, as the phantom[64] of the Roman bard accompanied Dante on his difficult & untried way.[65] [6][66] In these *Leaves,* every thing[67] is[68] literally photo-

42. "solitude" emended to "solitary"

43. Preceding ten words and comma inserted above "en" "barren" and "sea-beach and"

44. Preceding three words inserted.

45. WW apparently began: "Nor these only, for every where in these poems is the also" . The reading given emerges from a welter of unrecordable deletions and insertions. There is no main verb in the passage.

46. Paper identical with [3, 4], approx. 7⅛″ x 2¾″. Black ink with some black pencil emendation. Deleted: "of [*ins.*] the trade, the" ; inserted: "and"

47. Deleted: "sound & sight" ; inserted above: "noise and show"

48. Inserted above "fact" in "factories"

49. Inserted: "[*del.*] fill a [*del.*] you [*illeg. del.*] [*del.*] move page after page with you move" on two lines above "all the" and deleted "varied and" The emendations are indescribable.

50. Deleted: "varied and"

51. Deleted: "current life" [*formerly completed the phrase* "practical activity of" *above*] ; inserted: "[*del.* our ages] aroused[?] land and time. These occupy half [*del.*] to the book [*illeg. del.*] or more."

52. The emendations that follow are indecipherable. A "silent apparition," who evidently is the "dim form" at the bottom of the page, hovers among them. The reading of the next three words is tentative.

53. Sentence inserted.

54. Again, the preceding four words are the best that can be made of the MS.

55. Deleted: "facts"

56. Preceding four words inserted above "your life" and "[*del.*] but"

57. Deleted: "but [*illeg.*] of" ; inserted: "and again" above "[*del.*] of" and "many"

58. Inserted in black pencil.

59. Deleted: "not only"

60. Inserted. Deleted: "but" ; inserted: "and"

61. Inserted.

62. Inserted.

63. Preceding two words inserted above "accompanies"

64. Deleted: "spirit" ; inserted in black pencil above deletion: "phantom"

65. At top of the page preceded by an asterisk. Brought down to asterisk after "Dante"

66. Identical with [3, 4, 5], approx. 5⅛″ x 3⅞″. Black ink with some black pencil emendations. Deleted: "All is as it is in life" ; inserted above: "In [*two words del.*] this book [*ins.* above the deletion] these *Leaves of Grass* [*two words deleted, comma inserted*]"

67. Inserted above "y" in "every"

68. Deleted: "actually" ; inserted and deleted above: "faith" ; inserted: "literally" above "is" and before the deleted "faith"

graphed.[69] Nothing is poetized,[70] no divergence, not a step, not an inch, nothing for[71] beauty's sake[72] no euphemism, no rhyme.[73]

That[74] such a course gives offence to many[75] good people—That[76] it violates the established[77] conventions of[78] poetry is[79] certain. But is there not something secretly[80] precious to the soul in this[81] awful[82] adherence to the truth? [7][83]Is[84] there[85] not an inference that puts us all to shame in[86] the unmitigated and all-comprehending faith of these poems.[87] [8][88]Indeed the qualities which[89] characterize[90] Leaves of Grass are[91] not the qualities of a[92] fine book or poem, or any work of art, but the qualities of a living and full-blooded[93] man, pride, ama-

69. Deleted: "Not [*illeg.*]"
70. Inserted: "[*del.*] not no divergence . . . inch," above "Nothing . . . nothing for"
71. Deleted: "beat"
72. Inserted.
73. Deleted: "We do not wonder at the reception of this author"
74. Deleted: "he" ; inserted and deleted above: "this" ; inserted: "such a course [*del.*] must" above the deletions and "gives"
75. Deleted: "in certain." ; inserted: "good people.—" above "many" and "[*del.*] in certain" ; uppercase in "That" not reduced, not printed here.
76. Deleted: "he" ; inserted above: "it"
77. Inserted above "the" and "con" in "conversations"
78. Deleted in pencil: "parlors and"
79. Deleted: "also"
80. Deleted: "sweet &"
81. Deleted: "faithful the"
82. Inserted after a space and in two lines: "adherence to the truth"
83. Paper identical with [3–6]; approx. 4¾" x 4". Black ink with some pencil emendation. Cancelled passage: "[*ins. and del.*] This After [*del.*] all every [*ins.* above deleted "all"] thing is admitted against [*ins.*] it [*two words del.*] this book [*ins. and del.* above deleted "book" them] [*two words del.* there remains] from the points of view of [*del.* the] [*ins. and del.* above the deleted "the"] polite literary [*del.*] canons [*ins. and del. above*] taste [*del.* the] or of what is suitable [*preceding five words ins. and del. above the deleted* "polite . . . groups of" [*preceding three words del.*] polite groups of ladies and gentlemen in drawing rooms [*preceding three words ins. above* "tlemen" *in* "gentlemen" *and* "of" *and* [*del.*] the"] & the discriminations of clergymen [*preceding five words del.*] clergymen in their pulpits [*preceding three words ins. above deletions*] or the literary taste of them on a kindred plane."
84. Deleted: "Is" ; inserted: "Is" ; uppercase in "There" not reduced, not printed here.
85. Inserted above: "not" ; inserted and deleted: "not left" above the deletion; deleted: "something" ; inserted: "an inference" above "ething" in "something"
86. Deleted: "this [*ins.*] the tremendous [*ins.*] treatment" ; inserted in pencil: "the unmitigated" above "tremendous"
87. Deleted: "? which seem" ; period inserted.
88. Two pasted-up scraps of white laid paper totalling approx. 3¼" x 3¹⁵/₁₆". Scrap 1 is like [3–7], 2 has blue lines ⅜" apart on recto. Black pencil with some emendations in black ink. On the verso is the beginning of an unrecorded letter of July 5, 1871 from 107 North Portland Ave., Brooklyn, to a Mr. Dillingham (mentioned in "sent Press of the 22d.") A few cancelled words at torn-off top of scrap. Inserted: "Indeed" ; uppercase "The" not reduced, not printed here.
89. Deleted in black ink: "eminently"
90. Inserted in pencil: "[*del. in black ink*] these Leaves" ; inserted in ink: "of Grass" above "[*del.*] these"
91. Deleted in pencil: "more the"
92. Deleted in black ink: "book" ; inserted in black ink: "fine book or poem or any work of art" on two lines above "a ? but"
93. Preceding four words inserted in pencil on two lines at the right.

tiveness, adhesiveness, [9][94] curiosity yearning for immortality, joyousness and sometimes of[95] uncertainty.[96] You do not read it as some one in action in war, or on a ship, or climbing the mountains, or racing along and shouting aloud in pure exaltation.

A certain vagueness, almost passing[97] into chaos it remains to be acknowledged[98] is in[99] a few[1] pieces or passages; but this is apparently[2] done by the deliberate intention of the author.

W. W. is now fifty-two years old. No worldly aim has engrossed his life. He is still unmarried. None of the usual ardors of business ambition, of the acquisition of money, or the claims of society, pleasure, nor even the attractions of culture or art seem to have enslaved him. The thought of and the making of this work has spanned, as it were, the whole horizon of his life, almost since boyhood.[3]

94. White laid paper, approx. 4⅝″ x 4″. Blue lines 3″ apart. Pencil with some emendations in black ink. Deleted in pencil: "meditation"

95. Preceding three words inserted in black ink above "uncertainty"

96. Succeeding sentence is conjectural.

97. Deleted: "running" ; inserted above: "passing"

98. Preceding five words inserted in black ink above "is in . . . pieces"

99. Deleted: [illeg.]

1. Deleted: "of"

2. Inserted above "this is" and into the margin. Deleted in black ink: "certainly" ; inserted: "done" above "by"

3. The preceding paragraph is Bucke's addition in N&F.

Personal.

Text from a printed sheet in LC (Feinberg). Printed in black ink on white wove paper, 12″ x 6½″. The type, as Furness points out (157–158), is identical to that of *LG* (1876), and it was probably printed after the book had been printed. Two earlier printings in Texas carry WW's emendations. The first, called "Separate" in notes below, of provenance unknown, is on a leaf 9¼″ x 6⅞″. WW's emendations in black ink agree with the readings of the LC/Feinberg copy, but it is further emended in pencil. The second, called "Rossetti" in notes, was cut into two leaves and pasted by WW into a copy of *LG* (1876) which he sent to William Michael Rossetti. His emendations in black ink agree with the readings of LC/Feinberg, with one additional emendation of the first word.

The copy of *LG* (1876) was sent by WW to Rossetti on March 29, 1876, in addition to a copy which he had sent on the 15th (*Corr.*, III, 29, 33). WW corrected the title page of the March 26 copy for a London imprint and inserted into the Table of Contents five titles which also appear on one of his printed slips pasted at the end of the Contents, which he struck out. He also inserted a title for *"PERSONAL."* at the head of the Contents and inserted "Wound" in the title "The Dresser." He also enclosed full instructions for the printer and proofreader (*"To getter up"*). As he wrote Rossetti on March 29: "As it may be that out of this hubbub, some one in London may take a notion to rush & crudely reprint my books—I send you (same mail with this) full & corrected copies of my two volumes, prepared for the printers, for a London edition, with especial Preface note—& altogether as I should like to have the books brought out, for permanent reading & investigation in Europe."

The "hubbub" was one that WW had stirred up himself. On January 26 the *West Jersey Press* of Camden had printed a long and detailed account, certainly written by WW himself or under his close supervision, which presented a touching picture of the total failure of *LG* in America, the "denial, disgust and scorn of orthodox American authors, publishers and editors" (Allen, 469–470). WW was in a pathetic situation, it is true, for his powers were failing, he had been unable to sell any poems recently, and he was sick and lonely. He had been or was soon to be passed over in favor of Sydney Lanier for Centennial poet. He was also the greatest poet America had yet produced and he had to publish his own books. However, he was comfortably, though not ideally, housed with his brother and sister-in-law and had been able to put together and finance a handsome (by the standards of 1876), two-volume edition, which was just appearing.

WW promptly sent the *Press* clipping to Rossetti, who published it in London. Robert Buchanan fired a blast in the London *Daily News* attacking the United States for its neglect of its greatest writer and suggesting a British subscription. In response to cabled reports of Rossetti's and Buchanan's protests, the American press, especially the NY *Tribune*, attacked WW without mercy or honesty. Within three days of the American publication of the London protests, WW was backpedalling vigorously in a letter to Rossetti (*Corr.*, III, 29–30).

The two Texas copies seem to be early issues, just as the copy of *LG* appears to be early. Wells and Goldsmith, 20–21, describe a chaotic textual history for the Centennial Edition, and the copy in the Spenser Research Library, University of Kansas, shows all revisions in the Table of Contents except the insertion of *"PERSONAL."* The text of the Texas copy and the Kansas copy have not been collated.

Furness (163–164) printed *"PERSONAL."* from what he said was a proof in LC. Dr. John C. Broderick, Chief of the Manuscript Division, reports, however, that no copy, other than that in Feinberg, is in LC. Furness evidently worked from a later issue identical with Feinberg or an emended copy like the Texas Separate.

PERSONAL.

U.S. America:
Camden, N. Jersey, April, 1876.

To the Foreign Reader, at outset:

Though[1] there is many another influence and[2] chord in the intentions of the following Recitatives, the one that for the purpose of this reprint doubtless o'er-dominates the rest is to suggest and[3] help a deeper, stronger, (not now political, or business, or intellectual, but) heroic,[4] artistic, and especially emotional, intertwining and affiliation[5] of the Old and New Worlds.

Indeed,[6] the peculiar glory of These[7] United States I have come to see, or expect to see, not in their geographical or even[8] republican greatness, nor wealth or products, nor military or naval power, nor special, eminent Names in any department, (to shine with, or outshine, foreign special names, in similar departments,)—but more and more in a vaster, saner, more splendid[9] Comradeship, typifying the People everywhere, uniting closer and closer not only The American[10] States, but all Nations, and all Humanity. (That, O Poets! is not *that* a theme, a Union, worth chanting, striving for? Why not fix our verses henceforth to the gauge of the round globe? the[11] whole race?)[12]

1. Texas (Rossetti), inserted vertically in black ink at left: "(in caps" ; word double underlined in black ink.
2. Texas (Separate), preceding two words deleted in pencil.
3. Texas (Separate), preceding two words deleted in pencil.
4. Texas (Separate), deleted in pencil: "artistic" ; inserted in right margin: "human" in pencil.
5. Texas (Separate), preceding two words deleted in pencil.
6. Texas (Separate), preceding word and comma deleted in pencil; "t" capitalized.
7. Texas (Separate), deleted in pencil: "United" ; inserted in pencil in right margin: "American"
8. Texas (Separate), preceding word deleted in pencil.
9. Texas (Separate), preceding comma and two words deleted in pencil.
10. Texas (Separate), preceding word deleted in pencil.
11. Texas (Separate), preceding three words and question mark deleted in pencil.
12. Texas (Separate and Rossetti), omitted parenthesis inserted in ink in right margin. Evidently LC Feinberg is a corrected printing.

Perhaps the most[13] illustrious culmination of the Modern and of Republicanism[14] may prove to be a signal[15] cluster of joyous, more exalted Bards of Adhesiveness, identically one in soul, but contributed by every nation, each after its distinctive kind. Let me dare here and now[16] to start it. Let the diplomats, as ever, still deeply plan, seeking advantages, proposing treaties between governments, and to bind them, on paper: what I seek is different, simpler. I would inaugurate from America,[17] for this purpose, new formulas,[18] international poems. I have thought that the invisible root out of which the Poetry deepest in, and dearest to,[19] humanity grows, is Friendship. I have thought that both in Patriotism and Song, (even amid their grandest shows, past,) we have adhered too long to petty limits, and that the time has come to enfold the world.

While the following pieces, then, were put forth and sounded especially for my own country, and address'd[20] to democratic needs, I cannot evade the conviction that the substances and subtle ties behind them, and which they celebrate, (is it that the American character has enormous Pride and Self-assertion? ah, but underneath, living Goodwill and Sympathy, on which the others rest, are far more enormous,) belong equally to all countries. And the ambition to waken with them, and[21] in their key, the latent[22] echoes of every land, I here avow.

To begin, therefore, though nor envoy, nor ambassador,[23] nor with any official right, nor commission'd by the President—with only Poet's right, as general simple friend of Man—the right of the Singer, admitted, all ranks, all times—I will not repress the impulse I feel, (what is it, after all, only one man facing another man, and giving him his hand?) to proffer here, for fittest outset to this Book, to share with the English, the Irish, the Scottish and the Welsh,—to highest and to lowest, of These Islands—(and why not, launch'd hence, to the mainland, to the Germanic peoples—to France, Spain, Italy, Holland—to Austro-Hungary— to every Scandinavian, every Russ?) the sister's salutation of America from over sea—the New World's greeting-word to all, and younger brother's love. W. W.[24]

13. Texas (Separate), preceding word deleted in pencil.
14. Texas (Separate), preceding three words deleted in pencil.
15. Texas (Separate), preceding word deleted in pencil.
16. Texas (Separate), preceding three words deleted in pencil.
17. Texas (Separate), preceding two words deleted in pencil.
18. Texas (Separate), preceding comma and two words deleted.
19. Texas (Separate), inserted in right margin in pencil: "and most comprehensive" . A further word, possibly a preposition, may have been written off the edge of the leaf.
20. Texas (Separate and Rossetti), "e" deleted, apostrophe inserted in margin in ink.
21. Texas (Separate), preceding three words and comma deleted in pencil.
22. Texas (Separate and Rossetti), "s" deleted in black ink; apostrophe inserted in black ink. In Rossetti "latent" written in right margin.
23. Texas (Separate), preceding two words deleted in pencil.
24. A double line, the top one heavier, is printed across the leaf the width of the text.

(The Muse Invited.

Text from *Two Rivulets: Centennial Songs,* 4. WW was not invited to compose the Ode for the Centennial Exposition, perhaps fortunately, considering the failure of "Song of the Exposition" in 1871, but the Centennial Edition was his tribute. *Centennial Songs* was an eighteen-page pamphlet, copyright 1875, containing not only this note, printed as a Preface to "Song of the Exposition," and the poem itself, but also "Song of the Universal" and "Song for All Seas, All Ships," which was bound up in *Two Rivulets.* There seems to have been no separate publication.

(*The* MUSE *invited to* PHILADELPHIA.)

Song of the Exposition.

Applied to THE CENTENNIAL., *Phila.,* 1876—(*Originally recited for Opening the* 40th *Annual Exhibition* AMERICAN INSTITUTE, *New York, noon, September 7th, 1871.*)

STRUGGLING steadily to the front, not only in the spirit of Opinion, Government, and the like, but, in due time, in the Artistic also, we see actual operative, LABOR and LABORERS, with Machinery, Inventions, Farms, Products, &c., pressing to place our time, over the whole civilized world. Holding these by the hand, we see, or hope we see, THE MUSE, (radiating, representing, under its various expressions, as in every age and land, the healthiest, most heroic Humanity, common to all, fusing all,) entering the demesnes of the New World, as twin and sister of our Democracy—at any rate we will so invite Her, here and now—to permanently infuse in daily toils, and be infused by them.

Perhaps no clearer or more illustrative sign exists of the current adjustment and tendency than those superb International Expositions of the World's Products, Inventions and Industries, that, commencing in London under Prince Albert, have since signalized all the principal Nations of our age, and have been rife in the United States—culminating in this great Exposition at Philadelphia, around which the American Centennial, and its thoughts and associations, cluster—with vaster ones still in the future.

Ostensibly to inaugurate an Exposition of this kind—still more to outline the establishment of a grand *permanent* Cluster-Palace of Industry from an imaginative and Democratic point of view—was the design of the following poem; from such impulses it was first orally deliver'd.

To Getter Up.

Manuscript in Texas (Hanley). Inscribed in black ink with a broad-nibbed pen on white, wove, folded notepaper, 7½" x 4¾". Unprecedentedly, there are only two emendations. The MS doubtlessly refers to the London reprint of *LG* (1876), which WW tried to engineer in February and March of that year (see *"PERSONAL"*). The MS probably accompanied his letter of March 29 to Rossetti. See "D. W. Wilder." By March 30, however, WW had changed his mind about a shilling edition (*Corr.,* III, 35). H. Buxton Forman, however, also tried to publish a complete *LG* in 1872 and 1876. This was written in March, 1876.

To getter up of the books—Printer—& Proof-reader

remember this is to be a verbatim, entire & authentic edition, specially authorized by me, W.W. & representing me.

There are to be *two Vols.* each Vol. complete in itself.

My idea is of rather plain, solid looking books, ordinary 12 mo (of rather small)— Can't you make a book, (say paper covers,) that would sell for a shilling sterling, each Vol?—but that I leave to you—

You had better fix on a sized page *just the tally of these, so it will come in page for page.* (This book is in long primer—I should like well to have the same sized type & same general style[1] adhered to)

Proof reader—I depend much on you—please look over all the copy first, thoroughly, get my ideas, (perhaps *kinks*) & then see that they are adhered to, as the [*3; 2 blank*] proofs come in your hands— Of course read very carefully by copy, for punctuation, capitalization, &c— Particularly *mind the spaces* (leads or white lines) *between the verses,* (or between the passages in prose in *Two Rivulets*)

The little extra top heads *Leaves of Grass,* as on pp. 7, 29, &c. can be left out, if desired, for condensing

The little figures to first lines of verses must go in, just as in text[2]

(get this name below[3] cut, wood (or as you choose) to go on title page of *Leaves of Grass* Walt Whitman)

1. Preceding four words inserted above "type adhered to"
2. Following entry enclosed on left by a large parenthesis.
3. Preceding two words inserted above "this cut" . A hand points down to "this"

The Name of This.

Manuscript in Duke (19, #7). Inscribed in black ink on nine scraps pasted together or mounted as four, as follows. [*1*] Dark tan wove irregular, lower corners clipped, approx. 5¾" x 6¼", numbered "1" in red crayon in an unknown hand (Bucke?). [*2*] Similar to [*1*], approx. 9¼" x 6¼", numbered "7" in black pencil (by WW?), "2" in red crayon by an unknown hand. [*3*] Three scraps pasted together: [*A*] similar to [*1*] and [*2*], 5¾" x 5¾", numbered "8" in black pencil (by WW?), "3" in red crayon by an unknown hand; [*B*] same paper, approx. 5⅝" x 5¾", numbered in black pencil circled "4" (by WW?), "3a" in black pencil by an unknown hand; [*C*] white wove, carefully trimmed at the upper left to cut out words, approx. 2¾" x 5¼". [*4*] Three scraps: [*A*] dark tan scrap as above, 1⅛" x 6⅛", numbered "4" in black pencil by an unknown hand; [*B*] dark tan, approx. 1⅝" x 6⅛", on which is pasted [*C*] inscribed and printed white wove scrap, approx. ¹⁵/₁₆ x " 6¹/₁₆". All pasted on [*D*], fourth brown backing scrap. The paper unfortunately gives little or no clue to the date. With the MS is a note probably in hand of Horace Traubel calling attention to Bucke's note in *N&F*, 62: "Seems to be a rejected passage from *My Book and I*, printed in Lippincott, January, 1887, and afterwards largely used in *A Backward Glance*, annexed to current edition of *Leaves of Grass*." The MS is related to the complex of MSS leading to "A Backward Glance O'er Travel'd Roads" (1888), although it does not fit the pattern described in Sculley Bradley and John A. Stevenson, eds., *Walt Whitman's Backward Glances* (Philadelphia, 1947), and *Prose 92*, II, 711–732, 768–773. Rather than a rejected passage from "My Book and I," it seems to be a draft preface, perhaps to a projected edition of *LG*. The printed slip at the end is the last sentence of "A Backward Glance on My Own Road." See *Critic*, 4, NS (January 5, 1884), 2. The date, therefore, is between 1884 and 1888. First printed by Bucke in *N&F*, 62 (Pt. II, #33; *CW*, IX, 17–19).

The name of this[1] tells[2] much of the story— Before and afterward How the whole purport, history, results, of Book or Life, range between and within those words! *Before*—[3] that nebulae of thoughts and plans and misty[4] hopes![5]—those

---

1. Preceding four words inserted above the deletion following and "tells" ; deleted: "mere name of which" and a preceding passage of unknown length trimmed at top. Deleted from insertion: "Preface"
2. Deleted: "most" ; inserted: "much" above "of"
3. Deleted: "the" ; inserted above: "that"
4. Deleted: "shapes"
5. Deleted: "the ardor — the ["—those" *ins. but not del.*] toils and struggles of baffled impeded articulation —(most curious resumé of all!)"

startings out, urging, cleaving, beating flights of wings,[6] uncertain where you [2]'ll[7] soar, or bring up—or whether you will soar at all—[8] to end perhaps in ignominious fall and failure!— Those toils and struggles of baffled, impeded articulation—[9] those moods of proudest ambition and daring, quickly follow'd by deeper moods of qualm, despair, utter distrust of one's-self—[10] All carried along and[11] merged in the *Afterward*—the way things work— the apparent terminations—the results so unexpected,[12]— Finally,[13] the looking back[14] out of the[15] pensive evening—the—a[16] [3] procession of ghosts in arriere[17] in the soul's twilight, of all those angry wrestings, those absurd trusts, those high-sounding calls, those contrasts,[18] expectations, rejections, hauteurs, shames, loves, joys.[19]

Accordingly,[20] the reader[21] of the[22] ensuing book will be ushered into no palace hall, or banquet, or the Company of[23] gentlemen and ladies of[24] highest[25] refinement. It is probable—nay certain—that the[26] well-established, Gœthean, Emersonian,[27] Tennysonian[28] doctrine or principle[29] of verse-writing[30] to carefully[31] select & express the beautiful, with the most exquisite[32] metre, polish,[33] & verbal elegance, will view the bulk of these writings[34] with dismay & indignation.

6. Deleted: dash.
7. The page break is in the middle of "you'll" . WW did not indicate break by a hyphen.
8. Deleted: "or" ; inserted above: "to"
9. Preceding eight words inserted above "fall . . . moods"
  10. Deleted: "—those years of venture, and, at best, [*preceding two words del.*] callow, formation!—unfoldings so capricious, often inopportune [*preceding five words del.*]—so many failures ——so much unsatisfactory—a meagre dash or dot of genuine light at best—the vast mass of stolidity—the fortunes, misfortunes, happenings, surprises through many, many years"
  11. Preceding four words inserted above "Merged in" . WW did not reduce "Merged" to lowercase.
  12. Deleted: dash.
  13. Inserted above "the" and "lo" in "looking"
  14. Deleted: "from" ; inserted above: "out of"
  15. Deleted: "soothing and still" ; WW did not delete succeeding "and"
  16. Inserted above "—the" ; deleted: "resumé"
  17. Preceding two words inserted above "ghosts in"
  18. Inserted above "se" in "those" and "ex" in "expectations"
  19. First pasted-on scrap follows.
  20. Deleted: "if"
  21. Deleted: "enters upon" ; inserted: "of" above and before "the"
  22. Deleted: "following pages he or she will" ; inserted: "ensuing book" above "[*del.*] following pages"
  23. Deleted: "the [*illeg.*]"
  24. Deleted: "the"
  25. Inserted and deleted above "highest" : "pos"
  26. White, wove, pasted-on scrap begins.
  27. Inserted above "thean" in "Gœthean"
  28. Deleted: "old, well-established"
  29. Preceding two words inserted above "of" and into the right margin.
  30. Deleted: "as an art principle in art,"
  31. Inserted above "to select"
  32. Deleted: "rhyme" ; inserted above: "metre"
  33. Deleted: "metre"
  34. Preceding five words inserted above "will view with"

[4][35] have long been directing[36] admiration and awe[37] to something in others[38] other days. In the following book the reader is pointed in the main, and quite altogether, to him or her self, the existing day.[39]

Finally I think the best and largest songs yet remain to be sung.[40]

35. Brown scrap pasted on smaller brown backing. Deleted: "Poems" . No paragraph indentation in the MS.

36. Deleted: "their readers"

37. Deleted: "at" ; inserted above: "to"

38. Below this word with a finer-nibbed pen seems to be "No" in WW's hand. The entry was smeared while the ink was still wet.

39. Second brown scrap pasted on the brown backing scrap; text on white pasted-on scrap. Inserted and deleted in black pencil: "Then" ; inserted: "Finally" . Remainder of text clipped from *Critic.*

40. Deleted: printed "WALT WHITMAN"

Scatter'd, I Myself.

Manuscript in Morgan. Inscribed in black ink on two scraps of gray-brown paper: [1] approx. 9⅝" x 6"; [2] 4" x 6⅜". O'Connor's remark was made in a letter recorded in Bucke, 88. The date must be after 1883. Printed in part by Furness, 187.

scatter'd,[1] I myself hardly know where. Indeed if[2] there is any thing worth while to offer in my messages, it is effused[3] at random, obedient to the passing mood[4] moment.[5] Has not the Chaos of my pages,[6] its enclosing purport[7]? its clue or[8] formulation? No—no more than Nature has. Or if[9] it has,[10] it is not in the usual way, and you Reader dear,[11] may need to search long for it.[12] Upon the whole, it[13] evades me[14] more than anybody. . . . . . Indeed, I give you warning in advance Reader dear. The[15] vaunted result of[16] the now prevailing Religions, philosophies and[17] Poems[18] too,[19] something definite and certain—the telling of the tale to its climax and end— Something you can rest on for good, and no more beyond—

1. Deleted: "at random"
2. Deleted: "I have" ; inserted: "there is" above "have"
3. Deleted: "altogether by chance and mood" ; inserted: "at random" above "[del.] by chance"
4. Preceding two words inserted above "to the moment"
5. Deleted: "Have I then in [ins. and del.] Does" ; inserted: "Has not" above "the" before "Chaos"
6. Inserted and deleted: "then any enclosing" above "my pages" ; deleted: "no [illeg.]" ; inserted: "its enclosing" above the deletion and "purport"
7. Emended from "purpose" ; deleted: "no"
8. Inserted above deleted "no" and "form" in "formulation"
9. Deleted: "I have" ; inserted and deleted: "they" above "[del.] have" ; inserted: "it has" above "ve" in "[del.] have" and "R" in "[del.] Reader"
10. Deleted: "Reader dear"
11. Preceding two words and comma inserted above "you may"
12. Deleted: [illeg.]
13. Deleted: "puzzles and"
14. Deleted: "as much as" ; inserted: "more than" above "[del.] as much"
15. Deleted: "final" ; inserted: "vaunted" above deletion and "re" in "result"
16. Deleted: "all the good systems of" ; inserted: "the" above "[del.] all" and "now prevailing" above "[del.] systems of"
17. Deleted: "the great"
18. Emended from "Poetry"
19. Deleted: "hitherto" ; inserted and deleted: "[illeg.] pervading" above "something"

must not be look'd for in the following book[20] pages.[21] I would [2] liken[22] it more to the[23] awakening of thoughts, and views really fit for imaginative[24] America—or[25] sounding through camp at some day-break on[26] our Western humanity's journey,[27] "the signal,"[28] to use William O'Connor's[29] words, "of a great march—

20. Written above, possibly as an alternate.
21. Deleted: "I like"
22. Deleted: "them" ; inserted above: "it"
23. Deleted: "first"
24. Inserted above "for" and "Am" in "America"
25. Deleted: "sounded" ; inserted and deleted: "sounded some at the for or" ; inserted: "sounding [*del.*] some through camp (or [*del.*] the" above "humanity's journey"
26. Deleted: "or" ; inserted: "our"
27. Deleted: "at some daybreak," . Space for at least a line and a half before the next inscription.
28. Deleted: "as" ; inserted: "to use" above the deletion and "Wi" in "William"
29. Deleted: [*illeg.*]

For Criticism L of Grass.

Manuscript in Duke (45, #19). Inscribed in pencil with revisions in red and black ink on white, wove, pocket notebook paper with rounded corners, 6¾" x 4⅛". Blue rules ¼" apart. The first draft of *"Two suggestion points"* (see headnote especially). Written vertically in left margin in black ink: "Sent to Dr. Bucke." This MS and its final version were possibly written to keep Bucke on the right track in his *Walt Whitman;* thus, this MS can be dated between 1880 and 1883, when Bucke was working on the project, or even later, for on the verso are two stanzas from Tennyson's "The May Queen," which was published in *Tiresias* (1885). Printed in *N&F,* 55 (Pt. II, #44; *CW,* IX, 28–29).

for criticism L[1] of Grass[2]

—We have had Man indoors & under artificial relations—[3] man in war, man in love, (both the[4] natural universal elements of human lives)—man in courts, bowers, castles parlors—man[5] in personal haughtiness & the tussle of war, as in Homer,[6] or the passions, crimes, ambition, murder, jealously love, carried to extremes as in Shakes. We have been[7] listening to divine, ravishing tales[8], plots of   [9] valuable,[10] hitherto, (like the Christian religion) to temper & modify his prevalent perhaps natural ferocity & hoggishness—[11]

but never before have we had *man in the open air,* his attitude *adjusted* to the seasons &[12] as one might[13] describe it, adjusted to the sun by day & the stars by night.

1. Written over "of"
2. Small circled numeral "1" at upper right corner of MS after "Grass"
3. Preceding six words inserted on two lines above "had man in"
4. Deleted: "prevalent"
5. Inserted in black ink: "in personal haughtiness & the tussle of war," on two lines above "as in" and "Hom" in "Homer"
6. Inserted in black ink: "or the passions, . . . to extremes as in" on several lines above "Shakes" and into the right margin.
7. Preceding three words inserted above "listening"
8. Deleted in black ink: "of passion"
9. In the empty space of several lines: "each individual all other individuals [*preceding five words in red ink*] [*del.*] man inexpressibly"
10. Inserted and deleted: "but" above "hi" in "hitherto"
11. A note in red ink crowded in and written partially over following paragraph: "as the Universal comrade each nation courteously saluting all other nations" . Deleted: "but here we have"
12. Deleted: "to"
13. Deleted: "say"

Two Suggestion Points.

Manuscript in Duke (49, #36). Inscribed in black ink on three scraps of white wove paper: (1) 1¼" x 7⅞", (2) 2¼" x 7⅞", (3) 3½" x 7⅞". Glued on backing sheet (by WW?). See "for criticism L of Grass," which is a version of this MS and can be dated between 1880 and 1883. The MS was probably written to keep Dr. Bucke on the true way in his *Walt Whitman*. (Duke also holds seven portions of revised MS of Bucke's book—Trent *Cat.*, pp. 63ff.) See also *Walt Whitman. Walt Whitman's Autograph Revision of the Analysis of Leaves of Grass* (NY, 1944).

Two suggestion points for letter[1]

We have had man in love and war, (perhaps indeed[2] the most merely[3] natural, universal elements of human lives, human interest)—man in courts, bowers, castles, dungeons—man in personal haughtiness, and contests of strength, as in Homer—or passion[4] crime, jealousy, morbid infatuation, carried to extremes, as in Shakspere—humanity in divine ravishing tales, always with an indoor atmosphere, and under artificial and feudal relations. But never before have we so thoroughly[5] had Man in the open air, confronting, and a part of, Nature and the seasons, and so squarely[6] adjusted as one might describe it, to the sun by day,[7] the stars by night, and affiliated to their own spirit,[8] as in these poems.[9]

He turns Nature,[10] with its *ensembles*, always in human relations. It is not only the infinite and relentless Queen, unspeakably mysterious and separate; it is[11] our Mother, holding us with undying ties, affections. Tenderly she gave us birth—is ever ready for us through life, with health, with silence, with consolation; tenderly receives us at death. Then the singular problems of the subjectiveness of

1. In blue crayon. Trent *Cat.*, 49, suggests that it is a later addition.
2. Inserted above "ps" in "perhaps" and "the"
3. Inserted above "st" in "most"
4. End of first scrap.
5. Preceding two words inserted above "we had"
6. Preceding two words inserted above "and" and "adj" in "adjusted"
7. Deleted: "and"
8. Preceding six words inserted above "as in these poems"
9. End of second scrap.
10. Deleted: "into" ; inserted above: "with its"
11. Deleted: "also"

Man in the objectiveness of[12] the Universe—"thou art so near, and yet so far"[13]—
Whitman unhesitatingly grapples with,[14] and I think solves them as far as they
are capable of solution

12. Deleted: "Nature" ; inserted: "the Universe" above "of" and "[*del.*] Nature"
13. Alfred Tennyson, *In Memoriam* (1855), xcvii.
14. Deleted: [*illeg.*] ; inserted above: "and"

For Dr B's Criticism.

Manuscript in Duke (45, #20). Inscribed in pencil and black ink on two leaves of white wove paper (corners clipped), 6½" x 4½" and 6" x 4½". *FC&I*, 52, identifies it as a note for the proposed revision of Bucke's *Walt Whitman* (1883) and calls attention to a fuller, probably earlier, version in *SD* (*Prose 92*, I, 1–3). The date is, therefore, probably later than 1883. First printed in *FC&I*, 52.

for Dr B's criticism

as far as it may be stated the[1] purpose object[2] of *Specimen Days*[3] was to combine[4] & weave for them it & for me in one pattern (for those at all interested in it, or caring to pick it out, and for my own satisfaction,)[5] certain variegated[6] record-threads of my personal experiences early years, young manhood in New York City and Brooklyn, with what I had seen[7] of the Secession War 1861–'5,[8] hospital Scenes and interiors,[9] the actual rank and file from all the States,[10]— afterward, for four or five[11] years; notes and jottings of simple out-door rural Nature, as playing upon the emotions of a convalescent, a half-paralytic, and played upon in return—some [2] of my reflections in the mean time,[12] on literary characters, especially Carlyle,—with a "Collect" of various pieces, comments on[13] my time and spirit of the time, especially as in "Democratic Vistas")—[14] all scooped

1. Capital not reduced in MS, not printed.
2. Written above "purpose"
3. Deleted: "those"
4. Inserted and deleted in black ink: "or" ; inserted and deleted in black ink: "& weave for those who were interested in [*del.*] them [*ins.*] it or cared for [*del.*] them [*ins.*] it & for one certain variegated" ; inserted in black ink: "& weave for them . . . certain variegated record-threads"
5. Parenthetical passage in black ink at top of page. Point of insertion indicated by asterisks not shown here. Pencil, deleted in black ink: "various threads" ; inserted in black ink: "certain variegated record-threads"
6. Deleted in pencil: "life" ; inserted: "experiences"
7. Deleted: "and"
8. Deleted in pencil: "the Sec" ; preceding ten words and comma inserted in black ink.
9. Pencil, deleted in black ink: "of the Secession War of 1861—'5—certain jottings of" ; black ink, deleted in black ink: "Abrah[?]" . MS continues in black ink.
10. Deleted: "than[?]—notes an"
11. Preceding five words and comma inserted.
12. Preceding four words and comma inserted.
13. Deleted: "the" ; inserted: "my"
14. Deleted: "some of" . Next word begins a new line and is indented.

and swept in together, indeed ([15] like[16] hauling a fish-Seine)—some[17] parts and pieces elaborated,[18] stated as I am content to have them—but a great deal of the book crude notes and diary-jottings, personal and perhaps trivial—my purpose being, (I suppose) to give[19] glints and glances into[20] actual life-happenings

15. Parentheses in purple crayon.
16. Deleted: "fish in" ; deleted in purple crayon: "the result of"
17. Deleted: "of the"
18. Deleted: "and"
19. Deleted: "some genuine"
20. Deleted: "a," "my"

It Is Not.

Manuscript not found. Text from Traubel, II, 105. When Traubel read it to WW on August 7, 1888, WW laughed and said: "That's when I lift myself by my suspenders and put myself on a pedestal of my own make. . . ." Then more seriously: "It is a kind of self analysis which may amount to much or little according to whose perspective it gets into. You know I said from the first that Leaves of Grass was not to achieve a negative recognition—was bound to be a howling success or a stupendous failure. When I wrote that paragraph I must have felt prosperous." No date can be assigned.

It is not when matched with other verse and tested by the ordinary intellectual or esthetic lineaments they compare favorably with that verse; probably by those tests indeed they do not equal the best poems. But the impalpable atmosphere which every page of Leaves of Grass has sprung from, and which it exhales forever, makes a spell, a fascination, to one capable of appreciating it, that certainly belongs to no other poet, no other poem, ever yet known.

I Only Take.

Manuscript in Texas (Hanley). Inscribed in purple crayon on an irregular scrap of faded white wove. Cancelled by WW. The writing and the use of purple crayon suggest a late date.

I only take the United States into my theme so far as bearing on such result. Though they have the greatest bearing— And in fact, deeply ciphered out, *that* (and not merely "good government" in the usual sense) forms the distinctive reason for being[?] of these States

I Hope to Go.

Manuscript not found. Text from Traubel, II, 108. Traubel says it was dropped from "A Backward Glance O'er Travel'd Roads" in the preparation of *NB* because WW wanted a blank space at the foot of p. 118. This was written in 1888.

I hope to go on record for something different—something better, if I may dare to say so. If I rested "Leaves of Grass" on the usual claims—if I did not feel that the deepest moral, social, political purposes of America are the underlying endeavors at least of my pages; that the geography and hydrography of the continent, the Prairies, the St. Lawrence, Ohio, the Carolinas, Texas, Missouri are their real veins and current concrete—I should not dare to have them put in type, and printed, and offer'd for sale.

On the Other Side.

Manuscript in Texas (Hanley). Inscribed in black ink with emendations in black pencil and red ink on tan wove paper, 7⅝" x 6¼". Furness, who prints the MS in part (123), says the phrase "parrot-like repetitions" is from one of Rossetti's first letters to WW (December 8, 1867: Traubel, III, 305). Although Rossetti used it in mentioning external eccentricities in *LG*—the numbering of separate stanzas, he was referring, actually, to the reiterated charges of eccentricity brought by critics. WW obviously took it seriously. The writing indicates a date much later than 1867, as does the reference to the *Collect* (1882). WW used the phrase in "Note at End," *CPP*, and in *Preface Note to 2d Annex Concluding L of G. —1891* in *LG* (1891–92). (See *Prose 92*, II, 733–734, 736.) The MS seems closer to the *GBMF* Preface. This was written between 1891 and 1892. First printed in Leon Bazalgette, *Walt Whitman. L'Homme et Son Oeuvre* (Paris: 1908), I, frontispiece, from MS given Bazalgette by Traubel.

on the other side[1] I have had serious doubts about[2] writing this letter—but have finally concluded to try it as[3] foregoing[4]—Thoughts and granulations—random[5] passages, as they follow each other—[6] not so much[7] in explanation or defence of[8] the Volume (for the only real explanation is in itself)[9] but kindred to or hinting of[10] the atmosphere both of its incipiency and fruition. A good deal that might strictly[11] belong[12] to[13] the present letter holds position already in *Specimen Days and Collect.** note[14] It is quite possible too there may be "parrot-like repetitions"—which danger, however, has not troubled me. But as the[15]

1. Preceding four words inserted above "I have had"
2. Deleted: "the good of a Preface at all to Leaves of Grass" ; inserted: "writing this letter" above "[*del.*] all to Leaves"
3. Deleted: "herewith" ; inserted above: "foregoing"
4. Inserted and deleted: "([*illeg.*])"
5. Deleted: "random and detach'd"
6. Preceding dashes and seven words inserted; deleted: "—suggestion—keeps, such as they are,"
7. Preceding two words inserted above "not in"
8. Deleted: "L of G" ; inserted over deletion: "the volume"
9. Parenthetical statement inserted above "fence" in "defence" and "but"
10. Preceding three words inserted above "d" in "kindred" and "to"
11. Deleted in black pencil: "base"
12. Deleted in black pencil: " 'd"
13. Deleted: "this essay" ; inserted above: "the present letter"
14. Red ink.
15. Deleted: "ensuing"

His Theory Is.

Manuscript not found. The "writer" and the "interlocutor" cannot, of course, be identified. The "intaglio frontispiece" might refer to *LG* 1860, 1876, 1885, or later editions. Published in "Walt Whitman: Unpublished Notes and Letters," *Wake,* 7 (Autumn, 1948), 10.

His theory is, in almost his own words, that there are two natures in Walt Whitman. The one is of immense suavity, self-control, a mysticism like the occasional fits of Socrates and a pervading Christ-like benevolence tenderness and sympathy (the sentiment of the intaglio frontispiece portrait, which I showed him, and he said he had seen exactly that look in "the old man," and more than twice during 1863–'65, though he never observed it before or since.) But these qualities, though he has enthroned them, and for many years governed his life by them, are duplicated by far sterner ones. No doubt he has mastered the latter, but he has them. How could Walt Whitman (said my interlocutor), have taken the attitude toward evil, and things evil, which is behind every page of his utterance in *Leaves of Grass,* from first to last—so different on that subject from ever writer known, new or old unless he enfolded all that evil within him? (To all of which I give place here, as not essentially inconsistent—if true—with my own theory of the poet's nature; and also because I am determined to take the fullest view of him and from all sides.)

But This Complete Rupture.

Manuscript in LC (Feinberg #705). Inscribed in pencil on white wove paper, approx. 7″ x 4¾″. Blue rules ⁵/₁₆″ apart. The writing does not look like WW's, but was accepted by Bucke, Edward Naumburg, and Feinberg. The date is not ascertainable. Published in *Wake,* 7 (Autumn, 1948), 16. (Gene Edward Veith, Jr.)

But this complete rupture with the customary rules and definitions offends most readers at first sight. One tries too much to appraise Wh. by the flank of critical reason. But whoever comprehends him rightly will find that his effect upon the reader is not as much[1] intellectual as moral. To speak in Wh. language I would call the influence of these poems in a high, if not in the highest degree a physiological one. He himself demands, among other things,[2] that a poesy, which[3] pretends to satisfy the[4] wants of[5] the American republic, must make it's appearance in the spiritual as well as in the physical being of the reader, like healthy nourishment or pure air.

1. Deleted: "as"
2. Deleted: "of" ; inserted above: "that"
3. Deleted: "arrogates to itself"
4. Deleted: "claims" ; inserted above: "wants"
5. {*Illeg.*} marks or deletion.

And Here in This Article.

Manuscript in LC (Feinberg #705). A scrap of white wove paper, approx. 3¼" x 4⅜", inscribed in ink, pasted onto a scrap of bright blue wove paper, approx. 2½" x 5", inscribed in pencil. The MS might have been written at any time after 1870, and the writing suggests a date after 1873. (Gene Edward Veith, Jr.)

[1] And here in This article,[2] which is written to present[3] truthfully,[4] & plainly one side of the story[5] indispensable to the examination, (now[6] just seriously beginning)[7] of[8] Walt Whitman's writings,[9] may[10] perhaps not improperly be given in the brief,[11] the spinal idea of[12] Walt Whitman's[13] & poetry.

Much has been written about it. We doubt if a single article has yet penetrated or stated it.

1. Deleted false start: "All this" ; inserted and deleted: "For" above "And" ; inserted: "And" and "[del.] so here in" above "his"
2. Inserted and deleted: "be it remembered" above "ticle" in "article" and "[ins.] which is written" ; inserted: "which" above "is"
3. Deleted: "truth"
4. Deleted: "& as far as it goes, one" ; inserted: "& plainly [del.] a one" above "as far as it" and "g" in "goes"
5. Deleted: "of grave importance" ; inserted: "indispensable" above "[del.] of grave"
6. Deleted: "for seri"
7. Deleted: "in a few, (real minds"
8. Deleted: "Leav"
9. End of first scrap.
10. Inserted and deleted: "here" above "p" in "perhaps"
11. Preceding three words inserted.
12. Deleted: "these writings" above wordspace and "the"
13. Deleted: "writings"

III.   Attempts to Define the Poet's Role and Tradition.

One Obligation.

Manuscript not found. Text from *N&F,* 124 (Pt. III, #141; *CW,* VI, 149–150). The thought and the punctuation suggest the Preface of 1855.

One obligation of great fresh bards remains . . . the clink of words is empty and offensive . . . the poetic quality blooms simple and earnest as the laws of the world.

The audible rhyme soon nauseates . . . the inaudible rhyme is delicious without end.

Of This Broad.

Manuscript not found. Text from *N&F,* 104 (Pt. III, #70; *CW,* IX, 108). The imagery is not unlike the Preface of 1855, *LG CRE,* 711, l. 60ff. The date is probably before or shortly after 1855.

Of this broad and majestic universe, all in the visible world, and much in the greater world invisible, is owned by the Poet. He owns the solid ground and tills it and reaps from every field and harvests cotton and grain and clover. All the woods and all the orchards—the corn ear and stalk and tassel, the buckwheat its white tops and the bees that hum there all day—the salt meadows . . . .

Ferdusi.

Manuscript in NYPL (Berg). Inscribed in black pencil on faded white butcher paper, 2⅜" x 7⅝". The paper appears to be the same as that in "Hans Sachs" and "Author of the Neibelungen Leid." "Dante" and "Boccacio" were possibly part of the same MS list, but it was impossible to compare the paper. According to Stovall, *AL,* 26 (1954), 361, the phrases are from Carlyle's *Critical and Miscellaneous Essays* (edition and volume not cited). The writing and the fact that it was a Bucke MS suggest that this was written before 1860. First printed as part of a jumble of phrases in *N&F,* 167 (Pt. III, #51; *CW,* X, 14).

"Ferdusi, and the primeval mythologists of Hindostan"/
"The wayward mystic gloom of Calderon,"
"The lurid fire of Dante,"
"The auroral light of Tasso"
"The clear icy glitter of Racine"[:]Carlyle

Paths of Rhyme.

Manuscript in LC (#63, sheet #286). Inscribed in pencil on blue Williamsburgh tax blank, 8⅞" x 4¾". Published in Herbert Bergman, "Whitman and Tennyson," *SP,* 51 (July, 1956), 500. The date is 1857 or later.

paths[1] of rhyme, with Spenser, Dryden, Tennyson, and the rest
—Let them[2] in choice phrases, with rich fancies and imagery,[3] depict so well the events and characters they have chosen
Let them write "poetry" according to the models, and[4] according to the criticisms of other lands.—

1. Original opening word deleted: "roam"
2. Deleted: "tell"
3. Deleted: "all then tell" ; inserted: "depict"
4. Deleted: "as the"

Friday April 24, '57.

Manuscript in Duke (45, #21). Inscribed in black pencil on scrap of thin brown paper, approx. 7¾" x 4½". At one time a newspaper clipping was pasted to the upper left corner. First printed in *N&F*, 57 (Pt. II, #17; *CW*, IX, 57).

Friday April 24, '57.
True vista before

The strong thought—impression or conviction that the straight, broad, open, well-marked true *"vista before,* or [1] course of public teacher, "wander-speaker,"— by powerful words, orations, uttered with copiousness and decision, with all the aid of art, also the natural flowing vocal [2] luxuriance of oratory— That the mightiest rule over America could be thus—as, for instance, on occasion, at Washington to be, launching from public room, at the opening of the session of Congress— perhaps launching at the President, leading persons, Congressmen, or Judges of the Supreme Court— That to dart hither or thither, as some great emergency might demand—the greatest Champion America ever could know, yet holding no office or emolument whatever,—but first in the esteem of men and women

—*Not* to direct eyes or thoughts to any of the usual avenues, as of official appointment, or to get such any way— To put all those aside for good.— But always to keep up living interest in public questions,—and *always to hold the ear of people.—*

1. Three preceding words inserted above "course of"
2. Inserted above "lux" in "luxuriance"

The Florid Rich.

Manuscript in Duke (35, #27). Inscribed in black pencil on two pasted scraps: [1] pocket ledger paper, approx. 2¼" x 2¾", horizontal rules approx. ⅜" apart, vertical red rules for accounts; [2] pink wove paper, approx. 4⅞" x 5½". First printed in *N&F*, 98 (Pt. III, #54; *CW*, IX, 96). The paper suggests a date between 1855 and 1860.

The florid rich, first?[1] phases of poetry, as in the Oriental Poems,—the Bible[2]—Arabian Nights, Tales of the Genii, Ossian, the Indians of America, (Logan,)[3]—Song of Spring from the Persian[4]

The primitive poets, their subjects, their style, all assimilate.— Very ancient poetry, of[5] the Hebrew prophets, of[6] Ossian, of[7] the Hindu[8] singers and extatics, of the Greeks, of the American aborigines, of the old Persians and Chinese, and the Scandinavian sagas,[9] all resemble each other

1. Query written above "first"
2. Preceding two words inserted above dash before "Arabian"
3. James Logan (ca. 1725–1780) was a Mingo chief. A letter from him to Lord Dunmore refusing to make peace was much admired as a specimen of eloquence, most notably by Jefferson in his *Notes on the State of Virginia*.
4. End of pocket ledger paper.
5. Inserted above wordspace between "poetry" and "of"
6. Inserted above wordspace between "prophets" and "Ossian,"
7. Inserted above wordspace between "Ossian" and "the"
8. Deleted: "fathers" ; inserted and deleted above: [*illeg*.]; inserted: "singers and extatics, of the Greeks ["s" *ins*.] [*del*.] states of" above "the American aborigines,"
9. Preceding seven words inserted above "the old . . . other"

The Word.

Manuscript in Duke (11, #26). Inscribed in black ink on a brownish slip. A slightly incorrect quotation of John *i*.14, "The Word was made flesh and came to dwell among us." WW may simply have jotted down a central Biblical statement, but it seems likely that he is using it as a metaphor of the inspired nature of poetry. See " 'Still lives the song." First printed in *N&F,* 167 (Pt. IV, #52; *CW,* X, 15).

The Word is become Flesh.

Literature It Is Certain.

Manuscript not found. Text from *N&F,* 143(Pt. III, #189; *CW,* IX, 143). This probably was written in the 1850s.

Literature it is certain would be fuller of vigor and sanity if authors were in the habit of composing in the forenoon—and never at night.

What We Call Literature.

Manuscript in Duke (16, #39). Inscribed in black pencil on white laid paper, approx. 2⅜" x 7¹³/₁₆". Brown rules ⅜" apart. Since it was a Bucke MS, the date is probably in the 1850s. First printed in *N&F,* 69 (Pt. II, #56; *CW,* IX, 33).

What we call Literature is but[1] the[2] moist and wobbling cub,[3] just born and its eyes not open yet in many days.[4]— You are[5] a living man, and think; in that alone is a more heightless and fathomless wonder than all the productions of letters and arts in all the[6] nations and periods of this earth.—

1. Deleted: "a [?]"
2. Deleted: "blind" ; inserted above: "moist"
3. Deleted: "new" ; inserted above: "just"
4. Deleted: "I am" ; inserted above: "You are"
5. Deleted: "an" ; inserted "a"
6. Deleted: "years" ; inserted: "nations and periods" above "[*del.*] years" and "of"

In Those Days.

Manuscript in Middlebury. Inscribed in black pencil on white wove scrap, approx. 3½" x 5". The writing indicates a date in the late 1850s.

In those[1] days the bards were the only historians.— They were far more.— All that[2] all times lives in[3] men and women, the feelings, the aspirations, pride, majesty, delicacy, adhesiveness, amativeness, the dread of being thought mean, the demand for[4] a vague more[5] and better, than practically life affords[6]—urged[7] audiences for the singers and poets of those rude[8] races, and made[9] the bards who spoke to them sacred and beloved.

1. Deleted: "early times" ; inserted: "days" above "[del.] times"
2. Deleted: "at"
3. Deleted: "all"
4. Inserted: "[del.] the a vague" above "more"
5. Deleted: "than"
6. Preceding four words inserted on two lines above "better," . Deleted: "these"
7. Deleted: "the"
8. Deleted: "nations"
9. Deleted: "them" ; inserted: "the bards who spoke to them" on three lines.

What Shall the Great Poet.

Manuscript in Duke (17, #40). Inscribed in black pencil on white laid paper, approx. 1½″ x 5⅜″. The writing suggests a date in the 1850s.

What shall the great poet be then? Shall he be a timid apologetic person, deprecating himself, guarding off the effects he won

Is Literature Forever.

Manuscript in LC (Feinberg #835). Inscribed in black pencil on pink paper (wrapper?), 6⅜" x 5". The paper suggests a date in the late 1850s.

Is Literature forever to propose no higher object than to amuse? to just pass away the time & stave off ennui ?—[1] Is[2] it never to be the courageous wrestle with[3] live subjects—[4] the strong gymnasia of the mind—[5] must it offer only things easy to understand[6] as nature never[7] does.

1. Sentence written at top of leaf. Deleted: "I do not propose to amuse you, except in that highest amusement the n [*preceding two words del.*] (but that is truly worthy men [*preceding three words del.*] perhaps the [*del.*] truest [*ins.*] true amusement for [*preceding five words ins.*] American men, American women.)"
2. Written over "It" . Deleted: "consists in the is" ; inserted above: "it never to be"
3. Deleted: "strong"
4. Deleted: "real the" ; inserted and deleted: "the" above "[*del.*] the" ; inserted: "It is [*preceding two words del.*] the strong" above "[*del.*] the" and "gymnasia"
5. Deleted: "I have no [*preceding three words del.*] do not [*preceding two words ins.*] cannot offor offer you the easy most" ; inserted: "must offer only"
6. Deleted: "any more than" ; inserted: "as" above "[*del.*] than"
7. Inserted above wordspace before and above "does"

Taking En-Masse.

Manuscript in LC (Feinberg #19). Inscribed in black ink with some corrections in black pencil on Williamsburgh tax blank. The paper and writing indicate a date after 1856. The writing, indeed, resembles that more often found in the 1860s.

[1][1] Taking en-masse[2] what is called literature, we have this to say: Of heroes, history, grand events, premises, myths, poems,[3] &c. &c. the few drops[4] known must stand as representatives[5] for oceans of the unknown.[6] So Busy, on this beautiful and thick-peopled earth, has all life,[7] all action been for tens of thousands[8] perhaps hundreds of thousands, of years[9]. —with but here and there, as accident has had it, a little sample specimen[10] put in record—[11] which them we have received[12].— How sparse! How puny! How much we have never rec'd[13] never heard of![14] —A little of the Greeks and Romans —A few Hebrew [2] canticles —A few death-odors, as from graves, from[15] Egypt;[16] —what are they,[17] to the long and copious retrospect of antiquity—many of its nations, perhaps the[18] greatest of them preceding all we have heard, perhaps[19] a greater literature,[20] —even the names of those nations and their works[21] quite unknown to us.—

1. Deleted at top of page: "Of all heroes"
2. Inserted above "what"
3. Inserted above "ths," in "myths,"
4. Deleted: "are"
5. Deleted: "of the" ; inserted: "for" above "[del.] of" . WW deleted a redundant "pre" in "representatives"
6. Deleted: "Here is the thick" ; inserted above: "So [del.] This Busy on this"
7. Preceding two words inserted above "has all"
8. Preceding two words inserted above "ds," in "hundreds," and "of"
9. Deleted: "and" ; inserted above: "with but,"
10. Inserted in black pencil above "sample" ; deleted: "has been"
11. Deleted: "and" ; inserted above: "which them"
12. Deleted: "it"
13. Deleted: "have"
14. Preceding sentence inserted above "How . . . —A"
15. Deleted: "dead"
16. Deleted: "a-but w"
17. Deleted: "after all but [ins. and del. above deleted "all in"] shreds in comparison"
18. Deleted: "best"
19. Deleted: "with"
20. Deleted: "perhaps—the very" ; inserted above deleted "the very" : "even the"
21. Deleted: "at all"

It Is Not That.

Manuscript not found. Text from *N&F,* 68 (Pt. III, #48; *CW,* IX, 30). The bracket may indicate a lacuna in WW's text, such as appears elsewhere in his notes. The ideas suggest that WW wrote this in the 1850s.

It is not that the realities of all these things are in the books themselves—in the poems etc. The realities are in the realities only, in the earth, water, plants, animals, souls, men and women. Poems are to arouse the reason, suggest, give freedom, strength, muscle, candor to any person that reads them—and assist that person to see the realities for himself in his own way, with his own individuality and after his own fashion.

Names. The Biblical Poets.

Manuscript not found. Text from *N&F,* 166 (Pt. IV, #51; *CW,* X, 13), as part of a number of scraps grouped together by Bucke. First published in *N&F.*

Names. The Biblical poets—David, Isaiah, the Book of Job—etc. Also the New Testament writers. Merlin. Thomas the Rymer, Scotch, lived during 13th century, died 1299—supposed 80 years old. Hafiz. Sadi—Persian—about the year 1000 A. D. Eschylus. Sophocles. Euripides.

I Think All.

Manuscript not found. Text from *N&F,* 93 (Pt. III, #38; *CW,* IX, 87). The date, like that of many of WW's notes on his reading, is probably in the late 1850s.

I think all the peculiarities of poets (perhaps of all marked persons) are to be taken calmly and in a spirit of latitude, not criticised and found fault with. *Those traits were the men*—facts in nature the same as facts in the landscape, in mathematics, in chemistry. This must of course be applied to Milton, Pope, Tennyson etc., just the same as any.

We Know of No Beginning.

Manuscript not found. Text from *N&F*, 102 (Pt. III, #63; *CW*, IX, 105–106). Bucke inserts "[know]" in the second sentence. This probably was written between 1855 and 1860.

We know of no beginning in universal literature any more than in chronology. We only [know] what is first to be mentioned.

The first literature to be mentioned is doubtless Assyrian literature and the literature of Egypt and Hindostan. Many, many thousands years since, books, histories, poems, romances, Bibles, hymns, works illustrative of mechanics, science, arithmetic, humor, Government, war, manners, manufactures and all the principal themes of interest to civilized life and to men and women, were common in the great Asiatic cities of Nineveh and Babylon and their empires, and in the empire of Hindostan, and in the African Memphis and Thebes and through Egypt and Ethiopia. Cheap copies of these books circulated among the commonality or were eligible to them. Vast libraries existed; there were institutions in which learning and religion grew together. Religion had a deep and proportionate meaning, the best fitted to the people and the times. Astronomy was understood—with which no nation can be degraded nor any race of learned persons remain without grand thoughts and poems.

. . . . As the Highest.

Manuscript in Rollins College. Inscribed in black ink on five, pasted-together, faded, white, wove scraps, overall 14″ x 5″. The content is characteristic of almost any of WW's theoretical statements. The writing appears to be of the 1860s.

[1] . . . . As the highest achievements of the modern genius in Literature and Art[2] are to furnish a yet unknown & undreamed of development for the masses[3] of the people, the[4] broadest avenue toward that result is probably to be the entrance by common humanity, in due time, upon entirely different & far more spiritual views of Death.[5]

What a spectacle will that be of future New World philosophs & poets—successive dynasties of them—depicting[6] such life &[7] such Death[8]—making of average Man a God—embodying in superior poems the whole genius of Democracy,—arrived at last—[9] justifying its slow progress, & its long & varied developments through History[10]— illustrating by works[11] ahead of any yet its culmination in These States—pourtraying new &[12] per[13]fect races of Women—& finally developing, beyond all hitherto, & adjusted to Science & the modern, the ideas of the Immortal, & of that viewless & Unknown Experience,[14]—that[15] stage & sphere[16]

---

1. Deleted paragraph: "In my opinion it is [*illeg. ins.*] [*illeg. ins. and del.*] the idea of Immortality, above all other ideas, [*preceding four words and comma inserted*] that is to enter essentially into, & give final coloring to Democracy."

2 Preceding four words inserted above "genius are to"

3. End of first scrap.

4. Deleted: "[*illeg.*] primal &"

5. Preceding three words inserted above "more spiritual" . End of second scrap. Words have been trimmed off, possibly the three inserted words.

6. Deleted: "heroic" ; inserted above: "such"

7. Deleted: "spiritual" ; inserted above: "such"

8. End of third scrap.

9. Preceding three words and dash inserted above "racy" in "democracy" and "ju" in "justifying"

10. Deleted: "& Time"

11. End of fourth scrap.

12. Preceding two words inserted above "ing" in "pourtraying" and "per" in "perfect"

13. End of fifth scrap.

14. Deleted: "which all that goes before" ; inserted above in two lines: "—that stage & sphere which all that goes beyond"

15. Inserted and deleted: [*illeg.*]

16. Deleted: "of"

which all that goes beyond & all we know or view, or fancy we know or view,[17] is doubtless [18] not only for itself but for identity, for preparation.

17. Inserted and deleted: [*illeg*] ; inserted: "[*ins.*] or fancy we know or view" ; inserted and deleted: "and all that you [*illeg.*]"

18. Deleted: "mainly the preparation" ; inserted above: "not only for itself but [*del.*] for" ; inserted and deleted: "Still more for a Preparation [*illeg.*]" above following insertion; inserted: "for identity, for preparation."

Poet! Beware.

Manuscript in Pennsylvania. Inscribed in black ink on white wove paper, 5½″ x 7¾″. The writing suggests a date in the 1860s. First published in *N&F,* 58 (Pt. III, #21; *CW,* IX, 10).

Poet![1] beware lest your poems[2] are made in the spirit that comes from the study of pictures of things—and not from the spirit that comes from the contact with real things theselves

1. Deleted: "are" ; inserted: "beware lest" above the deletion and "your"
2. Deleted: "not" ; inserted above: "are"

That There Should Be.

Manuscript in LC (#58, sheet #260). Inscribed in black ink on brown wove paper, approx. 9″ x 5¾″. Carelessly trimmed left and bottom edges. At the beginning is deleted: "Yes, Poetry may be considered, among the rest, [*preceding six words and comma ins. on two lines above* "Poetry as"] as a *rounded orbic whole, inclusive of every thing* [*preceding four words ins. on three lines at the left following* "whole"]." The writing suggests a date after 1860.

That there should be a good deal of waste land and many[1] sterile spots, is an inherent necessity of the case—perhaps that the greater part of the rondure should be waste. Nature sows countless seeds, makes incessantly crude attempts—[2]— thankful to get now and then a something approximately good.

1. Inserted above "nd" in "and" and "st" in "sterile"
2. Preceding four words and dash inserted above "countless seeds" "thankful"

A Modern "Poem."

Manuscript in Yale. Inscribed in black ink on white laid paper, 6⅝" x 8". Blue rules ⁷/₁₆" apart, red-blue-red margin 1⅜" from left edge. The writing seems to be between 1860 and 1873.

A modern "poem" is as if a proper & fashionable suit of clothes, well made, good cloth, fair linen, a gold watch,[1] etc. were to walk about, demanding ? audience[2]— The[3] clothes are all well enough; but the objection would be, there is no man in them—no virility there.

1. Deleted: "& &"
2. Inserted in small script in space left blank. Question mark above.
3. Deleted: "objection would be"

Poets—Shakespeare.

Manuscript in Texas (Hanley). Inscribed in pencil with emendations in black ink on a half-sheet of white wove notepaper, 8¹/₁₆″ x 4⅞″, torn off from a larger sheet at right. Tan-shaded embossed upside down at lower right. Blue rules ⁵/₁₆″ apart. Upper margin at bottom. The embossing suggests a date during the War (see "take (Marg. D Valois"). First printed by Edward G. Bernard, "Some New Whitman Manuscript Notes," *AL,* 8 (March, 1936), 62.

Poets—Shakespeare Orientalism[?] Poe *Tennyson* soul's procession[1] Orientalism Conclusion of lectures on Poems

From the point of view of Humanity's and the Ages' ensemble[2] *for all that*[3] the Civilization, history, politics needing their[4] myriads of influences &[5] long cycles of time to unfold, are best defined &[6] expressed by a few comparatively short poems each [*illeg.*] or cluster of [*illeg.*] or series of influences[7] [*illeg.*] [*illeg.*] [*illeg.*]

The dreamy[?] meditative transcendentalism of Asia in the[8] Zend & Sanscript—and all[9] that lies beneath the tremendous chronology & vast conception of India in the Ramayana & Mahabarata

—the Syrian canticles, the Book of Job and the other books & emerging from them the idylls of the life of C[10]

1. WW projected a poem of this title in 1869 or later.
2. In black ink.
3. Deleted: "[*illeg.*] phi" ; inserted in ink following: "the"
4. Inserted above "myr" in "myriads"
5. Deleted: "[*illeg.*] centuries" ; inserted above in ink: "long cycles of time"
6. Preceding three words inserted in ink above "are" and "express" in "expressed"
7. Preceding four words inserted in ink above first two illegible entries.
8. Deleted: "L"
9. Deleted: "the history of" ; inserted: "that lies beneath" above "all" and "[*del.*] the history"
10. Presumably "Christ"

Of Late—That.

Manuscript in Texas (Hanley). Inscribed in black pencil on faded white laid paper, 7⅝″ x 4¾″. Blue pencil line down left margin. Although the writing is somewhat cramped, as compared to the running script of the 1860s, the MS may date from the late 1860s, when WW, as *DV* shows, was concerned about the dangers of Culture.

of late[1]—that there is a line beyond which even real art, refinement, "education" poetry &c. do deadly harm to the character

1. Deleted: "—or think I see"

—How Different.

Manuscript in LC (#231). Inscribed in black pencil with corrections in black pencil and black ink on white laid scrap, embossed "Philp and Solomon Washington DC" at upper left. Blue rules ½" apart. The writing and the use of this paper suggest a date in the late 1860s.

—How different[1] the[2] more cultivated, more mathematical,[3] cold & continent &[4] in[5] important respects far[6] more valuable, European intellect & aesthetic[7]— Yet in religion & poetry the old[8] Asiatic land dominates to this day and will until[9] above the world shall[10] rise[11] peaks still higher than the Hebrew[12] Bible[13] the Ionian Iliad, & the psalms[14] & great epics[15] of India.[16]

1. Deleted: "with"
2. Deleted: "far"
3. Deleted: "far more"
4. Deleted: "[*illeg.*] this"
5. Deleted: "most" ; inserted above: "important"
6. Inserted in ink above and preceding "move"
7. Preceding three words inserted above "valuable,—Yet" ; inserted and deleted: [*illeg.*] following "aesthetic"
8. Inserted above wordspace between "the" and "Asiatic"
9. Inserted and deleted in ink: "to above" above "the" ; inserted: "above" under deleted "above"
10. Inserted above "rise"
11. Deleted: "two"
12. Inserted in ink above "Bi" in "Bible"
13. Deleted in ink: "& the song of India"
14. Preceding six words inserted in pencil above "[*del.*] & Ionia" . Inserted in ink, deleted in pencil: "& the chants" under "& the psalms & great epics"
15. Preceding two words inserted in ink following "& the psalms &"
16. In ink. Inserted and deleted in ink: "& the Ionian epic" following "India"

Amid the Vast.

Manuscript not found. Text from *N&F,* 61 (Pt. II, #31; *CW,* IX, 15). The bracketed words are Bucke's. The material seems to be related in subject and tone to the MS Introductions written in the late 1860s and 1870s.

Amid the vast and complicated edifice of human beings many accomplishments and fitments and furnishings—the results of History and civilization, as they have come to us—the various conventions, social, ecclesiastical, literary, political—the resistless and precious accretion, always treated by him [the poet] with respect and even reverence. Amid this edifice or complex mass of edifices he builds, as it were, an impregnable and lofty tower, a part of all with the rest, and over-looking all—the citadel of the primary volitions, the soul, the ever-reserved right of a deathless Individuality—and these he occupies and dwells, and thence makes observations and issues verdicts.

(Personalism.

Manuscript in LC (Feinberg #17). Inscribed in black ink and, as noted, pencil on white wove paper, 4¾" x 7¾", cut from the bottom of a longer sheet. Blue rules on recto ½" apart. Left edge appears to have been torn from a pad of binding. In his card catalog, Feinberg dates the MS in 1856 and calls attention to "The Song of Prudence" (1856), which is derived from the 1855 Preface. The writing, however, which is larger and more flowing than other MS written in 1855 and 1856, suggests a date in the 1860s. The topics also suggest a date closer to *DV* (1871). The second part of *DV* (*Prose 92*, II, 291–403, ll. 894–1275) was published separately as "Personalism" in the *Galaxy* (May, 1868). One of the leading topics of *DV* is the inadequacy of "Culture." See also "I do not feel to write" and "of late—that." The date is more likely ca. 1867.

(¹ Personalism

Culture, as used, means human knowledge acquirements.² -Announce
    that the Devout Spirit,³ Conscienciousness A sense of immortality the spirit-
    ual sense the spiritual prudence
-spiritual prudence⁴
nearly altogether omitted in modern formulas, & in the atmosphere of poems & all the literary products.

1. Curved line at left of and below word.
2. Inserted in pencil.
3. The following four attributes of culture are in column under "Devout Spirit"
4. Phrase emphasized by a pointing fist at beginning and end and line around the whole.

In a Brief Passage.

Manuscript in LC (Feinberg #835). Inscribed in black ink on white wove paper, 8⅛″ x 5″. Blue rules ⅜″ apart. The rounded right corners suggest a leaf neatly removed from a bound notebook. The paper and the loose writing suggest a date in the late 1870s or the 1880s.

In a brief passage give a description of—& do justice to—Modern Literature, its best leading features.

The Bible Shakspere.

Manuscript in Folger Shakespeare Library (Black Box 106 Whitman). Inscribed in black pencil on yellow wove paper, approx. 12″ x 10½″, folded lengthwise to right of inscription. It is not clear whether this is an inventory or a project for a lecture series. Since Symonds's *Studies of the Greek Poets* appeared in two series in 1873 and 1876, this MS cannot be earlier than 1873. It is probably later, for WW's copy of Symonds is dated 1880 (Feinberg *Cat., #* 384).

The Bible   Shakspere[1]   Homer[2] (Iliad, Odessey, Hymns &c T.A Buckley's literal translation) Eschylus, Sophocles, Euripides Pindar. Dante's INFERNO: (literal prose trans by Dr. J. A Carlyle.)[3] OSSIAN   Walter Scott's BORDER MIN-STRELSY   Robert Burns. (Macmillan's Alexander Smith's edition)[4] Emerson Bryant Longfellow Tennyson J A Symond's GREEK POETS. Resumés and partial transla-tions of the MABHABHARATA,[5] RAMAYANA, NIBELUNGEN, Shah NAMEH, &c &c. &c. &c &c. &c.

1. See "Homer and Shakespeare."
2. Ibid.
3. John A. Carlyle, tr., *Dante's Divine Comedy. The Inferno* (London, 1849).
4. London, 1868.
5. WW's knowledge of Asian literature is outlined by Stovall, *Foreground,* 165–166. He owned and used Alger's *The Poetry of the East* after 1860 ("See pp. 52–57"). T. R. Rajasekharaiah, *The Roots of Whitman's Grass* (Rutherford, N. J., 1970), 126–132, points out that a remarkable number of primary and secondary works on Hindu thought and literature were available in NYC libraries in the 1840s and 1850s. Unfortunately, the libraries which still exist have no membership records. Judging from his method of approaching the *Nibelungenlied* and Egyptology, for example, it is probable that he relied on Alger and other secondary sources, rather than on primary sources. (See "Our own account" and related MS and "Bunsen.") For a poet this would have been sufficient.

(These I Believe.

Manuscript in St. John's Seminary. Inscribed in purple crayon on white paper, 11⅛"
x 8½". Horizontal rules ⅜" apart; vertical margins at left and right. In G. H. Lewis, *The
Life and Work of Goethe* (Boston, 1856), II, 93, the quoted remarks are assigned to Fried-
erick Schiller. See also "Miss Harriett H Swallow" for another reference to Lewis' *Goethe*.
The date is probably in the mid 1880s.

(These I believe are Goethe's own words)

Goethe said[1]—(from Lewes Life of Goethe)   ?p 93
    The laws of propriety are foreign to innocent natures; only the experience of
corruption has given origin to them. But as soon as that corruption has taken
place, & natural innocence has vanished from manners the laws of propriety are
sacred, & moral feeling will not offend.[2] They have the same validity in an artifi-
cial world as the laws of nature have in a world of innocence.— But *the very thing
which constitues the Poet is that he banishes from himself every thing which
reminds him of an artificial & conventional*[3] *world, that he may restore Nature in
her primitive simplicity.* And if he has done this, he is thereby absolved from all
laws by which a perverted heart seeks security against itself. He is pure; he is
innocent; & whatever is permitted to innocent Nature is permitted also to him[4]
. . . . If thou who readest & hearest him art no longer innocent, & if thou
canst not even momentarily become so[5] by his purifying presence, it is thy misfor-
tune & not his . . . thou forsakest him. . . . he did not sing for thee

1. Inserted above "the" in "Goethe"
2. WW omitted Schiller's final word: "them"
3. Preceding two words inserted above "tificial" in "artificial" and "world"
4. The ellipses here and below are WW's.
5. Inserted above "e" in 'become'

Behind All Art.

Manuscript in Texas (Hanley). Inscribed in blue ink on at least eight scraps of white wove paper, two or three layers deep. No writing seems to be concealed. Two variants, one a very rough draft, are in Berkeley (not printed here): "Then the high" and "Of the Crowded." The former is on the verso of a letter dated July 5, 1879. At top of this MS is a deleted number, "233," in blue crayon; in the upper right corner in blue pencil, "278." Above and to left of title is "cap head" in red ink. The writing and layout suggest a rejected passage from *SDC* (1882).

BeHINd all art[1] *indeed.*[2]

Then the[3] deeper art behind the[4] art of all. "What is[5] Apollo," says Addington Symonds,[6] "but the magic of the sun, whose soul is light? What is Aphrodite but the love-charm of the sea? What is Pan, but the mystery of Nature—the felt and hidden want pervading all?" Of the crowded and massive[7] mythology of ancient Egypt,[8] Max Muller[9] says[10] "the silent battle between light and darkness forming the solar drama, and every detail thereof, acted every twenty-four hours forever" is almost[11] certainly the basis subject and plot—ideas of the whole complicated system.[12]

1. Deleted: "too" ; inserted above: "indeed"
2. Title in red ink. Marked "cap head" in red.
3. Inserted and deleted: [*illeg.*]; inserted: "deeper" . Both inserted above "the art" and "beh" in "behind"
4. Deleted: [*illeg.*]
5. Preceding two words and quotes inserted above wordspace between "all" and "Apollo,"
6. Deleted: "What is Apollo" . For Symonds see "D. W. Wilder."
7. Preceding two words inserted above "crowded" ; inserted and deleted above "myth" : in "mythology" [*illeg.*]
8. Deleted: [*illeg.*]
9. Max Müller (1823–1900), orientalist, student of mythology and religion. He was a proponent of the solar theory of mythology mentioned here.
10. Inserted and deleted: [*illeg.*] above "the"
11. Inserted and deleted: [*illeg.*] above "almost"
12. Preceding four words and final punctuation inserted on two lines.

Into the Study.

Manuscript in LC (#63, sheet #290). Inscribed in black pencil and some black ink on inside of envelope from Dr. Bucke, dated June 11, 1884. The writing is remarkably small and firm, so much so that the very heavy emendation has defeated attempts to transcribe it. It has no direct connection with "Robert Burns as Poet and Person," which had been published in 1882, although WW may have been thinking of the revisions to that essay to be made in 1886. The date is 1884.

Into the study of Poetry, as an ensemble with measureless contrasts, comparisons varieties of the divinest heroism of humanity, all lands, all ages, with few leading features, but adopting countless samples and elements from all,—a Catholic Ideal, limitless, subtle, refusing to be tabulated, needing comparisons and contrasts, evolutionary, and ready at any time for themes, standards previously unknown, perhaps the advent of Burns and his writings throws some illustrations rarer than from any other poet

Distinctive and Without Relation.

Manuscript in LC (#63, sheets #291, 291a, 291b). Inscribed in black pencil with black pen, blue crayon, and purple crayon emendations on three scraps of paper pasted together. Probably related to "Roundly considered." The writing and writing material are characteristic of WW's extreme old age.

Distinctive[1] and without relation[2] as they seem at first sight all the world's[3] Poets and all its[4] Poetry, of[5] all varieties—the Oriental, the Greek,[6] with what there is of Roman—[7] the oldest myths—the interminable[8] ballad romances[9] of the middle ages,[10] the hymns and[11] psalms of worship,—the great[12] epics,[13] and swarms of lyrics—poems from the British Islands[14]—or the Teutonic, old or new—or[15] modern French, and British

1. Uppercase "D" over lowercase. Deleted at top of page: "another point on which I & which [*illeg.*]" ; original opening deleted: "Divergent and"
2. Preceding three words inserted.
3 Preceding two words inserted.
4. Inserted; inserted and deleted: "all varieties"
5. Deleted: "all lands of the globe all times [*ins. and del.*] ages from [*del.*] the primitive times on and [*illeg.*] on to the [*del.*] prent present [*two words ins.*] day inclusive—all tongues all [*del.*] themes forms, all subjects all sizes or long [*illeg. ins. and del.*] or short" ; inserted: "the [*del.*] Asiatic"
6. Deleted: "the" ; inserted: "with"
7. Deleted: "the scandinavian, the older [*ins. and del.*] the Teutonic Walter of A or the B or the P from the British Islands [*end of 291*] [*illeg.*] lyric [*illeg. ins. and del.*] the myths—of old" ; inserted: "the oldest myths"
8. Inserted.
9. Inserted.
10. Deleted: "or of"
11. Deleted: "psla"
12. Preceding two words inserted.
13. Deleted: "or" ; inserted: "and [*del.*] innumerable swarms of"
14. End of [*291a*]. [*291b*] is probably a correction slip.
15. Deleted: [*illeg.*]

¶In General Civilization.

Manuscript in Morgan Library. Inscribed in black pencil with corrections in purple crayon on inside of opened-out envelope from *North American Review* dated October 9[?], 1890. The date is probably late 1890.

¶In general civilization[1]

A[2] real representative National Literature[3] formates itself (like language, or[4] "the weather") not from[5] any two or three influences, or from any learned sylla-bus, or criticism, or what ought to be, or from the minds or advice[6] of toploftical quarters,[7] & indeed not at all from[8] the influences and[9] ways[10] generally supposed, (though they too are adopted) but slowly, slowly,[11] from many more and deeper[12] mixings and siftings[13] and generations and[14] years and races,[15] and[16] from what largely appears to be chance[17]—but is not[18] chance at all

1. This "¶" might possibly be meant to precede "In general . . . ," which is indented, or "A," which is inserted above deleted "The" and also indented. It is also possible that what appears to be a title is a false start.

2. Deleted in black pencil: "special and" ; inserted: "real" above "al" in the deleted "spe-cial" and "and"

3. Deleted in purple crayon: "forms and" ; inserted in purple crayon above: "formates itself"

4. Deleted in black pencil: "like"

5. Deleted in black pencil: "one or" ; inserted above: "any [*del.*] one"

6. Preceding two words inserted in black pencil above "nds" in "minds" and "of"

7. Deleted in black pencil: "or even" ; inserted: "& indeed not at all" above "[*del.*] even" and "from" and "[*del.*] the"

8. Deleted in black pencil: "the" ; inserted and deleted following: "any" ; in-serted: "the" before "[*del.*] any"

9. Deleted in black pencil: "sources"

10. Deleted in black pencil: "at first" ; inserted above: "generally"

11. Inserted in purple crayon: "slowly, slowly," above "from many" ; inserted and de-leted: "(I hope surely" above "more"

12. Deleted in pencil: "and"

13. Preceding two words inserted in pencil above "mixings"

14. Deleted in pencil: "infinite"

15. Deleted in pencil: "and siftings"

16. Deleted in pencil: "what [*illeg.*]" ; inserted above: "from what"

17. Corrected to singular.

18. Deleted in pencil: "so" ; inserted above: "chance"

IV. Needs of American Literature.

American Literature Must.

Manuscript in Rutgers. Inscribed in black pencil and black ink on white wove scrap. Stovall, *AL,* 26, 352, thinks it was suggested by "Thoughts on Reading," *American Whig Review,* I (May, 1845), 483–496 (Bucke Clipping #439), and points out the close relationship of the last paragraph to the following sentence from the article (p. 495): "If they were wild and irregular, it was because nature was so. . . ." The whole article appears to have interested WW. There is some echo of this material in Preface 1855 and "Song of the Answerer." First printed in *N&F,* 130 (Pt. III, #169, 170; *CW,* IX, 161–162), with some differences.

American[1] literature must become distinct from all others.— American[2] writers[3] must become national, idiomatic, free from the genteel laws— America[4] herself appears (she does not at all appear hitherto) in the spirit and the form of her poems, and all other literary works—/
The great[5] poet submits only to himself.[6]

Is Nature[7] rude, free, irregular? If nature be so, I[8] too will be so.[9] Do you suppose Nature keeps has[10] nothing[11] under those beautiful terrible irrational forms?[12]

1. Bucke begins: "When American literature becomes . . ."
2. Bucke begins: "When American writers become national . . ."
3. Deleted: "of"
4. Bucke begins: "When America . . ."
5. Deleted: "est"
6. Preceding sentence in black ink.
7. Deleted in ink: "wild and" ; inserted above in ink: "rude, free,"
8. Inserted in ink, deleted in pencil: "& you to" above "too will"
9. Preceding sentence in black pencil.
10. Inserted above "ps" in "keeps"
11. Deleted: "more"
12. Preceding sentence in ink.

America Needs Her Own Poems.

Manuscript in Duke (20, #10). Inscribed in black pencil on scrap of faded white wove paper, $4^{15}/_{16}$" x $5\frac{7}{8}$". Faint blue(?) vertical rules $^5/_{16}$" apart. A slip from a sales catalog with the MS draws a parallel with paragraph four of Preface 1855. Although the nationalistic sentiments expressed are characteristic of WW's entire career, the writing, which is similar to that of the early notebooks, also indicates a date in the 1850s or earlier. Printed by Bucke, *N&F,* 67 (Pt. II, #46; *CW,* IX, 29). (Another copy, with slight variations in punctuation, is in *N&F,* 72; *CW,* IX, 43–44.)

America needs her own poems, in her own body and spirit,[1] different from all[2] hitherto—freer, more muscular, comprehending more,[3] and unspeakably grander.— Not[4] importations, or any thing in the spirit of the importations[5] aloof and in These States exiles;—not the superb chronicles, faultless,[6] rich, perennial as they are and deserve to be in their native lands[7] of the past events and characters of Europe—[8] not the current products of imaginative persons, with tropes, likenesses, piano music, and smooth rhymes[9]

1. Preceding seven words inserted above "different from all"
2. Deleted: "the rest" ; inserted: "hitherto—freer" above deletion and "more"
3. Preceding two words and comma inserted above "and" and "unspeak" in "unspeakable". Above this is inserted and deleted: "than any hitherto" . The intended location of this phrase is not clear.
4. Deleted: "the"
5. Preceding nine words inserted on two lines above "tations" in "importations" and "aloof . . . in"
6. Deleted: "and"
7. Preceding eight words inserted on two lines above "l" in "perennial" and "as they are" . Deleted: "from" ; inserted: "of the past events and characters of" above the deletion and "Europe" and "[*del.*] nothing"
8. Deleted: "nothing"
9. Erased: "—nor of" . Printed in *N&F,* 67.

Caution.

Manuscript in Duke (25, #29). Inscribed in pencil on white wove paper, 6⅞″ x 2¼″, vertical rules ¼″ apart. First printed in *N&F* (Pt. II, #47; *CW,* IX, 30). According to Bucke's note, the date is probably the late 1850s.

Caution

Not to blaat constantly for *Native American* models, literature, &c,[1] and bluster out[2] *"nothing foreign."* — The best way to promulge Native American models and literature is to supply such forcible and superb[3] specimens of the same that[4] they will, by their own volition, move to the head of all, and put foreign models in the second class—[5]

I to-day think it would be best *not at all* to bother with arguments against the foreign models, or to help American models—BUT JUST GO ON SUPPLYING AMERICAN MODELS

1. Inserted.
2. Preceding two words inserted on a line above *"nothing"*
3. Preceding four words inserted on a line above "ply" in "supply . . . of" . "superb" written over [*illeg.*]
4. Written over [*illeg.*]
5. The following is added at upper right, enclosed by vertical and horizontal line, and noted with a pointing fist, the fist above *"Caution"*

The Questions Involved.

Manuscript in Texas (Hanley). Inscribed in pencil on faded, white, laid scrap, approx. 7½″ x 2⁷/₁₆″. Clipped from a longer piece. Neat handwriting and the subject matter suggest an early date.

[1] The [2] questions involved is curious to discuss. What may be said,[3] and opens long long vistas in connection, about Poetry fit for the New World? and what are the probabilities?—but what of the future?[4] The foreigner rules here for the present with absolute sway.

1. Deleted: "[*illeg.*] Western point of view.— All"
2. Deleted: "points[?] are" ; inserted: "questions involved is" above "[*del.*] points[?]" and "curious"
3. Inserted: "and opens long long vistas" on a line above "may . . . connection"
4. Inserted and deleted: "while" above question mark after "probabilities" . Inserted and brought down with arrow: "The foreigner rules here for the present" on a line above "but what of the future?"

Why Need Genius.

Manuscript not found. Text from *N&F,* 103(Pt. III, #66; *CW,* IX, 106). Since it was a Bucke MS, the date is probably in the 1850s.

Why need genius and the people of These States be demeaned to romances? Let facts and histories be properly told, there is no more need of romances.

For Lect on Literature.

Manuscript in LC (#63, sheet #306). Inscribed in black pencil on tan (possibly faded white) scrap, 8¼″ x 4⅞″. Text cancelled. The left edge appears to have been torn from a binding. Hanging indentation. The writing appears to be that of the 1850s. First printed by Furness, 65.

for lect on Literature

or (Democracy)

What are these, called our literary men, poets &c/ Scintillations[1] at best of other[2] the literary men & literary needs of other lands—exiles here, &

1. Deleted: "at" ; inserted: "at best" above "[*del.*] at" and "of"
2. Deleted: "lands literary men"

You Cannot Define.

Manuscript in Duke (27, #37). Inscribed in black pencil on soft, faded, white (proof?) paper, approx. 7¼" x 5³/₁₆". Offset from printed page on verso. The writing suggests a date in the 1850s, as does the fact that it was a Bucke MS. First printed in *N&F,* 128 (Pt. III, #160; *CW,* IX, 158).

You cannot define too clearly what it is you love in a poem or in a man or woman.[1]

A work of a[2] great poet is not remembered for its parts—but remembered as you remember the complete person and spirit[3] of him or her you love.—/

When he becomes is[4] vitalized with nationality and individuality from top to toe—when he seizes upon life with[5] masculine power—when he stands out in simple relief, as America does—/

bully-poet.

1. Sentence in small writing crammed at top of leaf.
2. Inserted above wordspace between "of" and "great"
3. Preceding two words inserted above "n" in "person" and "of"
4. Written above "becomes"
5. Deleted: "simple and"

America Has Been Called.

Manuscript in Duke (36, #28). Inscribed in black pencil on white wove scrap, approx. 3½″ x 6⅞″. Blue rules, ¼″ apart. The writing suggests a date in the 1850s. For related MS see "Literature. The tendency." First printed in *N&F,* 146 (Pt. III, #195; *CW,* IX, 197).

America has been called[1] proud and arrogant.— It may be, but she does not show it in[2] her literature.— It is indirect, and therefore more effective.[3] Day by day and hour by hour, in[4] tragedy and comedy, in picture and print, in every importation of art and[5] letters, she submits to one[6] steady flow of discrepancy and one supercilious and ceaseless

bring in a[7] sockdologer on the Dickens-fawners[8]

1. Deleted: [*illeg.*]
2. Deleted: "her criticism or" ; inserted and deleted: "drama or" above "litera" in "literature"
3. Preceding sentence inserted above "ure" in "literature" and "Day by day and hour"
4. Deleted: [*illeg.*]
5. Deleted: "literature she" ; inserted: "letters" above "ature" in "literature"
6. Deleted: "ceaseless stretch" ; inserted above: "steady low"
7. Inserted in ink, squiggles above and below. Perhaps he meant only one sockdologer.
8. "Dickens-fawners" written below "a sockdologer" and slightly slanting.

Books, As Now Produced.

Manuscript in Duke (36, #28). Inscribed in black ink and black pencil on white laid scrap, 7¾" x 4¹³/₁₆". Vertical blue rules on verso, ¼" apart. Illegible embossed stamp at lower right. For related MS see "Literature. The tendency." First printed in *N&F*, 146 (Pt. III, #195; *CW*, IX, 198). The writing suggests a date in the 1850s.

Books, as now produced, have reached their twentieth remove from verities.[1] Our writers have apparently forgotten that there is any thing to be aimed[2] at,[3] except[4] Literary Literature. But in its profound relations, in its origin in great minds[5] this great medium & institute has only to do with thoughts, men, things, & even the Soul, at first hand.[6]

1. Inserted in ink at top of page, brought down on arrow. Paragraphs in pencil cancelled in ink:
   We have to state that [*preceding five words del. in ink*] the superfine an in any [*preceding five words del. in pencil*] Literature in [*del.*] any [*ins. above deleted* "any"] its profound relation, has to do with thought, [*illeg.*] men, things, &c at first hand/
   Most people when they speak [*del.*] of or write or write of Literature mean merely *Literary* Literature. Most people [*preceding seventeen words del.*]"
2. Deleted: "at"
3. Deleted: "further"
4. Preceding five words inserted above "Literary Literature" ; deleted: "but" before "Literary"
5. Preceding six words inserted above "profound relations"
6. Deleted in pencil: "Its special [*illeg.*] & the instruments & teaches them" , pointing fist, and "opposite page"

It Is Quite Indifferent.

Manuscript in LC (Feinberg #835). Inscribed in black ink on scrap of blue Williamsburgh tax blank, 5¾" x 4⅝". The exact order of sentences WW finally intended is difficult to determine. The text here presents the most coherent reading. As the paper indicates, the date is 1857 or after.

It[1] is quite indifferent whether you[2] please or displease[3] any Americo-foreign[4] coteries—for they[5] are to disappear, like the Royal[6] colonial governments of a hundred years since[7] have disappeared.—[8] What do you suppose a grand Literature really is—or is to be.— Not to make[9] polite paragraphs,[10] I assure you—nor handsome conceits or rhymes, or books which merly show that you have carefully read all preceding books.—' Something from yourself[11] is demanded—and conformity[12] with America is sternly demanded and for some days to come,[13]

1. Deleted: "I have also to insure you that it"
2. Deleted: "conform to satis"
3. Deleted: "the"
4. Deleted: "appetites"
5. Deleted: "will"
6. Deleted: "governors"
7. Preceding five words and deletions inserted on two lines above "you suppose"
8. Preceding sentence at top of leaf and down right edge and between ends of lines.
9. Deleted: "pretty" ; inserted above: "polite"
10. Deleted: "correct books, a fine artificial style, or"
11. Deleted: "and something"
12. Deleted: "to" ; inserted: "with" above "A" in "America"
13. "Come" written over deleted "y" . An arrow to top of leaf suggests that WW intended the preceding six words to be inserted there, but no appropriate location can be found.

There Is Something.

Manuscript in Duke (36, #28). Inscribed in ink on irregular white scrap. For related MS see "Literature. The tendency." Marked at top with fist pointing to "(good statement)." First printed in N&F, 146 (Pt. III, #195; CW, IX, 197). The date is probably in the 1850s.

There is something very bitter in the tacit adoption in[1] in our great democratic cities[2] of these[3] forms and laws[4] imported from the royal capitals of Europe,[5] the

1. Deleted: "the" ; inserted: "our"
2. Deleted: "of America"
3. Deleted: [illeg.] ; inserted and deleted: "imported"
4. Deleted in pencil: "and manner" ; inserted in pencil: "& the [preceding two words del.] imported"
5. Deleted: "involving[?]"

Literature.

Manuscript in LC (Feinberg #835). Inscribed in black ink and, as noted, black pencil on the four rectos of two folded sheets of notepaper, 8″ x 4¹⁵/₁₆″. [*1*] and [*5*] are embossed "J.H. Owen" in a horizontal cartouche at upper right. No other example of this paper has been seen. The references to "The Eighteenth Presidency!" make 1856 the earliest possible date that WW could have written this.

[*1*] Literature

pages 245–6
German Lit[1]

or?[2] [·]
I do not demand
(or)
It is not so much to be demanded
(or)
America may[3] not demand
? insist to-day[4] of literary expression that it should depict[5] life & characters here[6] with all[7] their own native[8] colors & idioms & the smack of atmosphere & soil,—[9] for life & characters here,[10] at present are individually crude; they are in transi-

---

1. The reference is to Joseph Gostwick, *German Literature* (Phila., 1854). See *"Neibelungen-leid* Song." Gostwick complains that there is no poet "who will tell how the German people were living, and what they were doing, in the nineteenth century." He continues: "History speaks of men as if they were the creatures of politics; it explores not their true nature, it considers men apart from all the influence of nature: history is full of half-truths: poetry should supply this defect. The true poet should be the interpreter and the illustrator of life, a companion to the historian, but doing more than the historian does. . . ." Although *"Literature"* is a restatement of WW's ideas on the matter and he does not develop Gostwick's comparison of literature and history, it is worth noticing that here he is using Gostwick as more than a source of information.

2. At left of waved line bracing the three tentative openings. Each is parenthesized or is written between the entries.

3. Inserted and deleted: "to" above "n" in "not"

4. Preceding question mark and two words inserted above "demand of"

5. Deleted: "her" ; inserted and deleted: [*illeg.*] above "t" in "depict"

6. Deleted: "in their"

7. "all" inserted above "th" in "their"

8. Inserted: "native" above "own"

9. Deleted: "in its pourtrayals"

10. Deleted in black pencil: "are with all their vehemence," ; inserted in black pencil: "at present" above "[*del.*] vehemence"

tional conditions?,[11] too rapid, too terrible,[12] too varied &[13] boiling & bubbling with[14] formative processes—they[15] are[16] persons & there is nutriment[17] here to-day for artist souls,[18] great[19] as humanity can know,—but the nutriment is[20] not[21] derived here & now[22] from picturesque individualities,—it is but[23] from the action of[24] humanity in larger far larger masses, than ever before, like the whirl-ing of mighty winds [3; 2 *blank*] impossible to resist, & to be carried along by which is glorious, &[25] derived from the general buoyancy & intensity of the spirit of life. So the portraiture of individual specimens of Character may not at present be demanded.[26]

But what[27] America[28] may well demand

is that[29] writers, here,[30] those[31]

who expect to be

of any account, should first

survey the whole area of[32]

the New World,—its[33]

scope

possibilities[34]

survey first its geographic[35] &

   hydrographic greatness only

11. Question mark above "conditions" perhaps related to slash through "c" in "conditions"

12. Deleted: "for"

13. Deleted: "discordant corrup"

14. Deleted: "agitations" ; inserted: "formative" above "tations" in "agitations"

15. Emendations not clear. Inserted in ink and deleted in black pencil: "these times" ; deleted in black pencil: "are"

16. Inserted in black pencil: "persons & [*del. in black ink*] events" above "are nutriment" ; inserted and deleted in black pencil: "they" "through" above "iment" in "nutriment"

17. Deleted "enough" ; inserted: "there is" above "enou" in "[*del.*] enough" ; inserted and deleted: "these times" ; "to" not deleted, not printed here. Deleted: "the inspirations of" ; inserted in black pencil: "here to-day for" above "ations" in "inspirations" and "of" and "ar" in "artist"

18. Inserted and deleted: "as" above "g" in "great"

19. Inserted and deleted: "nutriment" above "t" in "great" and "as"

20. Deleted: "in the"

21. Deleted: "here" ; inserted and deleted above: [*illeg.*]

22. Preceding three words inserted above "d" in "derived"

23. Inserted in black pencil above "is"

24. Deleted: "such unprecedented" ; inserted: "humanity in larger far larger masses than ever before" above "[*del.*] unprecedented" and on three lines at right following.

25. Deleted in black pencil: "it is from the" ; inserted in black pencil: "derived from" above "&" and "[*del.*] it"

26. Preceding sentence inserted in pencil on two lines above "But what America demands"

27. "what" inserted above wordspace between "But" and "America"

28. Deleted in pencil: "demands" ; inserted above in ink: "may well demand"

29. Deleted: "here"

30. Inserted above wordspace between "writers" and "those"

31. Deleted: "worthy of"

32. Deleted in black pencil: "this" ; inserted: "the" above wordspace following.

33. From this point the MS text, although consecutive, is broken into short entries, sometimes with hanging indentation, as WW lists the preparation of the poet.

34. Deleted: "not" ; inserted: "survey first" above the deletion and "its" and "geo" in "geographic"

35. Deleted: final "al"

—[36] its mines,[37] the teeming
richness of its products
from the soil,
survey &
estimate well[38]
its people, the intense
intellect & hard conscientious
fibre of the New England states,
with[39] their feverish industry & invention
estimate too[40] the[41] abandon egotism & electric passion
of the South precious[42] elements,
[43] like the lightning that may kill, but the universe
cannot[44] live without it[45]—
survey[46] the[47] amplitude & brawn of the West [5; 4 *blank*]
the prairies, &[48] the mighty generic[49] race that
is so swiftly[50] faring upon them—[51]
absorb [*illeg.*] soul the splendid prophecy of
the west, in its material facts
alone—survey these[52]—then
    the moral aspects
    the religious fervor, often grotesque
    the reformers, also grotesque,
    spiritualism
    the enthusiastic young men[53]
    (shun at present[54] the cities which are nowhere American[55] but dwell long
    as you[56] like on the[57]

36. Deleted: "not"
37. Deleted: "&" ; inserted above: "the"
38. Preceding four words inserted above "its people, the"
39. Deleted in black pencil: "all"
40. Preceding four words inserted in black pencil above "industry . . . to"
41. Inserted and deleted: "personal" above "andon" in "abandon" ; inserted following the deletion: "egotism"
42. Inserted above "elem" in "elements"
43. Deleted: [*illeg.*]
44. Deleted: "is not" ; "cannot" was probably inserted after the deletion.
45. Preceding thirteen words inserted in small writing below the line.
46. Inserted in black pencil.
47. Deleted: "vast brawn & calm"
48. Inserted in black pencil.
49. Preceding two words inserted in black pencil above "race that"
50. Preceding two words inserted in black pencil above deleted "rapidly"
51. Deleted in black pencil: "all" ; inserted in black pencil: "absorbed [*illeg.*] soul" above the deletion and "the"
52. Deleted: "& then as but"
53. Preceding five items in an indented column.
54. Preceding two words inserted in black pencil above "n" in "shun" and "the"
55. Preceding four words inserted in black pencil above "ies" in "cities" and "but dwell long"
56. Deleted: "choose" ; inserted above: "like"
57. Deleted in black pencil: "good"

average specimens
of the country,) dwell on the
great[58] idea—facts of[59]
Liberty, progress, the eligibility
of man to greatness & to
the best & highest, & to
knowledge,[60] to the Presidency
among the rest, which have
here there roots & sprouting growth,[61]
and out of this, & these surveys,
& these digestions?,[62] to form an American
spirit & write in it—

(this last is not complete)[63]

[7; 6 *blank*][64] I fully join in the complaint that—for years past, men of capacity, honor, & dignity have been altogether driven from politics, & have left that important & vital field to[65] the low & wily & (expand—get the printed "address to young men" & extract from it)[66]—
—I fully join in this complaint[67] & would suggest that[68] an indispensable part of[69] the remedy to be applied[70] must consist in the better men who should enter the field of practical politics, must begin by making themselves at home with the masses of the people,[71] must habituate themselves to direct contact with them, & not be so much afraid, must if needs be mix with them in their haunts, even the lowest. Are the people to be rached? Then go where they are ([72]make this statement clearer

58. Deleted in black pencil: "moral real" above "ogress" in "progress"
59. Preceding seven words and the deletion above inserted in black pencil above "Liberty, progress, the eligibility"
60. Deleted: "&"
61. Preceding eight words inserted in black pencil on two lines following "the rest"
62. Question mark inserted above "digestions"
63. Below the body of the text.
64. Deleted: "I"
65. Deleted: "most"
66. Judging from the context, the reference is to "The Eighteenth Presidency!" which is addressed "to each young man in the Nation," especially the opening denunciation of American politics.
67. Deleted: "but [*two words del.*] wish to feel that [*two words del.*] an impor a serious hiatus [two words ins. above "hiatus"] has existed exists in the"
68. Not deleted, not printed here: "a" ; deleted: "great" ; inserted: "an indispensable" above "a" and "[*del.*] great"
69. Deleted: "this"
70. Deleted: "consists in the"
71. Deleted: "or" ; inserted: "must habituate themselves to" above "ple" in "people" and "[*del.*] or" and "direct contact"
72. Deleted: "expand &" following brace. The statement, which is crammed into the lower right corner on two lines, is probably an insertion.

Literature Means.

Manuscript in LC (Feinberg #835). Inscribed in black ink, black pencil, and blue crayon on pink wrapper stock, approx. 6¼″ x 5″. The paper indicates a date between 1855 and 1856.

[*1*] Literature means, (I say in the same[1] haste,) the[2] expression,[3] of the body and contents and especially the idiocracy & spirit[4] of a nation—and is its physiognomy, curious in itself, but principally curious from the play of physical, mental, and spiritual facts it rises out of (for[5] the face does not[6] mean the face[7] only, but the whole[8] body, & soul)[9]— Curious, also, from its look[10] shooting out wonderful attributes, may-be inexplicable, (although every one else[11] has a a[12] countenance, too,[13] and features partake in common,) which fix that identity to be remembered, different, not[14] merely part of a[15] crowd—rather, some divine idiomatic mask, individual,[16] symbol of life behind none but itself.—

[2] Such tests applied, we perceive the astonishing spectacle of These States, with the most heroic, copious, and original supply of their own native life-blood, life-motion, and life-material, but yet, (with the exception of censuses returns and cheap newspapers—though those are indeed[17] grand,) entirely without[18] any

---

1. "same" inserted at an angle to the right of "the"
2. Deleted: "exp"
3. Deleted: "taking their own [*illeg.*] sha [*ins. above deleted* "sha"] native permanent shapes"
4. Preceding six words inserted in pencil above "and contents of a"
5. Deleted: "literature" ; inserted above: "the face"
6. Deleted: "most"
7. Deleted: "itself"
8. "whole" inserted in blue crayon above "bo" in "body"
9. Two words inserted in blue crayon above dash.
10. Deleted: "containing" ; inserted: "shooting out" above "ns" in "contains" and "wo" in "wonderful"
11. Deleted: "too"
12. Deleted: "face"
13. Inserted above wordspace between "countenance," and " "
14. Deleted: [*illeg.*] ; inserted above: "merely"
15. Deleted: "general"
16. Inserted above "sym" in "symbol"
17. Inserted above "gra" in "grand"
18. Inserted and deleted: "any idiomatic" above "ly" in "entirely" and "without"

physiognomy of their own.—[19] What is here in such profusion—these numberless reprints, histories, essays, novels, poems—did you think they identified America, or celebrated her genius?— No; they identify Europe, kings, lords, eccle [3] siastics—all[20] standing for lands foreign to us, and a spirit foreign—no one the natural and free growth of our own soil—no one the new phases of humanity in The States.— Plenty of fine words—pages, paragraphs, verses, &c., mountain-piles, just as correct, just as genteel as the best of them;—But the spirit! ah, the spirit is wanting.—

19. Deleted: "What they have bears the stamp is only immigrancy features, importations before their own body.—"

20. Deleted: "bound up" ; inserted above: "standing for"

Literature. The Tendency.

Manuscript in Texas (Hanley). Inscribed in black ink on blue laid scrap, 5½″ x 7½″. Watermarked "Improved" in openfaced capitals, in an arc over US shield surrounded by stars. Blue rules, ⅜″ apart. Bucke prints this with "America has been called," "There is something," "In the pleantiful feast," and "Books, as now produced," with a note that they were intended for an unpublished essay. Despite his tendency to construct essays from scraps, he very possibly had here a bundle of MS pinned together by WW. In fact, the pinholes in "In the pleantiful feast" and "Books, as now produced" do match. The handwriting differs from MS to MS. This MS suggests that it was written in the 1860s, whereas others suggest they were written in the 1850s. First printed in *N&F,* 146 (Pt. III, #195; *CW,* IX, 197).

Literature.

The[1] tendency permitted to Literature,[2] has always been[3] & now is to[4] magnify & intensify its own[5] technism, to isolate itself from general & vulgar life, & to make a caste or order.

1. Deleted: "tence"
2. Deleted: "is to y"
3. Inserted: "[*del.*] & & now is" above "been"
4. Deleted: "it it it"
5. Deleted: "spirit, & proced" ; inserted: "technism" above "[*del.*] spirit,"

In the Pleantiful Feast.

Manuscript in Rutgers. Inscribed in black ink on white laid paper, approx. 9⅜" x 7⅞". Blue rules ½" apart; red-blue-red margin 1⅜" from left margin. Part of a larger leaf. (cf. Howells's objections), rather than "imaginative fiction" as written by Cooper, Poe, Melville, and Hawthorne. The writing suggests a date after 1860. For related MS see "Literature. The tendency." First printed in *N&F,* 146 (Pt. III, #195; *CW,* IX, 198).

In the pleantiful feast of romance presented to us, all[1] the novels, all the[2] poems, really[3] dish up[4] one[5] only figure[6]—various forms or preparations[7] of one only [8]plot, namely a sickly [9]scrofulous crude [10]amorousness[11]. True the malady described is the general one—[12] which all have to go through, on their way to[13] be eligible to Love, but this is not love.

1. In ink at top of leaf. Following text in pencil, cancelled in ink:

[*del.*] Literature
At present [*ins. and del. above* "the"] in [*ins. and del. following deleted* "in"] through the whole all of imaginative literature rises every where poems [*ins. above* "poems"] poetry it shows scenes ossified [*preceding eight words del.*] [*del. in ink*] All
Inserted in ink: "the" above wordspace between "All" and "novels"

2. Inserted in ink above "l" in "all"
3. Inserted in ink above "di" in "dish"
4. Deleted in ink: "by"
5. Deleted in ink: "f" ; inserted above in ink: "only"
6. Deleted in ink: [*illeg.*] ; inserted in ink: dash.
7. Preceding two words inserted in ink above "orms" in "forms" and "of"
8. Inserted in ink above wordspace between "one" and "plot"
9. Deleted in ink: "a desperate" ; inserted above in pencil: "scrofulous"
10. Inserted in ink above "amor" in "amorousness"
11. Deleted in ink: "miscalled love. It is a complaint [*ins.*] malady [*ins.*] it."
12. Preceding eight words inserted in ink; redundant "it" not printed.
13. Deleted: "real" above deleted "love. It is a complaint"

In Lectures.

Manuscript in Virginia. Title and first two entries in black ink, third in blue crayon on white wove scrap, 6" x 6¼". All entries except title in hanging indentation. At left of second entry in black ink is "? outset/ no/" . See "Really what has America." The writing suggests an early date, possibly as late as the early 1860s. First printed in *N&F*, 177 (Pt. IV, #118; *CW*, X, 32).

In Lectures on Democracy
? A course of 3 (or?[1] 5) comprehending all my subjects under the title)/
Come down strong on the literary, artistic, theologic, and philanthropic[2] coteries of These States, that they have not do not[3] at all recognized the one grand over-arching-fact, these swift-striding, resistless, all comquering, en-masse/[4]

boldly assume that all the usual priests,   &c are infidels/and the   are Faithful Believers

1. Question mark over "or"
2. Deleted: "classes"
3. Preceding two words inserted above "have not"
4. Rule in blue crayon three-quarters across page from left above final entry.

We Need Somebody.

Manuscript in Rutgers. Inscribed in black ink on white laid paper, approx. 9⅜″ x 7⅞″. Blue rules ½″ apart; red-blue-red margin 1⅜″ from left margin. Part of a larger leaf. On verso in pencil, possibly in WW's hand, what appears to be part of a legal opinion concerning the disposition of a cargo of cotton. Cancelled with a vertical stroke in black ink. The verso seems to pertain to the business of the Attorney General's office, rather than the Army Paymaster's or the Department of the Interior. The date of the recto is, then, probably after July 1, 1865, when WW was employed by the Attorney General.

We need[1] somebody or something, whose utterance[2] were like[3] an old Hebrew prophet's, only substituting rapt[4] Literature instead of[5] rapt religion—and the[6] amount of[7] that utterance crying aloud: "Hear, O People! O poets & writers![8] ye have[9] made literature[10] as the upholstery of your parlors, or the confections of your tables. Ye have made a mere ornaments, a prettiness.[11] Ye have feebly[12] followed & feebly multiplied the models of other lands.[13] Ye are in the midst of idols, of clay, silver & brass.[14] I come to call you to the[15] knowledge of the Living God, in writings. Its own literature, to a Nation, is the first of all things. Even [2] its Religion appears only through its Literature, & as part of it. Know

1. Deleted: "someth"
2. Deleted: "is" ; inserted: "were"
3. Deleted: "that a [*del.*] of"
4. "rapt" inserted above wordspace between "substituting" and "literature"
5. Deleted: "the"
6. Deleted: "spirit" ; inserted above: "amount"
7. Deleted: "which should be" ; inserted above: "that [*del.*] it utterance [*del.*] sh cry aloud:"
8. Deleted: "you"
9. Deleted: "supposed your" ; inserted above: "made [*del.*] of"
10. Deleted: "as an accompaniment, an adjunct, as of the same" ; inserted: "as the" above "[*del.*] same"
11. Preceding eight words inserted on two lines above "of your tables." ; deleted: "you" ; inserted above: "Ye"
12. "feebly" inserted above "ve" in "have"
13. Period changed to comma; deleted: "& put" ; inserted and deleted: "Yet" above wordspace between "other" and "lands"
14. Preceding sentence inserted on a line above "lands . . . to"
15. Deleted: "truth" ; inserted: "knowledge of the Living God, in writings" above "to the . . . [*del.*] Its liter" ; deleted: "Its liter"

ye,[16] Ye may have all other[17] possessions but without your own[18] Soul's Litera-
ture, ye are[19] but little better than[20] trading prosperous beasts. Aping but others,
ye are but intelligent apes. Until ye prove title by productions, remain subordinate,
& cease[21] that perceptual windy bragging. Far, far above[22] all else, in a nation,[23]
& making[24] its men[25] to move as gods, behold[26] the bards, orators, & authors,
born of the spirit & body of that nation.[27]

Its[28] Literature,[29] when it comes, is to be the most serious, most subtle, most
solid part of America, &[30] making[31] its conflicting elements homogeneous & the
States a Nation, & constituent; not[32] a Literature pinned on its breast, for a breast-
pin, or worn in the ears for ear-rings.

16. Preceding eight words and punctuation inserted above "ature" in "Literature," and "Ye
may have"
17. Deleted: "things" ; inserted above: "possessions"
18. Deleted: "grand" ; inserted above: "Souls"
19. Deleted: "as"
20. Deleted: "an[?]"
21. Deleted: "those" ; inserted: "that perpetual" above "windy"
22. Deleted: "also"
23. Preceding three words and comma inserted above "else, &"
24. Inserted: "[del.] all its" above "ing" in "making"
25. Inserted: "to move" above "as"
26. Deleted: "in a [del.] nation [ins. and del. above "nation"] race its original own poets" ;
inserted: "the" above "[del.] poets"
27. Deleted: "race" ; inserted: "nation"
28. Inserted.
29. Deleted: "is" ; inserted: "when it comes, is to be" above the deletion and "the most"
30. Ampersand inserted above "m" in "making"
31. Deleted: "The its most [ins.] to" ; inserted: "its conflicting elements homogeneous & [del.]
its the States a nation, &" above the deletion and "constituent; not [del.] pros"
32. Deleted: "pros to be" ; inserted: "a Literature" above "pinned"

Is It Enough.

Manuscript in Texas (Hanley). Inscribed in black pencil on tan laid scrap, 4^{11}/$_{16}$″ long, torn at both edges. The writing appears to be after 1870.

Is it enough to[1] keep on importing & [*illeg.*] [*illeg.*] the[2] first class productions of[3] foreign lands[?] and ages, poems and other & forever[4] humbly (with haply a few insertions of modern [*illeg.*] and dates)[5] repeat them—as if that were the finality?

1. Deleted: "merely" ; inserted and deleted above: "former [*illeg.*]" ; inserted: "keep on importing" above the deletions.
2. Deleted: "[*illeg.*] highest & Poetic [*illeg.*] literary" ; inserted: "first class" above the deleted [*illeg.*] and "highest"
3. Deleted: "other" ; inserted above: "foreign"
4. Preceding five words inserted above "ages humbly" . Deleted: "and" before "humbly"
5. Parenthetical statement inserted.

Roundly Considered.

Manuscript in LC (#63, sheets #289, 289a). Inscribed in black ink and black pencil with emendations in blue crayon on two scraps of tan wove paper. Possibly related to "Distinctive and without relation." The writing and writing material are characteristic of WW's extreme old age.

Roundly considered,[1] or [2]what there is in America, ([3]Bryant's for instance,[4] or Longfellow's or Whittier's)[5]—verse of all[6] tongues, all forms,[7] languages, subjects,[8] from[9] primitive times to[10] our own day, inclusive—really[11] combine in one[12] aggregate and[13] electric[14] globe or universe,[15] with all its[16] numberless parts and radiations[17] held together by [18]a common centre or vertaber,[19]—all having

1. Preceding two words inserted above "there is in Amer"
2. Inserted above "ed" in "considered"
3. Deleted: "Poe's" ; inserted: "Bryant's" above deletion and "for"
4. Deleted: "or Bryant's" ; "or Whittier's" inserted above; "or Longfellow's" inserted below. Inserted and deleted at top of page: "or Tennyson's [illeg.] or"
5. Inserted: "verse of" above "all"
6. Deleted: "subjects"
7. Deleted: "all" ; inserted: "languages" above the deletion and "su" in "subjects"
8. Deleted: "all [ins. and del.] all sizes or long or short—all the [illeg. ins. and del.] & lands of the [illeg.] ages"
9. Deleted: "the"
10. Deleted: "the present" ; inserted above: "our own"
11. Inserted above "com" in "combine"
12. Inserted and deleted: "disgusted" above and before "aggregate"
13. Preceding two words inserted above "in one" and "e" in "electric"
14. Inserted and deleted: "compact compact" ; inserted: "globe" above "ic" in "electric" and "or"
15. Deleted: "held together" ; inserted and deleted: "mark'd off from the rest." above "universe" and "[del.] held together"
16. Deleted: "now" ; inserted: "numberless parts and" above "its radiations"
17. Deleted: "in" ; inserted: "held together" above the deletion and "by"
18. Deleted: "one [illeg.] one central" ; inserted: "a common centre or" above "[del.] central" and "vertaber"
19. Deleted: "and" ; inserted above: "all" ; [end of LC 289]; deleted: "enough" ; inserted above: "having" . LC 289 and LC 289a both appear to have writing cut off.

(to the point of view,[20] comprehensive enough)[21] more[22] features of resemblance than difference, and essentially, like that planetary[23] globe itself,[24] compact and orbic and[25] whole.

20. Deleted: "ample enough"
21. Inserted and deleted above "comprehensive enough) [*ins.*] more features" : "but holding more" ; deleted: "having" before "[*ins.*] more"
22. Deleted: "points" ; inserted above: "features"
23. Inserted above "that globe"
24. Deleted: "rounded"
25. Preceding two words inserted above "d" in "and" and "wh" in "whole"

Difficult As It Is.

Manuscript in NYPL (MS Div). Inscribed in black ink on outside of slit-opened envelope of Scovel and Harms, Counsellors at Law, Camden, postmarked September 4, 1890.

Difficult as it is,[1] the final, all-diffusing, all-tending, all-justifying, all-con-certring, main[2] purport of American National Literature (and Art too) is better and superber development of men and women, consistently with our democratic and New World theories. There is no objection to merely fine books or other productions, but they[3] come under some[4] sharp and deep, doubtless western, pur-views, and may fail, with their finest finery.[5] We retain all the universal[6] tests of trial and then add some of our own[7] not so much for the United States but[8] for modern humanity.

1 Preceding four words and comma inserted above "The final all" . Following "The" not reduced to lowercase in MS.
2. Inserted above "pur" in "purport"
3. Deleted: "depend upon" ; inserted above: "come under"
4. Deleted: "high"
5. Preceding four words and final punctuation inserted above "may fail . . . retain"
6. Deleted: "les"
7. Deleted: "for the"
8. Deleted: "advanced" ; inserted above: "for modern"

Amer. Literature.

Manuscript not found. Text from Glicksberg, 162. No date can be assigned.

Amer. Literature

Out of every hundred books written in America, (or anywhere) what do we want, for real nutriment of ninety nine of them. All these books are written for exercises for the writers, to be plain about it—and to prove that he or she can achieve a literary diploma to serve for life if necessary.